The INCAS

CRAIG MORRIS AND ADRIANA VON HAGEN

The INCAS
Lords of the Four Quarters

With 189 illustrations, 49 in color

 Thames & Hudson

Ancient Peoples and Places
FOUNDING EDITOR: GLYN DANIEL

Half-title: Detail of the llama terraces at Choquequirau.
Frontispiece: A silver female figurine found on the summit of
Cerro El Plomo, Chile.

First published in 2011 in hardcover in the United States of America by
Thames & Hudson Inc., 500 Fifth Avenue, New York, New York 10110

thamesandhudsonusa.com

Library of Congress Catalog Card Number 2010935687

ISBN 978-0-500-02121-7

Printed and bound in China by Toppan Leefung

Contents

Preface

This volume, a comprehensive look at the rise and rule of the Incas, is the third book that Craig Morris and I wrote together in the more than two decades of our friendship. Craig died in 2006, before the completion of this book, and his thoughtful analysis and deep insight are much missed. While our earlier books were devoted to the ancient peoples and cultures of the central Andes, this one, fittingly, is about the Incas, the people to whom Craig dedicated his academic life. His landmark excavations at Huánuco Pampa, an Inca provincial center in the north-central highlands of Peru, and the pioneering analyses inspired by that work, feature among his lasting contributions to Andean studies. He later descended from the heights of Huánuco Pampa to the lush coastal valley of Chincha, where his work at the Inca settlement of La Centinela revealed the nuances of Inca rule among a collaborative conquered people. His final project focused on the Inca site of Tambo Colorado in the Pisco valley. The passion Craig felt about his discoveries at this site, and his authoritative understanding of the Incas, resonate throughout this book.

After an account of what we know of the rise of the Incas, we dedicate several chapters to politics, economics, and religion, as well as to art and technology. The second part of the book explores Cusco, the capital, and the empire's vast geographic expanse through the four *suyus*, the Incas' own quadripartite division of their empire. We reconstruct Cusco in its heyday, exploring the city's finely built palaces and temples, and survey the nearby Urubamba valley, where Inca rulers and their lineages established lavish estates such as Machu Picchu, the most famed of the royal enclaves.

Using the Inca road system to guide us, we take the reader to the empire's northernmost reaches in modern Ecuador, where Wayna Qhapaq, the last independent Inca ruler, was engaged in consolidating newly conquered lands when he received news of the Spaniards' arrival on the Pacific coast. En route, Inca settlements on the fringes of the tropical forest to the east and the Pacific coast to the west are explored. South of Cusco, we skirt Lake Titicaca and the famous shrine on the Island of the Sun and continue south to investigate what are today Bolivia, Chile, and Argentina, where rich mines spurred Inca interest in the region. Given space limitations, we could not possibly have included all the peoples and places absorbed or influenced by the empire. Nevertheless, we will reveal how the Incas governed the empire's many provinces, ruling some people directly and allowing others to maintain their traditional leaders, with little interference from Cusco. The concluding chapter is devoted to the end of the empire: the arrival of the Spaniards, the assassination of the Inca ruler

Atawallpa in Cajamarca, and the final years of the neo-Inca state in the tropical forests of Vilcabamba.

Assigning dates to particular events and spans of time to the reigns of Inca rulers before the arrival of Francisco Pizarro and his men in 1532 is particularly challenging. The Incas did not view the passage of time in a linear fashion; rather, they viewed history as cyclical. The Spanish chroniclers tried to dovetail this Inca view of "history" into the Western one, and some even tried to assign specific dates to particular events. Because the Incas had no writing as we know it, these chroniclers are often our only source of information. Although many aspects of what they wrote have been borne out by archaeology, many details have not. Nevertheless, we feel that their voices—especially those of Pedro de Cieza de León, Inca Garcilaso de la Vega, and Juan de Betanzos—add color to what would otherwise be a terse account based on archaeological excavations.

A note on the spelling of Quechua words: Quechua, the lingua franca of Inca expansion, was not a written language, and the first Spaniards to describe what they saw in a strange and foreign land transcribed what they heard—or thought they heard—in myriad ways. Thus, for instance, *waka* (shrine) is often spelled *guaca* or *huaca*. Although we have tried to use the Peruvian Ministry of Education's official orthography where feasible, in many cases we have opted for the most commonly recognized form to avoid confusion (i.e., Cusco rather than Qusqu). For archaeological sites, we have used the forms most regularly cited in the archaeological literature.

Finally, the authors are grateful to Warren Church, Lawrence Coben, David Drew, Heather Lechtman, Vincent Lee, Carol Mackey, Frank Salomon, Corinne Schmidt, Helaine Silverman, John Topic, and Gary Urton for their valuable comments and critiques of this book at various stages of its creation. We also thank Monica Barnes, Penny Berliner, and especially Sumru Aricanli of the American Museum of Natural History for their help with photographic material, as well as Sonia Guillén, Ricardo Espinosa, Jean-Pierre Protzen, Edward Ranney, Johan Reinhard, Vuka Roussakis, and Walter Wust for additional photographs.

Adriana von Hagen

Prologue:
The Road to Chachapoyas

A young girl, struggling to keep up with her family, stumbles on some paving stones. It is early morning and she is surrounded by dozens of families just like hers, carrying their belongings on their backs. There are llamas too, laden with cargo, gathered by the side of the road. A couple of days earlier an Inca official from Cusco had assembled the families in the plaza of their village in Lurín Wanka, on the banks of the Ango Yaku. In his hand he held a bundle of strings tied with knots, which he called a *khipu*, and announced that her entire village—some 100 families he reckoned, glancing at the knots—and their headman, the *pachaka kuraka*, would be relocated to the faraway land of the Chachapoya in the north to start a new life as *mitmaq* colonists. They were needed there, he explained, to set up a new village, where they would make pottery in the style of the Inca lords. The families would follow the Qhapaq Ñan, the royal road, for many weeks until they reached the provincial capital of Huánuco Pampa. Then, they would leave the royal road and head toward the rising sun, crossing a river so large that it was simply called the Hatun Mayu, "the big river."

Thinking of the village she has left behind, nestled on the flanks of a wide green valley covered in fields of maize, the girl wonders what her new home will be like. She had seen people from Chachapoyas city only weeks before: they too were *mitmaq* and were traveling with their families. They dressed differently and were with others from Chinchaysuyu, the northernmost quarter of the empire. She had also seen Cañari, people from even farther north, in whose homeland the great lord and emperor Wayna Qhapaq had waged fierce wars. But they were not being moved to weave or to make pots—they were being moved so that they would not rebel. It was said that the men were warriors and that some would serve as guards in the great palaces of Cusco.

As the girl and her *mitmaq* approach the outskirts of the great Inca city of Hatun Xauxa, near the Ango Yaku, the wide road is flanked by walls, and substantial stone houses and many fine temples come into view. The hills to the west are dotted with dozens of round storehouses filled with all manner of provisions including maize, potatoes, clothing, sandals, and feathers of brightly colored birds. From Hatun Xauxa the road begins to climb, passing the Yana Marka valley and a lake. Every so often along the road, flights of steps lead down to small streams crossed by stepping stones.

Eventually, the *mitmaq* reach Tarmatambo, with its array of beautiful buildings set among terraced fields, and settle for the night in a large thatched enclosure—a *tampu* (way-station)—flanking the plaza. Food is provided from the hillside storehouses. The next morning they set off early, loading the llamas and heading for the *puna*, the rolling grasslands, and Chinchaycocha, "the lake of the pampas cat." Again they follow the wide, paved road, climbing ever higher. In the distance they see herds of guanacos and vicuñas, wild animals that only the Inca emperor is permitted to hunt. *Pariwanas*, graceful, long-legged pink flamingos, pause by the lakeshore. Skirting the lake, the road passes above the marshy, reed-lined shore on a stone causeway. They journey on. When they reach Pumpu they cross on a rope bridge, high above a river that meanders from the lake; it sways and bounces under their weight. Pumpu is large and bustling. Smoke rises from the thatched roofs of houses set around an enormous plaza, much grander than anything they have ever seen.

The next few weeks seem endless as the *mitmaq* make their way along the Qhapaq Ñan, with the snow-capped mountains for company. They meet many people en route: other *mitmaq*, heading south; *mit'a* laborers, temporary workers destined for some imperial building project; soldiers marching in squadrons accompanied by their *kurakas*, bound for the wars in the land of the Cañari and beyond; road officials, *chaski* carrying messages encoded in their rolled-up *khipus*, running along the Qhapaq Ñan and leaving them far behind. There are llamas laden with all sorts of goods, headed for storehouses that provision *tampus* along the road. Every night the *mitmaq* sleep in a different *tampu*; these vary in size, and some have thermal springs. But as night turns to morning they must return to the endless cobbled road with its flights of steps and its bridges that swing high over rivers, or span streams on logs covered in earth and straw. It is said that Wayna Qhapaq designed this royal highway to be larger and wider than the road that his father had built.

Finally, descending a low hill they catch sight of Huánuco Pampa, a city so large that it is impossible to take it all in at once. On the hillside west of the road, the girl sees hundreds of round and rectangular storehouses. Officials oversee the unloading of llama trains and tally the goods stockpiled in the storehouses, noting the amounts on their *khipus*. As the Qhapaq Ñan enters the plaza, it passes by finely built stone structures. Facing the plaza is a compound that is home to hundreds of women who are responsible for weaving fine cloth in the style of their Inca masters and brewing *chicha* (maize beer) for the banquets and feasts held in the large plaza.

Towering over the plaza is an *ushnu*, a stepped platform made of exquisitely fitted stone, with carved pumas gracing the entryways. It is larger than the *ushnus* of Pumpu or Hatun Xauxa. This is where the lord Inca, carried on a litter covered in feathers and gold, reviews the troops or speaks to the people. The *mitmaq* rest in Huánuco Pampa for a few days, and observe people who serve the Inca lords. These people live in small windswept villages to the east, and every so often they come to the city, providing the lord Incas with their labor. They maintain the road and bridges, tend llamas, take turns at servicing the *tampus*, and supply Huánuco Pampa with pottery, weavings, sandals, and produce from the warm valleys to the east: aji peppers, cotton, coca leaves, feathers, honey, and dyestuffs.

Finally, the time comes for the *mitmaq* to leave Huánuco Pampa and continue the journey to their new home. They follow the Qhapaq Ñan briefly, but soon turn off along a narrower cobbled road that takes them down to the Hatun Mayu. As they descend, it gets warmer. Far below is the river, glinting in the hot sun like a giant golden snake. At this wide expanse of water the *mitmaq* must board flimsy rafts made of logs lashed together with rope, and cross into the land of the Chachapoya. They have left their llamas behind them, but on the opposite bank a new herd awaits them. Transferring their belongings, they begin the long trail up toward the dense forests. This is where they will establish their new home as potters, in the land of the Chachapoya.

• • •

Set in the early 1500s when the empire was at the height of its powers, this fictitious account of a journey along the Qhapaq Ñan—the imperial road that connected Cusco, the Inca capital, with its northern domains—highlights an important strategy of Inca expansion: the institution of *mitmaq* colonists, by which the Incas moved loyal communities to newly incorporated or unstable parts of the empire, and settled uncooperative peoples among more accommodating ones. As we will explore in the following pages, however, this was just one of numerous remarkable institutions that the Incas successfully developed to absorb, coordinate, and balance widely dispersed peoples and resources within their vast, expanding empire.

1 · Introduction:
Land of the Four Quarters

The Incas were neither the first Andean empire nor the first to develop the sophisticated mechanisms to manage and distribute ethnic diversity and exploit a variety of natural resources. Yet, even though much of their achievement was based on pre-existing technologies and institutions, the sheer scale of the Inca enterprise made it unique not only in the Andes but in the Americas as a whole.

From their capital, Cusco, in the south-central highlands of what is today Peru, the Incas emerged in the fourteenth century to ultimately build one of the ancient world's largest empires. On the eve of the Spanish invasion in the early 1530s, the empire extended northward from Cusco along the spine of the Andes to embrace most of modern Peru and Ecuador. Southward from Cusco, the Incas swept into Bolivia, north-central Chile, and northwestern Argentina. Inca domains also embraced the desert coast of western South America and parts of western Amazonia.

In Peru, heart of the Inca empire, the topography is especially complex. A combination of tropical latitude, imposing mountain ranges, and two ocean currents—the Humboldt and the El Niño—endow Peru with 84 of the world's 117 life zones. The country's ecoregions encompass the cold sea on the central and south coast and the tropical sea to the north, the coastal desert, the Equatorial dry forest to the north and the Pacific tropical forest farther south, the Andean foothills rising to the intermontane valleys flanked by the snow-capped Andes, the *puna* (high grasslands) in the south and the wetter *páramo* grasslands in the north, and the forested eastern slope descending to lowland Amazonia.

Unusually abundant in nutrients, the country's coastal waters spawn one of the world's richest fishing grounds, sustaining sea mammals and birds. In the winter much of the central coast is swathed in fog and bathed in a fine mist known as *garua*. By September—spring in the southern hemisphere—the desert is in bloom. In antiquity, these fog meadows, known as *lomas*, sustained forests and attracted deer and guanacos, the wild camelid ancestor of the llama. But overgrazing and deforestation have reduced the *lomas* to a few relict patches along the coast. While rainfall is minimal on the central coast and especially in the Atacama desert to the south, every so often the El Niño climatic event—named after the Christ child because its onset is usually noted at Christmas—alters oceanographic conditions and weather patterns across the Pacific, bringing torrential rains to Peru's coast, especially in the north.

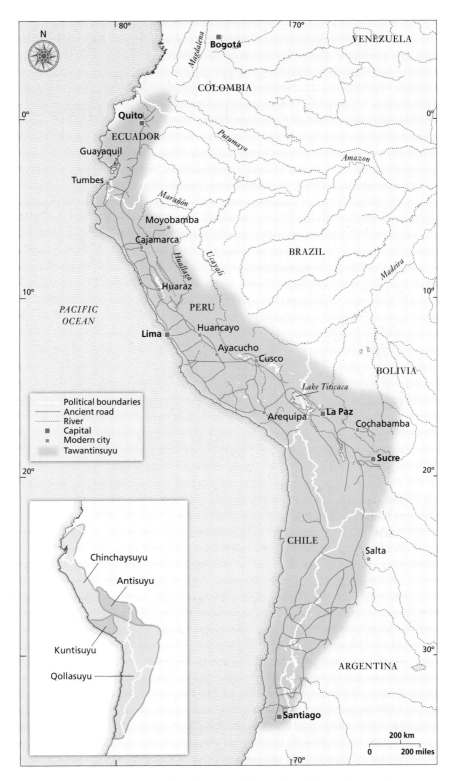

1 Tawantinsuyu at its height, showing the extent of the empire and the road system that linked Cusco, the capital, with its farflung domains. Inset: the *suyu* divisions of the empire.

Some fifty rivers cross the desert coast of Peru, tumbling down from the Andes to the east. Although hunter-gatherers exploited the seasonally inundated floodplains of the coastal rivers, it was only with the advent of irrigation agriculture—first recorded some 4,000 years ago—that people began farming this land, culminating in great coastal civilizations such as the Chimú that preceded the Incas. Pre-Inca peoples had domesticated all the crops grown in Inca times, including cotton and gourds, maize, manioc, peanuts, various species of beans, squash, chili peppers, and a variety of fruiting trees such as chirimoya that thrived along the irrigation canals and in the upper coastal valleys above the fog line. In addition, Andean peoples domesticated potatoes (2,500 varieties have been recorded) and other tubers, as well as Andean grains. Aside from camelids such as llamas and alpacas, the only domesticated creatures were guinea pigs, Muscovy duck, and dogs.

Climbing from the warm coastal plains, or *yungas*, one reaches the temperate western foothills of the Andes, ideally suited to coca (another species of coca thrives on the forested eastern slopes of the Andes). The terrain rises precipitously toward the Andes and the intermontane valleys, which at 7,500–10,500 ft (2,300–3,200 m) offer some of the most fertile farmland in the Andes. Often extensively terraced, they became the breadbaskets of the Inca realm, much of it devoted to maize for brewing *chicha*, maize beer. Terracing greatly increases the amount of arable land, as well as deepening soils, reducing erosion, creating microclimates (mitigating frost damage), and controlling

2 ABOVE Terracing in the Colca valley, Peru. 3 OPPOSITE, ABOVE Bromeliads growing on coastal sand dunes. 4 OPPOSITE, BELOW Irrigated river valley, Majes, Peru.

5 ABOVE Snow-covered peaks in the Cordillera Blanca, Peru.   6 BELOW Mist swirls in the cloud forests of northern Peru.   7 OPPOSITE A herd of llamas in the Colca valley, Peru.

moisture. Some terraces were irrigated by elaborate canal systems, enabling the Incas to shorten the growing season.

Higher still, at 11,500–13,000 ft (3,500–4,000 m), lies the *suni* or *jalca* zone, where farmers grow potatoes and other tubers such as *olluco*, *oca*, and *mashua*, as well as nutritious Andean grains such as quinoa and *kiwicha*. The *puna* grasslands, the highest habitation zone at 13,100–16,400 ft (4,000–5,000 m), are home to alpacas and llamas and their wild ancestors, vicuñas and guanacos. The camelids became one of the great sources of Inca wealth, providing the fiber to produce textiles, which were the most valued of Andean goods. Not only are camelids important sources of meat and fiber, but their dung served as fuel and their bones as tools. They were often sacrificed and their viscera used in divination. Llamas also served as pack animals, although they can only carry some 55 lb (25 kg).

While the snow-clad cordilleras overlooking the intermontane valleys and *puna* are far too high for human habitation, many of their summits were visited in Inca times, especially in the southern Andes, where the Incas sacrificed young women and children to appease the mountain gods. Sacrifices took place to mark times of upheaval such as drought or the earthquakes that so frequently rumble across the Andes. People identified mountains as sources of water and fertility, believing that they controlled rain, thunder, and lightning, and, by extension, the fertility of crops and herds. To provide rainfall and fertility, the mountains had to be lavished with gifts, especially the most precious gift of all, human life. Excavations of these high-altitude sacrifices provide some of the best evidence for Inca ritual practices (see pages 230–33).

Farther inland, on the eastern slopes of the Andes, is the cloud forest, where the Amazon's major tributaries rise. The eastern slopes and Amazonian low-

7

PL. 31

5

PLS 78–80

6

lands are especially moist because the Andes interrupt the westward flow of air. Although the Incas rarely ventured into the tropical lowland forest, they did establish colonists in key areas and tapped into existing exchange systems. From there came tropical forest products such as coca leaves, honey, exotic woods, medicinal plants and herbs, dyestuffs, and the feathers of colorful birds used to decorate the most sumptuous textiles. The region also provided important cultigens such as sweet potato, manioc, and peanuts.

The challenges posed by the empire's varied and rugged topography make the Inca achievement even more admirable. Yet, despite the empire's size and the Incas' impressive accomplishments, the lords of Cusco administered their realm without the help of writing as we know it. Instead, they relied on
PLS 72–74 complex, knotted string records called *khipus*. Because we cannot read *khipus*, much of what we know about the Incas and their empire comes to us through the Spanish chroniclers—the scribes, priests, soldiers of fortune, and officials who accompanied Francisco Pizarro and his conquistadors, and the later accounts by Spanish administrators and clergy. They described what they saw from a European point of view and a religion that ill-prepared them to understand a distinct culture in an unfamiliar landscape. Nevertheless, the chronicles and colonial administrative records, when critically read, and used along with ethnographic observations of the Incas' modern-day descendants and the science of archaeology, help elucidate the Andean past. Fortunately, the Incas left an impressive archaeological record in their monumental cities, tombs, and more modest domestic remains. The study of this archaeological record provides a counterpoint to the Spanish accounts. Together, the sources reveal a civilization as mighty and magnificent as the earliest eyewitnesses reported.

Many modern analyses cast the Incas in a very European light. Accordingly, some writers portray them as ruthless and totalitarian, while others see their empire as a benevolent socialist state. Almost all view it as an empire created by ambitious rulers and powerful armies without attempting to disentangle the objectives of the rulers or the character of the armies from Old World examples. We will probably never fully understand how the empire worked, or the processes changing it, but in this book we attempt to understand the Inca empire on its own terms, although within a comparative perspective. While emphasizing the differences, it is also important to consider the similarities between the Incas and other ancient imperial and urban societies.

As with all state societies, the Incas centralized power in a governing group controlled by a small number of individuals. And, as with all states, ancient and modern, wealth and privilege corresponded to rank, so that the elite were the primary beneficiaries of increases in production and more effective exchange systems. But the particular environmental conditions and the peculiarities in the historical circumstances in which certain social and cultural features emerged resulted in a state quite unlike the modern nation states most familiar to us. As we will see, the Incas developed unusual and remarkable political and economic institutions for coordinating and balancing widely dispersed peoples and resources across their diverse environment. While local and long-distance trade occurred, large marketplaces practically did not exist. People accomplished most exchanges through social and political mechanisms, some of which had ritual and religious components. Even warfare involved motivations and practices that went beyond simple notions of conquest, booty, and domination.

The Incas called their empire Tawantinsuyu, the "four parts together" or the "fourfold domain," and divided it into four distinct regions or *suyus*: the "upper" half included Chinchaysuyu and Antisuyu, while the "lower" half comprised Qollasuyu and Kuntisuyu. Chinchaysuyu, one of the largest quadrants, stretched west and north of Cusco to embrace the coast and highlands into northernmost Ecuador, while Antisuyu included the tropical forest northwest and east of the capital. Kuntisuyu, one of the smallest *suyu* divisions, extended southwest of Cusco to the Pacific coast, and Qollasuyu, the largest *suyu*, reached south of Cusco and included parts of Bolivia, Chile to a point just south of Santiago, the modern capital, and northwestern Argentina.

Scholars have long pondered the nuances of the name Tawantinsuyu, finding it a curious and misleading term to describe what they consider a unified and essentially despotic kingdom that had conquered a vast empire. We feel, however, that we should listen to the Incas and accept the empire's name as a reflection of their own understanding of the land they ruled. When we look closely at these four parts they appear quite different from each other, playing distinct roles in the magnificent totality assembled by the Incas. Inca expansion into the upper half of the empire—Chinchaysuyu and Antisuyu—found more centralized societies and a wide array of resources, and saw the almost immediate building of state infrastructure. Expansion and consolidation southward, on the other hand, especially into northern Chile and northwestern Argentina, encountered more scattered populations and resources, resulting in a more discontinuous approach. The Incas emerged in a land whose people had experienced centuries of balancing the many different parts of a complex Andean world. The empire they built reflected this experience.

Therefore we cannot view Tawantinsuyu as an empire in the traditional, Western sense of a European nation state with clear boundaries marked by conquests and alliances. Rather, it was based on shifting alliances, in which war and ritual played a leading, but not necessarily dominant, role. The process of empire-building had neither a clear beginning nor an end; that is until the early 1530s, when people with a very different set of customs and values arrived from the other side of the ocean. Their ignorance of the complex Andean environmental and cultural landscape and their endeavor to transfer much of the wealth to another continent toppled the great Inca empire.

2 · The Birth and Growth of Tawantinsuyu

The Incas' complex administrative, religious, and cultural traditions did not arise in a vacuum. In addition to their genius for absorbing contemporary cultures, the Incas may have drawn heavily upon the legacies of two earlier societies: Wari and Tiwanaku.

The large, ethnically and ecologically diverse regions controlled by both Wari and Tiwanaku foreshadow the scale of the Inca empire hundreds of years later. The Incas borrowed strategies of statecraft from both, creating a spiritual connection to Tiwanaku and its haunting stone monuments, and adopting Wari's novel scheme of far-flung urban settlements linked by a road system. The Incas later incorporated parts of this network into their own road network. Inca state installations, many built on virgin ground, follow a pattern similar to that established by Wari. Their system of integrated settlements and roads prefigured a new dimension of urbanism that extended beyond individual settlements into planned and coordinated networks of sites.

Wari and Tiwanaku: setting the stage for the Incas

The city of Tiwanaku, where major building was under way by AD 200 on the southern shores of Lake Titicaca, prospered for almost a millennium. Tiwanaku's residents lived in dense concentrations of houses with adobe (sun-dried mudbrick) walls, beyond the carefully planned ceremonial core of stone temples, sunken courts, gateways, and architraves embellished with the emblems of Tiwanaku religion.

North of Tiwanaku in the Ayacucho basin, a people from an ancient city now known as Wari began to extend their influence across the Andes in around AD 600. Large, high-walled rectangular compounds subdivided into patio groups characterize the city's remains. Its art style, with distinctive ceramics and textiles, spread across much of the central Andes. Intriguing similarities between the iconography of Wari and Tiwanaku suggest that either Wari borrowed some of its stylistic elements from Tiwanaku, or that the two cultures shared a common ancestral tradition.

8 The Gateway of the Sun at Tiwanaku, Bolivia, built *ca*. AD 500. Several centuries later the Incas drew inspiration from Tiwanaku mythology and monumental architecture.

While almost four centuries elapsed between the demise of Wari and Tiwanaku—provoked by a combination of environmental factors as well as social and political instability—and the onset of Inca expansion from the Cusco heartland, the two ancient cultures influenced many aspects of Inca ideology, aesthetics, and statecraft. Indeed, the differences between the largest divisions of the Inca empire—Qollasuyu and Chinchaysuyu—may reflect their respective Tiwanaku and Wari heritages.

It may be no coincidence that the Inca empire emerged in the Cusco region where the Wari had held sway, bordering on territory once controlled by Tiwanaku. The Incas were well positioned to benefit from the experience, knowledge, and legends handed down from both empires—and eventually to rule the former territories of both.

By the same token, not surprisingly, the Incas targeted the former Tiwanaku heartland as one of the first regions far beyond Cusco to conquer, and the Titicaca basin's herds of alpacas and llamas became one of the great sources of Inca wealth. The Incas also established a mythical association with Tiwanaku, assimilating the Titicaca region into one version of their origin myth.

16 From Wari, the Incas inherited valuable administrative tools and organizational models. They elaborated the Wari *khipu* (a string accounting device; see pages 34–35) for their administration. Other Inca devices may also have Wari roots. The discovery of a boulder pecked with regularly spaced compartments at the Wari site of Hatun Cotuyoq near Huaro, southeast of Cusco, recalls the Inca counting device known as a *yupana*.[1] The compartments apparently related to decimal units, and sums were tallied using kernels of maize or small stones. Researchers have recovered similar artifacts from Inca sites, and a seventeenth-century drawing by the native chronicler Felipe Guaman Poma
PL. 73 de Ayala shows a *khipukamayuq* (*khipu* maker/reader) holding a *khipu* with a *yupana* illustrated in the lower left-hand corner of the drawing.

A common language to link the diverse cultures of the central Andes may have been another Wari legacy. Like the Incas, the Wari may have employed Quechua as a lingua franca. Although many chroniclers would have us believe that Quechua originated in the Cusco region and owes its widespread usage today to far-flung Inca conquests, linguists in fact believe that it originated on Peru's central coast about a thousand years prior to the rise of the Incas.[2] Quechua's early diffusion may be linked to Pachacamac, a coastal pilgrimage center and oracle that first rose to pan-regional pre-eminence in Wari times.

The pre-imperial Cusco valley

The extent of Wari influence on the Inca society that arose in Cusco several hundred years later is not altogether surprising. Recent research in the Inca heartland of the Cusco basin shows that Wari peoples established themselves in the area around AD 600, slightly earlier than previously thought.

9 From their base at Huaro, where the earliest Wari settlements have been documented, Wari peoples built Pikillaqta in the Lucre basin, 11 miles (17 km) to the northwest. Pikillaqta covers almost one square mile (2½ sq km), and was the largest Wari center outside of Ayacucho. Intriguingly, Wari peoples neither finished building all the sectors at Pikillaqta nor occupied fully its completed sectors, and by 1100 they had abandoned the Cusco region. Nonetheless, 500 years of Wari settlement in the Cusco region left its mark.[3]

In the wake of Wari's demise, the Cusco region witnessed population increases, newly founded settlements, and the creation of terraces and canals on the north side of the Cusco basin, with much of the land probably devoted to maize agriculture.[4] The fall of the Wari polity around 1100 appears to have kindled rivalries among the numerous ethnic groups living in a 40-mile (60-km) radius around Cusco. Archaeological surveys reveal a mix of defensive settlements and unfortified villages, suggesting that some people co-existed peacefully in the valley of Cusco while others probably maintained hostile relations with their neighbors. These peoples, including the Anta, Ayarmaca, Mohina, Pinahua, and Huaro, among others, eventually became known in imperial times as "Incas-by-privilege." Although inferior in status to the Inca elite, who were presided over by the ruling Inca and the royal descent groups, these loyal, "honorary" Incas later served the expanding Inca state as low-ranking administrators and colonists.[5]

9 Aerial view of the Wari site of Pikillaqta in the Cusco valley, Peru. The Wari presence in the Cusco region pre-dated the rise of the Incas by several hundred years.

After the fall of Wari, local groups in the Cusco basin continued to build settlements based on the Wari model, but on a much smaller scale.[6] Excavations at the site of Chokepukio, 17 miles (28 km) southeast of Cusco, revealed a dense occupation following Wari times, spanning some 600 years. The site is dominated by large, niched structures that recalled Wari architecture at Pikillaqta and heralded the large halls that fronted Inca plazas.

Cusco itself was already an extensive settlement in pre-imperial times, perhaps as large as imperial Cusco. Pre-imperial wall remains unearthed

10

throughout the city and its suburbs point to a bustling occupation by peoples who used a pottery style known as Killke, or Early Inca. Because of extensive rebuilding in imperial Inca, colonial, and modern times, however, it is difficult to determine the exact size of pre-imperial Cusco. Even the famed Inca masonry styles—polygonal with its sunken joints and the regular rows of coursed masonry—may have developed a hundred or so years earlier than previously thought.[7]

The ceramic styles of Killke and Lucre influenced imperial Inca pottery, as did, perhaps, Titicaca basin pottery styles. Lucre-style pottery from the post-Wari and pre-imperial period documented in Chokepukio, for example, is technologically more similar to the imperial Inca style than Killke. The Incas, however, borrowed many design elements from Killke. Both Killke and Killke-related ceramic styles, dating to 1000–1400, have been found over a wide swathe of the Cusco region.[8]

10 Chokepukio in the Cusco valley, Peru. The large, niched structures that dominate the site heralded the vast halls that flanked Inca plazas.

By the mid-1300s, if not earlier, one group based in what would become Inca Cusco began to dominate its neighbors. They were the Incas. (The term refers to the king, known as the Sapa Inca ("unique Inca"), as well as to the ethnic group and the art style.) As the Incas developed into a regional power, they employed a mix of strategies that included political and economic alliances. Heralding the pattern of political rule and succession seen in imperial times, regional alliances often had to be re-established—with strategic marriages playing a key role—at the accession of each new leader. By 1400, the Cusco region was under their sway.[9]

Inca myths of origin and expansion

Two myths define how the Incas explained their own origins, social structure, the founding of Cusco, and their rise as a regional power. It is important to emphasize that these stories are not actual histories of events, but served to place the Incas and their ancestors in the natural world and to justify their own view of their special position of power and privilege. Mirroring the origin myths of other Andean peoples, the Incas believed that their ancestors emerged from a natural feature in the landscape.

The first of these myths, the tale of the Ayar siblings, traces the wanderings of Ayar Manco (later Manco Qhapaq, the founding member of the official dynasty) and his brothers and sisters, from their appearance at the cave of Tampu T'uqu near Paqariqtampu ("origin tampu" or "inn of dawn"), now the archaeological site of Maukallaqta to the southwest of the capital, to the founding of Cusco. The four brothers and four sisters, accompanied by the ancestors of the Tambo and Maras ethnic groups (who emerged from adjoining caves), set off in search of fertile land to claim as home, "making war on all those who do not receive [them] as their lords," in the words of the chronicler Pedro Sarmiento de Gamboa.[10] He based his account on interviews with more than 100 Cusco khipukamayuqs (khipu makers/readers) and recorded one of the most complete versions of the myth.

The siblings' journey was fraught with obstacles and challenges, and one of the brothers was entombed at Tampu T'uqu and converted to stone, while another brother was transformed into a stone pillar on the summit of Wanakawri, which became one of Cusco's most sacred shrines. Finally they reached the valley of Cusco and, after plunging a golden staff into the ground, deemed it fertile.

Near the site of the Qorikancha, later the Inca sun temple, they saw a heap of stones where yet another brother was turned into stone, serving as a "stone of possession" or "boundary marker." Sarmiento continues: "In the ancient language of this valley the heap was called cozco, whence that site has had the name of Cusco to this day."[11] There they settled, displacing the previous inhabitants, who had called their village Acamama. The original group of legendary settlers included Manco Qhapaq, his four sisters, a son, Zinchi Roq'a, who succeeded his father, and the ayllus (descent groups that claimed a common ancestry) that had accompanied them from Tampu T'uqu. The exploits of Cusco's mythical founders are enshrined in Cusco's ceque system (see pages 74–76), lines of

12

11

shrines that defined the city's ritual and economic organization, and include the place where Manco Qhapaq first settled and a field where one of his sisters first planted maize.

With the second origin myth the Incas explained their apparently sudden rise as a dominant regional power through the fabled exploits of Pachakuti, the ninth king in the official king list (a list of rulers compiled by various chroniclers; see page 29), and his victories in the Chanka wars. The Chankas were based in Andahuaylas, west of Cusco. There, from around 1100 to 1400, they lived in scattered villages perched on mountain tops and ridges, some surrounded by walls up to 6½ ft (2 m) high, and others by defensive ditches. Recent archaeological surveys in the Chanka heartland suggest that the Chankas were neither powerful nor cohesive, although they may have formed a loose confederation to contest burgeoning Inca power.[12] Although Andahuaylas borders on the heart of Wari territory, little but the memory remained of Wari's planned urban settlements and finely made pottery.[13]

The Incas may have perceived the Chankas as obstacles to expansion, since the only logical route from Cusco to what would become Chinchaysuyu, one of the quarters of the Inca empire, implied control of the approaches to the Apurímac and Pampas rivers. Conversely, alarmed by the expansionist tendencies of Cusco-based groups, the Chankas may have intended to regain a foothold in Cusco, thereby reclaiming the former glory of their Wari ancestors, who only centuries earlier had dominated Cusco.[14]

The gist of the legend is as follows: During the reign of Wiraqocha (the eighth ruler in the traditional Inca king list), the Chankas sent messengers to Cusco demanding the ruler's surrender. Rather than surrender, Wiraqocha abandoned the city with his designated heir, Inca Urco. As the Chankas marched on Cusco, another son, Inca Yupanki, called on the surrounding people to send troops, but they refused.

Then one day, while at a spring, Inca Yupanki had a dream vision in which the creator god (or Inti, the sun god) appeared and told him that he would be "greater than any of his ancestors...because he would conquer the Chankas who were marching on Cusco."[15] As the Chankas reached the northern outskirts of the city, the stones in the fields transformed miraculously into twenty squadrons of soldiers. With the aid of the *pururaucas*, as the stone warriors were called, Inca Yupanki defeated the advancing troops and pursued the Chankas to a place called the plain of Anta, west of Cusco. (As occurred with several of the founding ancestors, about a dozen or so of these *pururaucas* became enshrined in Cusco's *ceque* system.)

Inca Yupanki took the prisoners and spoils of war to his father. The old ruler refused to tread disrespectfully on them, as was customary, insisting that Inca Urco, the designated heir, do so instead. Rebuffed by his father, Inca Yupanki withdrew the spoils and prisoners and returned to Cusco as de facto ruler (some say he staged a palace coup and had Inca Urco murdered). Meanwhile, the Chankas had regrouped for a new attack. Forewarned, Inca Yupanki engaged the Chankas in a bloody melee, turning the battle site into Yawarpampa, or "field of blood." The Chankas fled west toward their home, many drowning as they attempted to cross the Apurímac river.

11 Located southwest of Cusco, these structures at Tampu T'uqu commemorate the mythical origin place of the Incas.

Following Inca Yupanki's victory he was henceforth known as Pachakuti, "transformer of the world." If these wars did indeed occur, their epic and legendary nature suggests that the events took place long before the Spaniards recorded them. Some scholars propose that the Incas invented the events outright to glorify Pachakuti, but the consensus is that some form of hostilities had

12, 13, 14, 15 Stylized portraits of Inca rulers by the native chronicler Felipe Guaman Poma de Ayala. From left to right: Manco Qhapaq, Pachakuti, Topa Inca, and Wayna Qhapaq.

probably taken place. They may have been ritualized battles (see pages 37–40). Pachakuti's legend is thus probably another example of Inca "rewriting" of history to lionize the deeds of particular rulers.[16]

Regardless of the extent to which the story is pure invention or mere embellishment, or whether the conflicts were wars as such or periodic ritual battles staged against a rival people, the story of the Chankas paved the way for and later justified Inca expansion northwest of Cusco. There, the Incas founded the important administrative center of Vilcaswaman, some say to commemorate their victory. Whatever the actual nature of these battles of conquest, virtually all the people who once inhabited Chanka territory were eventually dispatched as *mitmaq* colonists—an institution introduced in the Prologue and described in more detail in the following two chapters—to other parts of the empire, and replaced by *mitmaq* loyal to the Incas.

The king list

The chroniclers attribute early "conquests" beyond the Cusco heartland to several rulers who preceded Pachakuti. But the early kings' lives and exploits are filled with supernatural feats and divine intervention, lending a mythical tone to the accounts. As with the semi-legendary Chanka wars, their feats are also commemorated in Cusco's *ceque* system, where shrines include the house where the second Inca Zinchi Roq'a's body was displayed and a seat where the fourth Inca Mayta Qhapaq planned a battle. The traditional king list records

The Traditional Inca King List

1   Manco Qhapaq

2   Zinchi Roq'a

3   Lloq'e Yupanki

4   Mayta Qhapaq

5   Qhapaq Yupanki

6   Inca Roq'a

7   Yawar Waqaq

8   Wiraqocha Inca

9   Pachakuti Inca Yupanki

10 Topa Inca Yupanki

11 Wayna Qhapaq (d. *ca.* 1524/28)

12 Waskar Inca (d. 1532)

13 Atawallpa (d. 1533)

(with some variation) eleven kings, from the legendary Manco Qhapaq to Wayna Qhapaq, the last independent Inca ruler. The first five kings belonged to *hurin* (lower) Cusco and the following five to *hanan* (upper) Cusco.

The Spaniards learned that empire-building had taken place during the reigns of Pachakuti, Topa Inca, and Wayna Qhapaq, and that the half-brothers and sons of Wayna Qhapaq, Atawallpa and Waskar, were embroiled in a war of

14, 15

succession that coincided with the arrival of the conquistadors. Later, Wayna Qhapaq's son Manco Inca rebelled against the Spanish invaders and retreated to the jungles of Vilcabamba, where he and his successors Sayri Tupac, Titu Cusi, and Tupac Amaru hounded them until Tupac Amaru's capture in 1572.

Some scholars have suggested that the traditional kings, along with the descent groups of their ancestors and the kin groups of Cusco, may reflect institutions that regulated the social structure of Cusco rather than a chronological list of kings.[17] Even if we take the king list at face value and acknowledge that some rulers existed, the list was probably constantly modified and rewritten to erase those who had fallen out of favor with Cusco's elite, expunging some rulers and their descent groups known as *panakas* (royal *ayllus*) from official memory, and embellishing and glorifying the exploits of others, such as Pachakuti. Indeed, as well as his Chanka victory, Pachakuti is credited with inventing many of the institutions and policies for which the Incas are so famed, as well as the reorganization of religion and the rebuilding of Cusco to mirror its prominence as the center of an expanding empire.

The Spanish chronicler and soldier Pedro de Cieza de León, for instance, describing the men who recited or sang the official histories, said: "If there had been one among the Incas who was lazy, cowardly, given over to vices, and who took his pleasure rather than enlarging his power, [it was] ordered that little mention be made of such, or almost none. They put such care in this that if any mention of them was made, it was only so their names and successions would not be forgotten, but about all else they were silent, singing only of those who had been good and brave."[18]

In 1946, archaeologist John Rowe suggested plausible dates for the reigns of the Inca kings, based on the 1586 chronicle of Miguel Cabello de Valboa. This chronology, widely accepted by many scholars of the Incas, dates the final Chanka battle to 1438 and posits that the Incas expanded from Cusco, conquering and consolidating their rule over a vast territory, in under a century. Nevertheless, there is one question that has long perplexed students of Inca civilization: How could only the last three kings—Pachakuti, Topa Inca, and his son, Wayna Qhapaq—have created in such a brief period an empire that extended from just short of the Colombia–Ecuador border in the north to central Chile and northwestern Argentina in the south?

The king list probably reflects events and sequences that were compressed to fit a preconceived plan, and it reveals the Inca concept of time, which was cyclical, repetitive, and patterned. The chronicle of Juan de Betanzos appears to mimic how the Incas remembered their past, based on a sequence of events rather than on absolute chronology.[19] Thus, because of the way the Incas regarded their past, assigning absolute dates before the European invasion is risky. "They did not count their age in years; neither did they measure the duration of their acts in years; nor did they have any fixed points in time from which to measure historical events," remarked the Jesuit chronicler Bernabé Cobo.[20] Andean people, in fact, tracked peoples' ages by noting their stages in life, such as their physical condition and their ability to work.[21]

Empire-building

Attributions of when particular rulers conquered specific territories vary considerably according to each chronicler and his sources. If, for instance, Topa Inca, acting as military commander, conquered a province during his father's lifetime, then the conquest was attributed to both. At the same time, local informants often confused military leaders with Inca rulers.[22] In addition, many provinces took advantage of succession disputes to rebel, forcing new sovereigns to reconquer them, and so the conquests were credited to more than one ruler. Topa Inca's conquests were recorded on *khipus* in order of prestige rather than chronology, and so conquests in Chinchaysuyu and Antisuyu (the higher-ranking divisions of the empire) were listed before Qollasuyu and Kuntisuyu (the lower-ranking divisions).[23] Despite the inconsistencies in the chronicles, the various attributions of conquests are not mutually exclusive. As we will see in the following chapters, rapid expansion, rebellion, and reconquest were phases of the same process.[24]

Radiocarbon dates from Inca sites scattered across the empire suggest a rather different scenario from the traditional account. Obviously, Inca dates are much earlier in and around Cusco, but emerging evidence points to an unexpectedly early Inca presence elsewhere. The transition from pre-imperial to imperial Inca—marked by the appearance of the classic Inca ceramic and architectural styles—dates to around 1400, some forty years earlier than the traditional chronology. Radiocarbon dates from the coast of Peru, for instance, fall mostly in the early 1400s and span the fifteenth century. A date of around 1470 has traditionally been given for the onset of Inca dominion of the north coast, but carbon dating has revealed that there may have been an Inca presence some fifty years earlier. Surprisingly, some of the earliest radiocarbon assays come from northwestern Argentina and Chile, where dates for an Inca presence also begin around 1400, some twenty to seventy years earlier than the conventional chronology.[25] The early dates support the scenario of Inca expansion as a series of raids and reconquests before consolidation occurred.

Regardless of who conquered what or how long it took, bringing half a continent—and some twelve million people—under one ruler is an impressive achievement. The myth of the explosive expansion of an empire undertaken by Pachakuti and his two successors may have been largely political propaganda directed toward Inca allies and opponents, backing up the ruling group's position of superiority, while the antiquity of the mythical rulers who had preceded them added legitimacy to the Inca dynasty. As we will see in the following chapter, reality suggests a much more gradual process of empire-building based on traditional Andean practices.

3 · The Principles of Inca Statecraft: Feared Warriors, Generous Rulers

The Inca empire's extent and pace of expansion were extraordinary for the ancient world, an achievement made even more remarkable by its ethnic and geographical diversity. While technologically advanced in many areas, the Incas' lack of draft animals and writing as we know it hampered transportation and communication. Inca rulers used most of the wide-ranging strategies of expansion documented in other ancient empires: military force, diplomacy, claims of divinity, and marriage alliances. Yet the specific strategies they used to incorporate peoples into the empire were steeped in the particular landscape and customs of the Andes, giving Inca governance a special character.

In theory, the Inca ruler or Sapa Inca wielded absolute power and authority. Miguel de Estete, secretary to Francisco Pizarro, remarked on the deference that Atawallpa's subjects bestowed on him. As the son of the sun, the Inca ruler was treated like a living god, dressed in the finest textiles of the land, and bedecked in feathers and gold. He was carried on a litter "of finest gold, whose seat was a plank of the same and on top was a valuable woolen pillow adorned in rich stones."[1] Francisco Pizarro's cousin Pedro noted that all those who approached him had to enter the room barefoot, carrying a burden. All the things that Atawallpa had ever touched or worn—sumptuous clothing and left-overs from meals—were stored and then burned. Nevertheless, the ruler's power was curbed by local leaders, religious specialists, oracular pronounce-ments, members of the court, and the limitations placed on decision-making by the size of Tawantinsuyu.

Organizing an empire

16–18, PLS 72–74

The Incas' principal means of keeping records was the *khipu*, a device of dyed, knotted strings (see box overleaf). *Khipus* were not used to make calculations but rather to record information that had been calculated elsewhere (such as with a *yupana*; see page 22) by manipulations of pebbles or kernels of corn. Administrators, known as *khipukamayuqs*, used the *khipus* to record statistical information such as census counts, amounts of tribute, and storehouse con-tents. At the same time, *khipus* recorded information for narratives, including genealogies, histories, and even poems and songs. The information in these so-called literary or narrative *khipus* was recited by the Inca record keepers on ceremonial occasions. Each Inca ruler commissioned his own administrators who recorded and remembered the sovereign's deeds. The information kept by

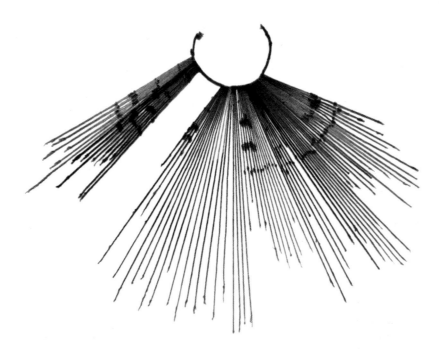

16 A cotton *khipu*. These knotted string accounting devices were vital to the management of the Inca empire.

bureaucrats at lower levels in the Inca administrative hierarchy was passed on to higher-level administrators, although the *khipus* themselves were probably stored at provincial capitals.

The Incas organized their empire into some eighty provinces, each divided into two or three *sayas*. Each *saya* was composed, ideally, of 20,000 to 30,000 households. At the highest level were four administrators in Cusco, each responsible for one *suyu*, or quarter, of the empire.[2] Inca imperial bureaucracy was based on a decimal system of organization. At the local level, groups of ten households were under a single administrative official. Ten such household groupings were placed under an official of 100 households—and so on, up through officials of 500, 1,000, and 10,000 households.

The decimal census was keyed to the use of the *khipu* account records,[3] but local surveys recorded by the Spaniards reveal that the need to fit existing, pre-Inca ethnic groups into decimal units resulted in only approximations of actual population counts.[4] Decimal organization was apparently never instituted evenly across Tawantinsuyu, and in many senses it was an ideal system; in the far northern and southern domains of Tawantinsuyu, for instance, the Incas may only have applied it to communities of *mitmaq* colonists.

While some sources speak of numerous state officials based in Cusco and in provincial centers, Tawantinsuyu was not a heavily bureaucratic empire. Instead, it echoed—albeit on a drastically expanded scale—the kinds of interaction

18

The Memory of Things

Although *khipus*—the knotted string devices used by the Incas to record everything from population counts to songs commemorating heroic kings—look relatively simple to the casual observer, they are in fact quite complex. Basically, a *khipu* (usually of cotton, rarely of alpaca) consists of a main cord from which dangle a series of pendant cords, studded with single, long, or figure-8 knots. "Although [the Incas] don't have writing, they recall the memory of things by means of certain cords and knots," observed Miguel de Estete.

Encoded in the strings and knots is information that apparently played a fundamental role in the "reading" of *khipus*: the type of fiber used, the color of the fiber (whether natural or dyed), the direction in which the fiber was spun, how the spun fibers were plied, how the colored cords were combined, how the pendant cord was attached to the main cord, and the position of the knot on the pendant cord. "Although to us it may seem strange and awkward," noted Pedro de Cieza de León, "it is a fine way of counting."

Nevertheless, and despite the many recent advances made in *khipu* studies, especially by Harvard University's Khipu Database Project, KDB, no one has been able to decipher a *khipu*. Many early Spanish chroniclers lauded the ingenuity of the string records and the skill of their makers and keepers, the *khipukamayuqs*, but not one explained exactly how *khipus* were read, made a drawing of a transcribed *khipu* (with knot and word equivalents), or, better still, left us an actual *khipu* with its transcription (a so-called Rosetta *khipu*).

In the early decades of the invasion, the Spaniards relied on knotted records for the fundamental economic and demographic data they needed to set up the colonial administration; *khipu* records proved especially key to the dozens of Spanish officials who crisscrossed the empire on fact-finding missions known as *visitas*. Information from *khipus* also fueled narratives such as the chronicle of Juan de Betanzos of 1551–57, and the 1570 account of Pedro Sarmiento de Gamboa, who based his history of the Inca empire on interviews with more than 100 *khipukamayuqs*.

In spite of early Spanish reliance on *khipus*, by the late 1570s information gleaned from *khipus* began to clash with the Spanish written word, especially in lawsuits (instigated by an increasingly savvy native population familiarized with the Spanish penchant for legal proceedings and bureaucracy). And so in the early 1580s, *khipus* were denounced as "idolatrous objects" and ordered to be burned.

This in part explains why fewer than 1,000 *khipus* are found today in museums and private collections; most come from looted Inca-period coastal burials where arid conditions enhance preservation. In addition, the sample is skewed because of poor preservation in the highlands, although a cache of thirty-two *khipus* from the cloud forest burial site of Laguna de los Cóndores in Chachapoyas (discussed below) is an exception.

There are two types of *khipus*: numerical and narrative. Numerical *khipus* recorded economic and demographic data such as, for example, the resources of newly conquered lands, their "pasture lands, high and low hills, plough lands, estates, mines of metals, salt works, springs, lakes and rivers, cotton fields, and wild fruit-trees, and flocks… All these things and many others he [the Inca] had counted, measured, and recorded," wrote Garcilaso de la Vega in the early seventeenth century, adding "they had special accountants for all the affairs of peace and war, for the numbers of vassals, tributes, flocks, laws, ceremonies, and all else that had to be counted." As Garcilaso observed, the knots on the cords of numerical *khipus* were arranged in order of units, tens, hundreds, thousands and so on, and, as modern research has shown, the types of knots and their position on the cord indicate numerical value. While *khipus* recorded the information, sums were tallied with kernels of maize or small stones on devices made of wood or stone known as *yupanas* (as seen in plate 73 by Guaman Poma de Ayala of a *khipukamayuq* holding a *khipu* in his hands; a *yupana* is shown in the lower left-hand corner). Equally important, the colors of the cords, as noted, played a key role in identifying what was being counted. Garcilaso, for instance, wrote that yellow signified gold, white denoted silver, and red stood for warriors, but this has not been proven.

Narrative *khipus*, on the other hand, recorded prose and poetry, but how the information was registered and how the *khipus* were read is a matter of ongoing debate. "Treating their knots as letters, they chose historians and accountants...to write down and preserve the tradition of their deeds by means of the knots, strings and colored threads, using their stories and poems as an aid," wrote Garcilaso. "Thus they remembered their history."

How did the Incas use *khipus* to administer their vast empire? *Chaski* messengers running in relay along the road network often carried *khipus*, conveying information from the capital to the provinces, and vice versa. *Khipukamayuqs* resided in every village, and their number was "in proportion to its population, and however small, it had at least four and so upwards to twenty or thirty," remarked Garcilaso. Information from the villages went to the capitals of each province and so on up the hierarchy to Cusco, the capital of the empire. Cieza noted that at the beginning of the new year the *khipukamayuqs* went to Cusco, "bringing their [*khipus*], which told how many births there had been during the year, and how many deaths. This was reported with all truth and accuracy, without any fraud or deceit." Most tellingly, Garcilaso noted that all the *khipukamayuqs* kept the same records, suggesting a system of checks and balances that has been borne out by recent breakthroughs in *khipu* studies.

At the small administrative center of Puruchuco near Lima, for instance, Harvard's KDB Project studied seven of twenty-one *khipus* found buried in an urn (one of the few excavated *khipu* caches with provenance). Their research revealed numerical matches among the *khipus*, indicating an accounting hierarchy and showing how information may have been passed from the provinces to the capital. Equally significant, the *khipus* share an arrangement of knots at their starting ends that may have denoted the place name, "Puruchuco." *Khipukamayuqs* were certainly among those buried at the looted cliffside tombs at Laguna de los Cóndores in Chachapoyas, where archaeologists uncovered some thirty-two *khipus* at two distinct burial sites. There, the KDB Project analyzed a particularly fascinating and apparent "calendar" *khipu* consisting of 762 pendant strings; 730 of the strings are divided into 24 groups of approximately 30 pendants each, suggesting that it covered a span of two years, perhaps a record of the region's labor quota. Two other *khipus* from the same cache match some of the numerical data encoded in the calendar *khipu*.

17 A *khipukamayuq*, described in this drawing by Poma de Ayala as the "Inca's noble accountant."

18 LEFT A provincial administrator holding a rolled-up *khipu* in one hand and an extended *khipu* in the other.

19 RIGHT A *tokoyrikoq*, charged with periodic inspections of the empire's domains.

common in Andean communities known as *ayllus*, kin groups who shared resources and a common ancestor. *Ayllu* leaders, called *kurakas*, managed most day-to-day affairs. Cusco officials usually played a significant role in the selection and confirmation of these leaders. Inspectors (*tokoyrikoq*) native to Cusco and often related to the ruler apparently handled most provincial administrative affairs. Some scholars assume that they lived in the provinces they oversaw, while others argue that they only performed periodic inspections. One *kuraka* from the town of Auqimarka in the Huánuco Pampa hinterland, for instance, testified to Spanish officials that an Inca administrator oversaw 10,000 households and visited the province annually; another witness described this person as a *tokoyrikoq*.[5] Given the nature of their duties, the inspectors were probably accompanied by *khipukamayuqs*,[6] while other record keepers likely resided locally.[7]

According to Juan Polo de Ondegardo, a sixteenth-century Spanish official versed in such matters, the inspectors ensured that workers placed produce from state fields in storehouses, recorded census data (such as births, deaths, and marriages), obliged subjects to fulfill their labor "tax" (levied on heads of household, who "paid" their "tax" by providing their labor to the empire), raised armies when required, and designated local *kurakas*. The inspectors also punished crimes and, as Bernabé Cobo put it, found "out everything that went on in his province in order to provide a remedy when it was necessary."[8]

War and ritual war as tactics of expansion

Given the Incas' penchant for casting themselves as valiant warriors, and the Spanish tendency to see everything through their own lens of war and coercive conquest, a picture has emerged of the Inca empire as a conquest state in a more or less European sense. The Spanish chronicles speak of armies composed of hundreds, even thousands, of soldiers, leaving the impression of a great military state formed through armed conquest.

Certainly, armed conflict played a crucial role in Tawantinsuyu's expansion. Yet it is difficult to evaluate the nature of this conflict and how Inca warfare compares with our own notions of combat and military conquest. Apparently, no Spaniard observed a battle between Inca and other local forces, and our evidence for strictly indigenous Inca warfare is based on the chronicles. Many scholars have noted the distinctive nature of Andean warfare,[9] and suggest that it differed substantially from European warfare.[10] We suspect that the emphasis on militarism in the sixteenth-century sources reflects the invading Europeans' own preoccupation with conquest warfare as they practiced it.

Although slings, padded helmets, and mace heads clutter museum shelves, archaeological excavations have turned up few conventional lethal weapons, and most Inca settlements do not contain apparent military installations. Star-shaped mace heads, in fact, may have served as badges of office as much as weapons and were, for instance, common offerings at the sanctuary of Catequil in Huamachuco and other sites related to the shrine.[11] The great "fortress" of Saqsawaman above Cusco served more as a theater for religious ritual than as a defensive bastion, and administrative cities such as Huánuco Pampa included thousands of buildings spread across an open plain with no defensive walls.

20 Felipe Guaman Poma de Ayala's rendering of a battle scene. The warriors on the left stand on a *pucara*, or fort.

In 1536, after having observed Spanish military practices for four years, rebellious Incas besieged Spanish-occupied Cusco. While their tactics showed considerable military sophistication, ritual practices intervened in this obvious effort to throw off the European invaders. With the Spaniards' food supplies running low and victory apparently near, the rebels abandoned the battle because their ritual calendar dictated that they pause to make sacrifices to the new moon and allow the soldiers to attend to their fields.[12]

Yet another dimension of indigenous Andean warfare is seen in historic and contemporary accounts of ritual battles. Despite successive government attempts to stamp them out because injuries and deaths brought them into conflict with European law, such battles have survived in the Andes for centuries. Known as *tinkuys*, these battles combine elements of politics, religion, economics, and war. While widely distributed, they are best known in the region of Cusco. The encounters take place during the rainy season, while the crops are in the fields. The spilling of blood onto the earth is believed to guarantee rainfall and ensure good harvests, underscoring the *tinkuys'* connections to both religion and the economy.[13] Community members not actively engaged in the armed contests provide a colorful backdrop of singing, dancing, eating, and drinking. Nevertheless, such conflicts are serious, accompanied by humiliating insults and casualties.

Modern-day ritual battles recall aspects of the indigenous fighting described in the chronicles. Cieza, referring to the legendary Chanka war, with an allusion to the Spaniards' own experience with the indigenous peoples, notes: "The Inca and [the Chanka leader] held a talk, but, as they were all armed for war, the interview was useless, for they grew more irate with their own words, and finally came to blows with terrific whooping and uproar, because these people are very noisy in their fights, and we fear their shouting more than their deeds."[14] The similarities between contemporary ritual battles and those the Incas may have fought are intriguing. Of course, the wealth and power of the Incas would have raised the number of soldiers, the splendor of their dress, as well as the tactics and strategic objectives to an imperial scale unimaginable to participants in recent ritual battles. In the same way that they magnified certain local-level institutions (see Chapter 4), the Incas may have employed many aspects of Andean ritual battles, but made them more structured and strategic, turning them into a ritualized form of imperial war.

As we saw in Chapter 2, the Chanka wars may have followed the pattern outlined above, signaling adjustments to an ongoing conflict with a neighboring people rather than outright conquest. The Incas used the myths and legends built around that war, complete with soldiers conjured out of stone, as a measure to glorify their ruler as a great warrior with divine attributes. Once they had gained their reputation, they became more likely winners in subsequent confrontations. The mythic histories of past battles may have been as important as the outcome of future confrontations. The size and ferocity of Inca armies as well as the strategic abilities of their commanders also played important roles.

Rebellion and reconquest were common themes in the history of Inca expansion, and Inca battles of conquest had to be refought, particularly when a new

21 The plaza at Saqsawaman, located between the zigzagging walls (*foreground*) and a stone outcrop, may have served as a setting for mock battles in Inca times. Today it serves as the setting for a re-enactment of the Inca winter solstice festival.

ruler came to power.[15] Part of their hegemonic strategy probably implies Inca manipulation and control of the endemic rivalries and conflicts that raged across the Andean highlands before the Incas established "pax Incaica." The frequent ritualized wars before Inca rule were probably fought between loosely related neighboring groups. In spite of the recurring, ritual nature of these fights, they were nonetheless battles, and as the empire grew the Incas normalized these encounters, converting many of them into battles between groups joined together in the state hierarchy. In effect, they became fights among "insiders," regulated by the Incas.

The Incas incorporated great plazas, analogous to those in Cusco, in many of the administrative centers they built throughout their realm. Chapter 8 explores one of the grandest of these centers, Huánuco Pampa, where the Incas 22 may have staged ritual battles in the central plaza, thereby establishing fighting not just as an act of conquest, but as a fundamental instrument of rule. Hosting

22 Huánuco Pampa in the north-central highlands of Peru. Ruined walls in the foreground are the remains of one of the estimated 500 storehouses that perch on a hill to the south of this large provincial Inca settlement.

and supervising ritual battles allowed the Incas to influence outcomes and to shift group relationships toward their own ends. The methods of Inca warfare were very different from those in the West, but they appear to have been quite effective in the Andean world.

Specialized soldiers: the Cañari and Chachapoya

Inca strategies for expanding, ordering, and controlling their empire shifted substantially over time. The lack of written history, however, makes it difficult to track these changes. The chronicles indicate that Inca reliance on a seasonal force of fighters, tied to the agricultural calendar and the system of labor tribute, may have been giving way to a standing army comprised of specialized warriors. Numerous chroniclers refer to two ethnic groups, the Cañari and the Chachapoya from northern Chinchaysuyu (the northwestern quadrant of the empire), who served as palace guards in Cusco and functioned as state-sponsored *mitmaq* colonists.

As the empire expanded, obliging soldiers and others fulfilling their labor obligation to travel longer distances from their homes, the rotating service staffed by male heads of households became increasingly inefficient.[16] Toward

the end of their reign, the Incas had established entire communities of soldiers, along with their families, in regions that required their service. The advantages to the Inca state of full-time "soldiers" are clear: they reduced the constant need to mobilize and deploy troops over great distances. These new military specialists served much as the farmers and craft specialists dispatched as colonists throughout Tawantinsuyu.

The choice of recent and reputedly adamant foes of the state, such as the Cañari and the Chachapoya, as trusted guards is difficult to comprehend. Scholars have assumed that these peoples, seasoned in their own conflicts with groups around the fringes of the empire, were chosen for their superior military skills. We know that at least the Cañari practiced ritual warfare,[17] which may have been a key factor in their being assigned critical roles as palace guards and warriors. It seems likely, however, that their bellicose character was embellished in official oral traditions. Their explicitly belligerent pose could have proven advantageous in the run-up to battle, creating fear and increasing the chances of "victory."

With their dual character as both ferocious recent enemies and trusted loyal allies, we cannot truly gauge the roles of the Cañari and Chachapoya as subjects and defenders of the Cusco overlords.

Mitmaq: a patchwork of interspersed colonies

Despite the importance of conflict and warfare in imperial expansion and in the management of incorporated groups, the Incas employed mainly non-military strategies to enlarge and administer Tawantinsuyu. Such policies encouraged peoples' submission without the loss of state resources resulting from the use of military force. The chronicler Juan de Betanzos, describing colonists dispatched to Cusco from the Quito area in far northern Chinchay-suyu, sketched the fundamentals of this system: "These Indians were young married men with their wives, their things, and seeds from their lands so they could be placed as *mitimaes* [*mitmaq*] in the valleys and lands surrounding Cuzco. [*Mitmaq*] means people from one province settled in another."[18] Cieza continues: "If the natives should rebel, and the [*mitmaq*] supported the [Inca] governor, the natives would be punished and reduced to the service of the Incas. Likewise, if the [*mitmaq*] stirred up disorder, the natives put them down. In this way these rulers had their empire assured against revolts."[19]

The seemingly contradictory but strategically advantageous aspect of *mitmaq* colonies was that the Incas settled less cooperative communities among more accommodating ones, and moved loyal, pacified communities to newly incorporated areas or regions of disquiet. As a result, the Incas created a heterogeneous socio-political landscape settled by peoples with various regional origins and political loyalties. Such fragmentation made it less likely that large groups could unite and oppose Cusco. While all empires establish colonies as a principal strategy of rule, the Incas relocated an astoundingly large percentage of the population great distances, thereby accomplishing the imperial objectives of creating and maintaining peace.

Royal generosity, service, and loyalty

Kings, their close relatives, and their highest representatives host sumptuous feasts and dignify important events with their presence. Rulers' ceremonial roles help maintain their royal status, encourage their subjects to honor them, and also ensure cooperation and warm sentiments. In the Andes, local chiefs and leaders provided feasts for the local community members who worked their fields, compensating the workers for their labor with food and entertainment. In the non-market Inca economy, the distribution of many highly valued goods depended on gifts and issues from the Inca and his representatives. Economic and political circumstances elevated royal hospitality to the pinnacle of imperial activity, creating a court filled with elaborate ceremony accompanied by great quantities of prestige food and drink.

In part, the importance of ritual events lay in their religious significance, since most feasts related to worship and the ceremonial calendar. But they also offered a context to instruct subjects in the empire's official myths, history, and ideology. People literally sang the praises of the Inca and his victories, creating the history of the empire. Cieza describes "banquets and drinking feasts, great *taquis* [dances], and other celebrations...completely different from ours, in which the Incas show their splendor, and all the feasting is at their expense, where there were vessels of silver and gold, and goblets and other things."[20]

23

23 An Inca jar used for serving *chicha*, maize beer, offered on ceremonial occasions.

Archaeological research has revealed ample evidence of feasting in Inca cities and settlements scattered across the realm. Outside of Cusco, at least, people did not dine off silver and gold dishes; rather, they feasted with Inca-style ceramic plates and jars, PLS 81–84 as revealed by the many tons of broken pottery now crowding museum shelves. Much of the tableware and serving dishes supplied by the state for feasts and ceremonies were fashioned in a highly standardized imperial style.

Great feasts and drinking bouts combined with lavish gifts provided the populace with scarce or locally unavailable luxury goods. The Inca and his representatives often gave gifts of cloth and other goods encoded with signs and symbols of the status and duties that the state envisioned for the recipients. This distribution of sumptuary goods in the name of the ruler combined important exchange functions with socio-political objectives: the state distributed goods and positions— along with a dash of prestige. Both the goods and the ceremonial settings provided by the rulers made local peoples feel important and contributed to their support as willing subjects. In hosting great ceremonies and issuing luxury goods, the Incas bought loyalty with royal generosity.

Roads and cities: the infrastructure of rule

With more than 25,000 miles (40,000 km) of roads, the Inca road network was 24 one of the most elaborate transportation systems in the ancient world. While technologically impressive, the roads served as much more than a monumental achievement of Inca engineering or a transportation link that enabled kings, soldiers, state officials, and the products of the imperial economy to circulate through the realm. They also symbolized domination and control, and served as a visible means of underscoring a newly incorporated region's place in Tawantinsuyu. Thus, the roads and the movement they organized were part of the essence of empire.

The road system linked hundreds of way-stations that provided temporary lodgings and supplies for official travelers. The largest administrative centers housed elaborate administrative palaces and buildings dedicated to ceremony and religion. Hundreds of people resided in the large centers year-round, not only to serve travelers but also to staff the temples, host ceremonial activities, work on state projects, manufacture cloth, and brew *chicha*, maize beer.

24 The Inca road near Huánuco Pampa. The high *puna* grasslands between the modern Peruvian departments of Huánuco and Ancash boast some of the best-preserved sections of the Qhapaq Ñan, the highland road that connected the capital Cusco with Quito in Ecuador.

The great Inca infrastructural network varied substantially from region to region. It is most impressive in the northern highlands, where the road between Cusco and Quito linked a series of major state-built cities. In contrast, installations along Inca roads in the south, in modern-day Chile and Argentina, are generally small. These striking differences reflect the distinct pre-Inca pasts of the regions, as well as variations in human and natural resources. Along much of the Peruvian coast, for example, an elaborate system of roads and urban centers flourished for centuries before the rise of the Incas, while farther south, in Chile and Argentina, populations tended to be relatively sparse, making a substantial administrative apparatus less necessary. As we shall see, more conceptual or ideological factors may also have been involved, leading the Incas to deliberately give the "upper" and "lower" parts of their empire distinct characters.

Religion as statecraft

Religion was a vital and complex part of life in Tawantinsuyu, inextricably linked to imperial governance. The Incas built temples to the official state religion throughout the empire. The state solar religion served two primary political purposes: first, as the ruler was regarded as the son of the sun, it underscored his divinity, and second, elaborate origin myths enhanced the legitimacy of the Incas and their rulers by linking them to both the natural and supernatural worlds.

Throughout history, shared religion and ideology have provided strong underpinnings to many states and empires. The Incas knew that religious ideology could help to cement their empire. They also recognized, however, the power of local religious traditions, and knew that religion could divide or forge regional identity. In some cases, the Incas associated themselves directly with local deities and oracles, encouraging their worship as an adjunct to imperial religion. In most cases, the ruling Incas honored local shrines (*wakas*), oracles, and ancestral mountain gods (*apus*), and took portable versions of the shrines to Cusco, where they served as "honored hostages." The Incas did not encumber their diverse empire with a single, simplistic, and dogmatic religion.

Ties that bind: kings, kinship, and royal alliances

In many states and empires, kinship ties between ruling families and local elites
are a common accessory to political power in provincial areas. Inca society was
no different. Extensive marriage links connected lesser royals and local elites,
and law and custom permitted the ruler and many other members of the elite to
take secondary wives. By around 1500, late in Inca times, the Inca took his full
biological sister as his principal wife, and his successor, in theory, was a son of
that marriage. Such royal marriages and successions concentrated power at the
top, but this vertical concentration did not rule out horizontal linkages. Marriage alliances strengthened and personalized alliances between local leaders
and their royal overlords. The "gift" of a bride—a royal relative or a woman
"chosen" for special privileges by the Inca—represented both a kinship tie and
the ruler's generosity. Referring to Pachakuti's generosity toward local lords,
the chronicler Betanzos explains: "He gave them many jewels of gold and
silver... He also gave each one two sets of the garments he wore, and to each
one he also gave a lady born in Cusco and of Inca lineage. Each of these women
was to be the principal wife of the Cacique [local lord] to whom she was given.
The children of these unions would inherit the domain of their father. Because
of these family ties, they would never rebel."[21]

Some categories of *aqlla*, women who were chosen to serve the Inca religion, were often given as brides. These highly prestigious women were obliged to remain virgins until they left the cloistered *aqllawasi* ("house of the chosen women"). As the friar Martín de Murúa noted in his early seventeenth-century chronicle,[22] the *aqllawasi* compounds served essentially as "storehouses" of women, many of whom were also distributed by the Incas as wives to important local elite men. As archaeology has shown, the "chosen women" of the *aqllawasi* at Huánuco Pampa wove fine cloth, brewed *chicha*, and probably awaited an appropriate marriage (see page 160). The range and intensity of their activities demonstrate their extraordinary importance to imperial objectives. Just as the Incas increased the value of cloth and food by storing them in royal storehouses and encoding the objects with state symbols, they also increased the women's importance by choosing them and housing them in *aqllawasi*. Women endowed the ruler with a unique capacity to grant prestige and intimate pleasure, resulting in important political and economic ties.

Establishing marriage links was very much a two-way street. Evidence from early Spanish administrative records demonstrates that the Incas dispatched many provincial elite women, particularly the daughters or sisters of new allies, to Cusco as secondary wives of the ruler. But women played an even larger role than that of marriage partners. Archaeology and colonial records suggest that the standard chroniclers, with their patriarchal backgrounds, underestimated and misunderstood the overall importance of women in Inca governance. The *Qoya*, or "queen," played an active part in important policy matters. Like her male counterpart, the *Qoya* too was accorded labor, land, and herds. On her death her mummy was worshipped and the cult sustained in much the same way as that of the ruler. The *Qoya* enjoyed joint rule with the emperor, and some of them even governed Cusco in the absence of their husbands.[23]

25 Poma de Ayala's drawing of an *aqllawasi*, which housed the *aqlla* or "chosen women." The *aqlla* spun and wove fine cloth and brewed maize beer for the rulers and the state religion.

The four parts: an empire united by division

As with all empires, Tawantinsuyu formed a composite of many different groups. These varied greatly in size and socio-political complexity, and many were themselves composed of multiple groups. The Incas fitted the various incorporated groups into a fourfold system in much the same way that these communities often organized geographic and social space. Unfortunately, early Spanish observers did not explore the concepts behind "Tawantinsuyu," and we are left to speculate whether the fourfold division simply organized and named geographic units, or whether in actual fact it had deeper and more complex meanings.

The oppositions, conflicts, and exchanges that characterize ritual battles echoed, in part, the traditional relationships between the parts, or halves, usually portrayed as "upper" and "lower" in Andean and other New World societies. As we explore Inca cities and towns in later chapters, we will see concrete examples of how division into ranked parts is often expressed in architecture and town planning. This spatial organization also reflects fundamental aspects of life in Inca settlements. Did the division of the Inca empire into four parts serve as more than a mere metaphor? Although no early chroniclers suggest such a notion, we suspect that the Incas envisaged Tawantinsuyu as an upper and lower empire and that the differences between them are more than superficial. Some of these contrasts reflect differing environments, resources, and population densities. The prevalence, for instance, of high-altitude human sacrifices in Qollasuyu, the lower empire, probably relates to the distribution of appropriate peaks. But the two great pre-Inca empires, Wari and Tiwanaku, left deep cultural imprints, respectively, on "upper" and "lower" Tawantinsuyu that need to be better researched and understood. Scattered throughout the written and archaeological records are clues to suggest that the four-part division constituted a grand vision of empire in which the differences formed an essential aspect of the empire's character.

The picture we have sketched of the political forces that created Tawantinsuyu portrays an empire of unusual temporal and spatial qualities. Inca rulers did not, and probably could not, insist on immediate submission and obedience from the peoples they incorporated. "Conquest" was an ongoing process that had to be regularly reaffirmed by rulers, particularly newly crowned rulers, faced with predictable rebellions.

As a result, imperial annexation was gradual and never fully completed. This is especially evident near the edges of the empire. The Incas searched for desired resources and cooperative peoples to compose their realm. But when outright conquest failed, they used other mechanisms to secure access to valuable resources controlled by restive peoples.

As we have seen, the Incas viewed their empire as a collection of parts. It was not cut from a whole tapestry spread evenly over the landscape. Much like its resources, it was discontinuous. Roads and conceptual lines linked its parts, but in between—and beyond—the rulers tolerated regions far from the reach of imperial control.

4 · The Wealth of the Empire: Land, Labor, and the Worth of Goods

The Incas accumulated such vast wealth that sixteenth-century Peru grew into a legendary source of gold and other "treasure," and the Spanish idiom "vale un Perú" ("worth a Peru") became synonymous with great riches. To the Incas, however, gold had no commercial value and did not function as a medium of exchange. Rather, cloth served as the most common and visible indicator of wealth and status. The Inca state invested heavily in the herds (the domesticated llamas and alpacas and wild vicuñas and guanacos) and cotton fields that provided the fiber, and in the labor that turned out fine garments, resulting in the cloth-filled warehouses that so amazed the conquering Spaniards. In addition, the Incas regarded *Spondylus*, the coral-colored spiny oyster, as perhaps the single most valuable commodity derived from nature, just as other Andean peoples had done for centuries.

These features of the Inca economy are but an inkling of several apparent contradictions between great wealth and a technology and economic organization that was very different from modern economies. Not only did Andean societies lack machines capable of replacing people and animals, but the Spanish chroniclers also seldom mention the existence of markets, as they frequently did in their accounts of Mexico. How did the Incas accumulate and "invest" such vast wealth, and how did they transfer it from one region and from one segment of the population to another?

Reciprocity as an exchange system

Harnessing and managing human energy on a large scale is one of the major Inca achievements, contributing to a new level of wealth in the Andes. The Incas shifted people from community-based subsistence production and transferred them to regions and into social positions where they produced more valuable foods, sumptuary goods, and invested in the physical infrastructure of the expanding empire. The changes in labor organization not only increased overall production but shifted the emphasis to goods that the Incas found more valuable for promoting imperial expansion.

Many societies have functioned without money or sizable markets, and some of them have devised ways of accumulating substantial wealth. They operate as drastically expanded small communities in which goods and services are obtained through rights to land and labor, and are distributed using principles

26 *Lomas,* fog meadows on Peru's central coast, bloom in September, spring in the southern hemisphere.

27 The coast of Peru boasts some of the world's richest fishing grounds.

28 OPPOSITE The Inca road approaching the Inca installation at Inkawasi in the Cañete valley on Peru's south coast.

29 ABOVE The roadside *tampu* (way-station) of Pariachuco on the highland Qhapaq Ñan, the royal road, near Conchucos, Ancash, Peru.

30 BELOW The Inca coastal road near Quebrada de la Vaca in southern Peru is a less formal construction than its highland counterpart.

31 Llamas and trekkers on the great Qhapaq Ñan, the royal road that connected Cusco to Quito, seen here at the pampas of Huamaín in Huánuco, Peru.

32 ABOVE Agricultural terraces follow the natural contours of the terrain at Pisaq above Cusco's Urubamba valley.

33 OPPOSITE, ABOVE The provincial Inca center of Huánuco Pampa in Peru's north-central highlands, viewed from the storehouse hill to the south.

34 OPPOSITE, BELOW Agricultural terraces cling to the forested slopes beneath Choquequirau high above the Apurímac river, west of Cusco.

35 Snow-clad Mt. Salcantay in the Cordillera Vilcabamba, Peru.

of reciprocal gift-giving and labor exchanges among friends and relatives. This so-called reciprocal system is intrinsically linked to the personal and social relationships between the people who make the exchanges. Thus, the value of the goods or the labor provided in any given exchange is not limited to the utility, quality, or rarity of the items; rather, the effect that the good or service has on the relationship must be calculated as part of the value exchanged.

In such societies, the items exchanged are as significant for their social and sentimental value as for their importance as needed or wanted goods and services. The social, and even the political, context of gift exchanges becomes important in establishing the value of goods or services acquired or given. For the Incas, this was particularly true of commodities such as cloth and items of adornment. But it was also critical for "luxury" foods, such as maize and *chicha*, maize beer. Indeed, as discussed in the previous chapter, in Inca times economic transactions, social relations, work, and authority or power relationships between rulers and subjects were closely linked. Economic matters were embedded in a complicated web of social, political, and even religious and military settings.

To understand the social and political dimensions of the Inca economy, we need to explore the social settings where goods were produced and items and labor exchanged. Indigenous Andean *ayllus*, localized descent groups, were largely self-sufficient.[1] On the coast, fertile valleys provided marine resources and irrigated farmland, but in the highlands, farmers cultivated dispersed pockets of crops adapted to a wide range of altitudes. Highland *ayllus* distributed lands so that their members had access to enough land to produce the necessary crops that grew at different altitudes. Communities often controlled and cultivated lands in more than one ecological zone.

To do this, they deployed members of their *ayllus*, either permanently or temporarily, to ecological zones often located two or three days higher up or at altitudes lower than that of the nucleus of the group. This strategy of scattering land and people, rather as islands, throughout the diverse, sharply vertical Andean landscape enabled people to exchange a wide variety of products through normal community relations. While small markets existed in some regions, and long-distance exchange specialists were known, especially in the far north, most exchanges were accomplished through direct exchange mechanisms within the dispersed, kin-based community. It is unclear when, how, or why this way of tapping into the diverse Andean environment developed, but regions where distinct environmental zones lie relatively close to each other are most easily exploited through this strategy of "ecological complementarity."[2]

Seasonal and full-time labor

The key to understanding the functioning of the non-market Inca economy is the role of labor. In most cases, people did not work to receive specific goods in return for their efforts. At least in the highlands, *ayllus* and their leaders organized labor so that community members received adequate food and other subsistence goods. In most cases, land appears to have been assigned to *ayllus* based primarily on their size and needs. Able-bodied members of the *ayllu* worked the fields, and some of the labor was performed communally. Local leaders redistributed the use of land periodically to adjust to the changing needs of the communities' families.

In much of the Andes, *ayllu* members tilled the fields assigned to the local leader, as well as those of the sick and other households that lacked able-bodied workers. These workers received food and drink from those who benefited from the labor. In the case of the leader—the *kuraka*, or head of the dominant *ayllu*—the hospitality was expected to be generous, and the work was often performed in a ceremonial context, with the host providing sumptuous feasts with large quantities of *chicha* beer. The crops that they produced and the basic technology used to grow them were those that had sustained Andean peoples centuries before the Incas appeared.

At the state level, Inca rulers managed their empire's enormous economy largely through a system of land assignments, labor "taxes," and royal gifts and hospitality that reflected the customs of local communities. Tribute in labor, rather than goods, supported the state and its ruling elite. The Inca rulers and the state depended on land and camelid herds tended by local *ayllu* members in fulfillment of their labor tax. The Inca rulers also endowed land and herds to the state solar religion, as well as to other shrines and oracles. Heads of households worked the lands of the Inca and the state religion, while women spun and wove for the Inca, using fibers provided from state lands, herds, and storehouses. In return, the ruler supplied state workers with food and drink, in the same way that local leaders provided sustenance for those who labored for them.

The general principle of exchanging labor for hospitality and gifts seems to have pervaded many aspects of the Inca economy, both state and local. Archaeologists have recovered evidence of large-scale feasting held in the residences of important local leaders and in regional palaces at major Inca state administrative centers.

36 A woman of Quehue, near Cusco, carries her quota of rope for building the suspension bridge illustrated on pages 94–95; some principles of Inca labor organization still persist in the Andes.

335

DEPOCITODELINGA
COLL CA

topa ynga
yupamqui

depocitos del ynga

como

37 ABOVE Storehouses at Huánuco Pampa. Some 500 storehouses poised on a hill south of the settlement stored luxury goods and foodstuffs that Inca rulers lavished on subject peoples.

38 LEFT The Inca ruler Topa Inca inspects storehouses and consults with a provincial administrator, who is holding a *khipu*.

They have also excavated dozens of storerooms in warehousing complexes adjacent to major provincial capitals, where some rooms still contained remains of maize, potatoes, and other foodstuffs. These huge state stores enabled Inca officials to fulfill their obligations, maintaining and rewarding the many people who tilled the state fields, wove cloth for elaborate costumes, produced imperial gifts for the populace, fought wars, and built roads and cities. The Incas did not simply provide minimal rations; rather, they lavished people with maize beer and luxury foods that could not easily be obtained at home. The meals, and perhaps the work itself, took place in a context of celebration and shared accomplishment, accompanied by music, dancing, and ritual performances.

37, 38

59

The men and women who worked for the state fell into several categories based on whether they worked full-time or seasonally, and whether their service removed them permanently from their native communities. Probably the most common labor category was called *mit'a*, comprising able-bodied heads of household who worked seasonally. They retained ties to their local communities even though many traveled substantial distances from their homes. The Incas also used this system of rotating service to recruit soldiers.

In contrast to the rotating workers, female *aqlla*—weavers, brewers, and religious officials—and male *yana* (personal retainers) performed full-time service and usually lost the ties to their communities. *Yana* have often been equated with slaves, but this is a serious oversimplification, and their loss of community ties should not be compared with enslavement in the European sense. The state supplied them with food and other needs, and many *yana* and *aqlla* occupied privileged positions; indeed, the Incas elevated some *yana* to *kuraka* status. While *yana*, at least, existed in parts of the Andes before the Incas ascended to power, the numbers of *yana* and *aqlla* probably increased under the Incas since they provided vital services in tending camelid herds and producing cloth, products of special value to the empire's political and economic growth.

Mitmaq formed the most unusual category: entire communities relocated to new areas that required their services. The Incas transferred experienced maize farmers, for instance, to newly terraced valleys to increase production. Unlike the other labor groups, whose subsistence needs were assured by the state's storehouses, most *mitmaq* cultivated their assigned lands to provide their own food. They also provided strategic services to the state, in addition to their economic functions (see page 42). The Incas moved loyal groups to areas of rebellious peoples, and dispersed less compliant communities among more reliable ones.

The economic and political dimensions of the *mitmaq* were intricately entwined. The increasing demand for silver and gold adornments among the growing state elite prompted the deployment of skilled Chimú smiths from Peru's north coast to Cusco and administrative centers. Weavers and potters were also resettled, often moving great distances. The maize fields of Cochabamba, Bolivia, provide perhaps the most dramatic example of the Inca use of the *mitmaq* institution. There, Atawallpa's father Wayna Qhapaq transferred the local population to other regions and replaced them with 14,000 workers to grow maize in the state's fields. Although not all these workers were *mitmaq*, the Cochabamba maize fields are another example of how the Incas carefully managed and transformed traditional forms of labor to meet new levels of imperial needs and ambitions. Exactly how communities were persuaded to relocate is difficult to fully comprehend, and no doubt they often refused and rebelled. The *mitmaq* institution, however, becomes more comprehensible when viewed as a response to a varied environment.

In contrast to typical highland patterns, coastal groups rarely established members of their own communities in highland satellite settlements. On the desert coast, the lord of Chincha, who became an important Inca ally, ruled a kingdom comprising groups of specialized farmers, fishermen, and long-distance traders. The lush, irrigated valleys supplied ample crops, while coastal waters provided fish, making these communities more self-sufficient than the highland ones. Of course, although the coastal communities could ensure their subsistence needs, they lacked substantial quantities of luxury camelid fibers, some metal ores, certain feathers, and other sumptuary goods. Coastal societies obtained non-local luxury goods through exchange networks or alliances with highland societies. The north-coast Chimú, for example, produced mostly cotton cloth and acquired pre-spun and dyed camelid fiber from the highlands, using it sparingly.[3] The Incas' particular interest in Chincha and its trading specialists may point to an emerging emphasis on more efficient exchange mechanisms, particularly for goods from faraway sources. At the same time, however, it was in the Inca state's best interests to gain or retain control over such highly valuable goods as *Spondylus*, certain fibers, and feathers and other components of high-status goods. The ever-growing importance of sumptuary goods linked to prestige and status in the expanding empire emerges as a key motivation for expansion itself. The search for mineral ores, warm lands to sustain maize crops, shells, feathers, and other components of luxury goods will be a constant theme in later chapters as we survey Inca influence and expansion into new territories.

Terraces, breweries, and warehouses

The Incas inherited a wide range of domesticated plants and animals from their Andean predecessors, as well as a broad range of agricultural techniques, land improvement methods, and a detailed understanding of the environment. As we have seen, Inca leaders enhanced these inherited technologies and resources with new initiatives and innovations that boosted and refocused human efforts to improve production and increase wealth.

Inca investment in their elaborate road system and in urban infrastructure supported a whole range of economic and political ends. Even more important than the system's practical benefits for travelers were the facilities in the centers along the roads that housed work areas for cloth and beer production. In addition to actual production amenities, the largest administrative centers provided urban settings and impressive ceremonial backdrops for political and economic activities. As we know from both ancient and modern cities, the attractions of bringing people together in new and exciting circumstances are themselves motivators for economic and political action. Life in Inca settlements had an urban vitality that allowed commoners the opportunity to observe and associate with an economic and social elite.

The Inca state supported its cities and other imperial installations from its fields and warehouses. Many of the cities were artificial and built far away from areas of intensive agricultural production. The state built a massive and technologically advanced warehousing system to provide food and other goods where they were needed. As Cieza recounts: "They had…many lodgings and great storehouses filled with all necessary supplies… Certain depots were filled with fine clothing, others, with coarser garments, and others, with food and every kind of victuals…nothing, from the most important to the most trifling, but could be provided."[4]

39 Agricultural terraces at Moray overlooking the Urubamba valley near Cusco. Builders took advantage of limestone sinkholes to create these terracing systems.

In Cusco, and particularly in the administrative centers along the Cusco–Quito road, the storehouses supplied the needs of a rich urban lifestyle and the raw materials required for production. Some scholars have interpreted Inca warehouses as evidence of a benevolent socialist state.[5] While the aims of the storage system reflect the Incas' political and economic agenda, it seems likely that the populace benefited from the stored staples during years of poor harvests. As Cieza noted: "If there came a lean year, the storehouses were opened and the provinces were lent what they needed in the way of supplies."[6]

Cloth, shells, silver, and gold

Since the Incas organized their imperial economy largely without markets, the value of various goods, except for certain staples such as potatoes, was established through their role in a complex system of social relationships and rituals. The Incas made production choices to supply these needs and to reward citizens for their labor and their loyalty to the ruler.

But how did value enhancement work in the Inca economy? In the case of the highly valued spiny oyster (*Spondylus princeps*), harvested in deep waters off the coast of modern-day Ecuador, its distant source and difficulty of acquisition made it rare, while the coral-hued shell turned it into an easily recognizable object of adornment. However, the shell's fundamental attribute may relate to its association with life-giving rain—a quality so important that the shell became the favored food of the gods—and fertility. Its religious connotations enhanced the importance and status of those who possessed it. PL. 85

Shiny precious metals, mainly gold and silver and their alloys, also underscored the social basis of value. Centuries before the Incas, Andean metallurgists had developed techniques that enabled them to create large shiny objects containing relatively small amounts of gold or silver. This emphasis on glitter and color contrasts with the interests of Old World metallurgists, who focused primarily on a metal's hardness to produce weapons and tools.[7] Adornments with glittering surfaces formed part of the ritual paraphernalia of important persons, placing them at the heart of ceremonial life. They not only increased the spectacle of the ceremony, but their use by already powerful and important people mutually enhanced the value of the objects and the status of those who wore them. PLS 86, 87

Among the most important gold objects were the ear spools that royal men wore in their pierced ears. Both the size and materials used for ear ornaments varied according to the social hierarchy: "Each one, according to rank, pierced his ears as law required."[8] The Spaniards referred to noble men as *orejones* ("big ears"), since even when the ornaments were not in place the elongated earlobes drooped. According to the chronicler Garcilaso de la Vega,[9] the materials used for ear ornaments ranged from a symbolic stick, wood, and various metals, to large gold or gold-covered ear spools, and the size of the ruler's ear perforations was at least twice that of anyone else's.

Perhaps the most significant royal gifts were the paired sets of wooden, ceramic, or metal drinking beakers called *keros* or *aquillas*, which the Inca ruler offered to the leader of a group he wished to incorporate into his empire. The act of offering the beakers, often made of precious metals, customarily initiated 40, PL. 81

40 A pair of wooden Inca-style *keros* or ceremonial drinking cups, found at Laguna de los Cóndores in the cloud forest of northern Peru. *Keros* such as these were commonly issued to lords of 100 households.

the process of "conquest," and, if accepted, and following the appropriate toast, a friendly relationship began. If it was refused, the consequences could be dire.[10] At Huarco in Peru's coastal Cañete valley, for instance, "[Topa Inca] advanced with his troops in orderly fashion, and sent…emissaries, at times with gifts, at times with threats and menaces," but the people of Huarco resisted for many years until they finally capitulated. Topa Inca, however, decided to use the people of Huarco as an example and "ordered his troops to kill all of them, and with great cruelty they carried out his command and killed all the nobles and most honorable men…the huge piles of bones bear witness."[11]

PLS 88–91   Fine garments and other extraordinary cloth objects were regarded among the most valued manufactured objects in the Andes centuries before the rise of the Incas. Textiles featured in virtually every social situation, from birth to death, and exchanges of cloth underlay practically all significant relationships.[12] The state controlled the production and distribution of many classes of garments, particularly those bearing designs symbolizing rank and position.[13] The Inca rulers and their officials issued or bestowed fine cloth to various members of the society. Since the Incas controlled cloth production and distribution, they used such "gifts" to confer and define the social status of the recipients. To enhance and control production of the finest cloth, the Incas maintained groups of specialized weavers, such as the famous cloistered *aqlla*, as well as male weavers, called *qumpikamayuq*.

The Incas also imbued maize with ceremony; indeed, the ritual uses of maize, combined with the inebriating effects of maize beer, endowed it with a value far greater than its nutritional benefits. Brewers, mainly women, transformed a large portion of the grain into beer, which in turn figured as the key elixir in feasts and ceremonies. The importance of maize and beer to Inca rule is mirrored by the enormous investments they made in expanding maize production, through terracing systems and warehouses. Unlike major food staples such as potatoes, other tubers, and root crops, maize featured as a luxury ingredient in official feasts and rituals critical to the expansion of the state and its economy.

The Incas left most of the day-to-day needs of their subjects in the hands of *ayllus* overseen by local leaders. In the empire's final years, however, the state and its elite became increasingly intrusive in local affairs by appropriating more and more land for Cusco's objectives. Labor too became increasingly redirected to serve the Inca and the religion, especially long-term state service through institutions such as *aqlla* and *yana*, leaving people with less time to tend their fields. But the state, with its enormous ritual apparatus centered in Cusco and other imperial cities, focused mainly on the goods to which it could add value. Although it did not fully control fine cloth, maize beer, the mildly narcotic coca leaf, or *Spondylus*, it did monopolize their production and distribution.

Religion played a vital part in virtually all the rituals and ceremonies organized by the Incas as part of their economic and political initiatives. We turn to the complex world of Andean religion under the Incas in the following chapter.

5 · Religion and Ideology: The Sun, the Moon, the Oracles, the Ancestors

At the edge of the Lurín valley, south of modern Lima, a vast walled city of adobe rises from the desert sands overlooking the Pacific Ocean. Its highest structure, a five-tiered Inca sun temple once painted deep red, crowns the summit of a low hill, flanked to the west by wetlands bordering a broad beach. Near the Inca temple stands another building, the much older temple of Pachacamac, richly adorned with murals depicting men, fish, birds, and plants. It housed, the Incas believed, Pachacamac's oracle, "in a very dark chamber with a close fetid smell. Here there was a very dirty idol made of wood and they say that this is their God who created them and sustains them."[1]

The city of Pachacamac, one of the most important Andean pilgrimage centers of its time, highlights the tensions between imperial and provincial ideologies. For its walls not only enclosed an Inca sun temple but also the temple of Pachacamac, a pre-Inca oracle so powerful and influential that the Incas allowed it to function alongside the shrine devoted to the imperial solar cult. "It is said," wrote Cieza, "that he [Topa Inca] was very desirous of having there only a temple to the sun; but as that shrine [Pachacamac] was so venerated by the natives, he refrained, and contented himself with having a great temple to the sun built."[2]

The Inca attitude toward Pachacamac demonstrates, once again, the flexibility of imperial strategies in governing conquered lands and their gods. By forging an alliance with a regional pilgrimage center and oracle, the Incas not only formed a spiritual pact with an incorporated region but also manipulated its ideology. Nonetheless, the Incas expected conquered peoples to acknowledge the sun and the moon as superior, and the Inca ruler and his sister-consort, the *Qoya*, as their offspring. Inca state religion focused on Inti, the solar deity, whose principal temple was the Qorikancha in Cusco. In his role as tutelary god, Inti served as both an ancestor of the ruling Inca and as a symbol for the expanding Inca state.

Confused and contradictory accounts reflect attempts by the Spaniards to simplify the Inca religious system. Even Juan de Betanzos, an astute and well-versed sixteenth-century observer, fluent in Quechua and married to Atawallpa's niece and consort, showed his bewilderment and Christian convictions when he wrote, "Sometimes the devil [said] he was the Sun and in other places he said he was the Moon. He told others he was their god and creator. He told others he was their light who warmed them and shined on them, and thus they would see him in the volcanoes of Arequipa."[3]

"Glad words"—the voice of oracles

Oracles—large and small, regional and local—and their predictions played a central role in the pre-Inca Andes, as well as in imperial religion and politics. Not only did oracular shrines (often regarded as ancestors of descent groups) give prophecies, but their opinions, especially those of regional oracles and revered, royal ancestors, allowed them to contradict the power, authority, and divinity of the ruler.[4] As part of their strategy in winning over conquered provinces, Inca rulers allied with strategic provincial shrines (as in the case of Pachacamac). They also consulted oracles before embarking on major military and administrative matters. Atawallpa's father Wayna Qhapaq, for example, sought advice from an oracle on whether he should widen "the Quito road," ordering it "built larger and wider than his father [Topa Inca] had made."[5]

Every year the sovereign summoned portable versions of the empire's leading *wakas* (shrines), accompanied by their priests (who acted as mediums) and their *kurakas*, to Cusco for an oracular congress, expecting to receive "glad words." The Willaq Umu, the high priest of the sun and the empire's highest-ranking medium, presided over the congress and "had power over all the shrines and temples, and appointed and removed priests."[6] He served as the voice of the sun: "He talked on his own behalf and as himself, and other times in place of the Sun, as if the Sun were a man."[7]

Officials kept track of the oracles' predictions, and rewarded those whose prophecies came true with gold and silver, fine cloth, and llamas. Especially "honest" or accurate oracle-*wakas* and heads of provinces and lineages such as Pachacamac, Coropuna, and Catequil received gift-bearing processions known as *qhapaq hucha*, headed by young boys and girls destined for sacrifice. The power and prestige of oracular shrines rose and fell according to the veracity of their auguries, and the Incas punished the shrines whose predictions did not bode well. Catequil, for instance, an important oracular shrine and mountain deity located in the northern highlands of Peru (people believed he created lightning bolts and thunder by hurling stones with a sling) predicted that Atawallpa "would have an unfortunate end"[8] in the war of succession with his brother, Waskar. An enraged Atawallpa climbed up to the sanctuary and "gave the idol such a blow in the neck with the battle-ax he carried that he cut off the head. They then brought the old man, who was held as a saint and who had given the idol's reply...[and he] also beheaded him with his battle-ax."[9] Atawallpa was also displeased with Pachacamac's prediction that Waskar would emerge victorious in the war of succession between the two brothers, and he encouraged the Spaniards to ransack the sanctuary.

Imperial sun temples

People believed that the reigning Inca king, the Sapa Inca, not only descended from Manco Qhapaq, the mythical founding ancestor, but was also the human manifestation of Inti, the sun. Because of the primacy of Inti and his human manifestation in the Inca ruler, the Qorikancha, Cusco's sun temple, ranked as the empire's most important shrine, followed by those at Lake Titicaca and Pachacamac. Aside from the Qorikancha, the Incas dedicated three other

41

41 A wall of beautifully built andesite blocks formed the enclosure wall of the Qorikancha, the temple of the sun. Spanish clergy built the church of Santo Domingo on the site of the sun temple.

temples in Cusco to the sun. Some of these may also have functioned as solar observatories and included Saqsawaman, which Cieza described as a "house of the sun," Mantocalla, and Puquín, where recent excavations uncovered finely made ashlars. Puquín may be the "Poquen" referred to by Cieza, who calls it a house of the sun and adds that it housed painted wooden panels illustrating the origin myths and the genealogy and life history of each Inca ruler.

Nonetheless, the Qorikancha served as the conceptual model for a network of sun temples across the realm. Sun temples received endowments of religious specialists, *aqlla*, land—much of it devoted to maize cultivation—as well as pastures to sustain large herds of camelids. As with all pilgrimage centers, only the most devout could enter the Qorikancha's inner sanctum after fasting and abstaining from salt, meat, hot peppers, and sex for a year; and they could only enter barefoot and carrying a burden, as a sign of submission and reverence.

The ruler's main wife, or *Qoya*, served as the human manifestation of Quilla, the moon. "The Moon was the sister and wife of the Sun and…mistress over the sea and winds, over the queens and princesses, and over [childbirth]; and she is queen of the sky."[10] Aside from her temple in the Qorikancha, Quilla had several shrines dedicated to her on the outskirts of Cusco, where Miguel de Estete, an early eyewitness, observed "many life-sized statues and figures of gold and silver, all cast in the forms of women." She was fêted at Qoya Raymi, the September equinox festival that coincided with the onset of the agricultural cycle and the rainy season. Because of the chroniclers' patriarchal bias, they often ignored lunar worship and its obvious links to women, and their patchy references to it belie its importance.

The Incas regarded Illapa, the lightning god, who apparently also had a shrine devoted to him in Cusco's Qorikancha, as the sacred force controlling thunder and, by extension, all celestial phenomena, such as rain, hail, and the rainbow. "They imagined that he…lived in the sky and was made up of stars, with a war club in his left hand and a sling in his right hand. He dressed in shining garments which gave off flashes of lightning when he whirled his sling, when he wanted it to rain."[11]

The revered ancestors

The Incas and other Andean peoples venerated natural features in the landscape from which they believed that their ancestors had emerged, and called these origin places *paqarinas*. "Their [*paqarinas*] have different shapes and names, according to their provinces: some had stones, others springs and rivers, others caves, others animals and birds and different kinds of trees and plants."[12]

Ayllus, or kin groups, not only adored their *paqarinas* but also venerated founding ancestors, frequently envisaged as upright stones. Some important ancestor mummies, called *mallkis*, often became *wakas* and oracular shrines. The Incas commemorated especially important *paqarinas* by building elaborate constructions near them. One such example is Maukallaqta, the original Paqariqtampu ("origin tampu"), near the Tampu T'uqu cave where the Incas' founding ancestor Manco Qhapaq and his siblings emerged from below ground. Maukallaqta is said to have housed Manco Qhapaq's oracle.[13]

42 The summit of Wanakawri overlooking the Cusco valley was one of the Incas' holiest shrines, linked to the wanderings of their mythical founding ancestors, Manco Qhapaq and his siblings.

Mountain *paqarinas* were especially influential and often regarded as the abodes of powerful weather gods. People identified mountains as sources of water and fertility, believing that they controlled rain, thunder, and lightning and, by extension, the fertility of crops and herds. To provide rainfall and fertility, the mountains had to be appeased and lavished with gifts. Offerings of child sacrifices to mountains provide some of the most compelling evidence for Inca ritual practices.   78–80

Wanakawri, a mountain near Cusco, marked the site where one of Manco Qhapaq's siblings was magically transformed into stone, and became Cusco's   42 second most important *waka* after Tampu T'uqu. Badly eroded structures near the summit of Wanakawri pinpoint the location of the ancient shrine, where the Incas worshipped a "medium-sized, un-carved and spindle-shaped" rock.[14] There, according to Cieza, "on certain days women and men were sacrificed."[15] Sacrifices and pilgrimages to Wanakawri were part of Qhapaq Raymi, the summer solstice rite, which was "the most serious and solemn festival of the whole year"[16] and also featured the initiation rites of noble Inca youths.

The sacred origins of kingship

In Chapter 2 we described one Inca origin myth that tells how Manco Qhapaq, the founding Inca, and his siblings emerged from a cave near Paqariqtampu, south of Cusco, and underwent a series of travails before founding Cusco. This myth may reflect early Inca times in the Cusco basin and provide justification for their dominion over the many ethnic groups living in and around Cusco.

Another origin myth centers on Tiwanaku, the important pre-Inca center near Lake Titicaca, and on the lake itself. It tells of a creator god, Tiqsi Wiraqocha, and his role in the creation of humans, as well as the birth of the sun, the moon, and the stars. "For many days they were without light, and when they were all in darkness and gloom, there arose from this island of Titicaca the sun in all its splendor, for which reason they hold the island to be a hallowed spot."[17] People living in the Titicaca basin worshipped the sun long before the Incas and regarded the Island of the Sun as its birthplace. After they had conquered the region, the Incas appropriated the local solar origin myth and fused it with that of their own founding ancestors, creating the hybrid myth recorded by some chroniclers. This composite version describes how the Inca ancestor-founder Manco Qhapaq and his sister-consort emerged from the waters of Lake Titicaca and traveled underground to emerge in Paqariqtampu and found Cusco.

The hybrid myth evokes Inca ideology as the empire began expanding beyond Cusco, conquering other peoples and grafting local and regional origin myths and gods onto their increasingly elaborate mythology and cosmology. Although imperial manipulation of religion was apparently gradual, it eventually allowed the Incas to create a mythology that legitimized their rule and served as a rationale for expansion, "[magnifying] their origins."[18]

Astronomy and the ritual calendar

Across the empire, scores of public and private ceremonies punctuated each month. An extremely accurate calendar, based on solar, lunar, sidereal, and planetary observations, regulated the empire's annual cycle of religious festivals, as well as the agricultural year. "They know the revolutions the sun makes, and the waxing and waning of the moon. They counted the year by this and it consists of twelve months, by their calculations."[19]

Religious specialists tracked the movements of the sun, moon, and stars to program the most important rituals in Cusco and Tawantinsuyu, recording their calendrical observations on a special *khipu* known as a *quilla wata khipu*, or lunar year *khipu*. As the empire grew ever larger, it became increasingly important and complicated to coordinate ritual activities. The Incas employed different forms of calendar reckoning, taking into account solar, lunar, stellar, and planetary rhythms.[20]

The twelve-month lunar calendar consisted of 354 days—eleven days short of the solar year of 365.25 days; possibly an intercalation month was added to reconcile the two calendars.[21] Commoners used the simpler lunar calendar as well as stellar and solar observations. Cusco's elite, however, established a new calendar fixed and determined by solar observations. There are indications

43 The Inca pilgrimage center on the Island of the Sun in Bolivia ranked among the holiest of the empire's shrines. These walls formed part of a precinct that included a sun temple, an *aqllawasi*, and storerooms.

that, as sun worship spread, the traditional lunar calendar was being replaced or dovetailed with the new solar calendar. The solar calendar not only entrenched ritual authority in Cusco, but also underscored the special link between the reigning Inca and the sun.

In Cusco, pairs of rectangular stone pillars placed on the western and eastern horizons framed summer or winter solstice sunrises and sunsets, and tracked the movement of the sun across the horizon from solstice to solstice. The number of pillars reported by the chroniclers ranges from eight to sixteen, and they must have been tall enough to be seen by those gathered in Cusco's main square. Archaeologists have uncovered evidence for similar pillars on Lake Titicaca's Island of the Sun, where participants could observe the June solstice setting-sun framed between pillars positioned 105 ft (32 m) apart on a ridge northwest of the plaza.[22]

Andean peoples perceived solar and lunar eclipses as terrifying calamities. Although the Incas observed eclipses, they did so "without understanding their

44 A carved rock surrounded by a curved wall at the so-called Torreón, Machu Picchu.
The structure may have served as a celestial observatory.

causes."[23] They believed that solar eclipses signaled the sun's anger and foretold
"the approach of some grave punishment." During a lunar eclipse, "they were
seized with fear and sounded trumpets, bugles, horns, drums... They tied up
their dogs...and beat them with many blows and made them howl."[24] They
believed the moon would take pity on the dogs and "awake from the sleep
caused by her sickness,"[25] for they thought the moon had died or fallen ill.

Thousands of people congregated in Cusco's main plaza to observe important sunrises and sunsets. Cusco's political and religious elite may also have
attended private rituals involving shadow- and light-casting devices in the
Qorikancha. Similar rites may have taken place at the famous settlement of
Machu Picchu, where the so-called Torreón may have served as a celestial
observatory. One window in the Torreón framed the rise of the Pleiades in the
fifteenth century, while stone pegs on the exterior of the temple possibly held a
shadow-casting device. This device would have cast a shadow on the edge of a
flattened rock within the Torreón that may have marked the June solstice
sunrise in the fifteenth century.[26]

44

People observed the Milky Way, especially its "dark cloud" constellations (formed by patches of interstellar dust) in which they saw a llama, a fox, a tinamou (a small game bird), a toad, and a snake, among other images. "In general [the Incas] believed that all the animals and birds had their likeness in the sky."[27] In addition, they observed stars of differing magnitudes—including the Pleiades, which they called *qollqa* (storehouse)—to determine the onset of the maize harvest.

Imperial rites and sacred occasions

When the Incas conquered a province, they took a portable version of its leading *waka* to Cusco, where they kept it as an honored hostage. Although the *wakas* eventually returned to their places of origin after the provinces had accepted Inca rule, once a year the empire's foremost *wakas* were required to return to Cusco, accompanied by their *kurakas* and priests, to participate in an oracular congress.

During another festival known as the Citua, "evils" were expelled from Cusco. All non-Incas and people with physical defects had to leave the city, while the nobles and citizens of Cusco observed the new moon from the Qorikancha. Once the moon had been seen, squadrons representing Cusco's royal and non-royal lineages ran off in the directions of the four *suyus* until they reached a large river where they washed, allowing the river to carry the evils and sickness to the sea. People in Cusco also washed, and those who had been required to leave the city were allowed to return.

Subsequently, all "the things that were to be offered in the sacrifice were brought [to Cusco's main square]." These included 200 children aged four to ten, gold and silver figurines, fine cloth, seashells, and feathers and llamas of all colors. "They entered into the main square where the Inca sat on his golden stool. The statues of the Sun, Lightning and Thunder and the embalmed Incas with their priests processed around the square twice, bowing before the statues and the Inca."[28] The Inca ruler then consulted the *wakas* and asked them to make predictions. "[They] announced…whether there would be abundance or scarcity; whether the Inca would have a long life, or might, perchance, die that year; if enemies might be expected to invade the country from some side, or if some of the pacified peoples would rebel… And this was asked not of all the oracles together, but one by one."[29]

Later, "the Inca ordered the distribution…of the sacrifices that had to be offered at the guacas [*wakas*] of the city and at the provincial guacas from throughout his kingdom."[30] Once all the *wakas* of Cusco had been served with sacrificial offerings, the "provincial priests took what had been allotted to the guacas of their lands."[31] Known as *qhapaq hucha* (or capacocha, meaning "sacred obligation"), these rituals were not bestowed on all the *wakas* but only on those "who were heads of provinces or lineages."[32] Pachacamac featured among the chosen provincial *wakas*, lavished each year with "human beings, both female and male, from [Tawantinsuyu], the four quarters of the world."[33]

While there is some confusion in the chronicles regarding when the *qhapaq hucha* took place, there is a consensus among scholars that cyclical and extraordinary as well as regional and imperial ones occurred. Annual *qhapaq huchas* were dedicated to the health, long life, and prosperity of the Sapa Inca and his *Qoya*, while unscheduled events marked times of upheaval, such as the death of an Inca ruler, drought, or an earthquake. On his deathbed, Wayna Qhapaq, for instance, "ordered that great sacrifices be made for his health in all the land and at all the *wakas* and temples of the Sun."[34]

PLS 75–80, 85, 89, 92 The *qhapaq hucha* ceremony is one of the few Inca rituals described in the chronicles that has been borne out by archaeology: sacrifices of young boys and girls or young *aqlla*, found in mountaintop sanctuaries, accompanied by offerings of gold, silver, *Spondylus*, fine cloth, coca, and feathers—objects harvested or produced under imperial supervision, with limited circulation.[35] As Juan de Betanzos records, "They sacrificed many boys and girls, whom they interred alive and sumptuously dressed. The [children] were buried in pairs of male and female, and with each pair they buried silver and gold household utensils... These children were the sons and daughters of caciques [lords] and chiefs."[36]

Sacred processions accompanied the young children designated as offerings to the provincial *wakas*. "They went straight toward the place where they were going without turning anywhere, going over hills and through ravines until each one reached his land. The children who could walk went on foot, but they carried the very tiny ones on their backs, along with the gold and other things."[37] The child sacrifices discovered at high-altitude sanctuaries, many of them on the summits of snow-clad volcanoes over 16,500 ft (5,000 m) high, are found mainly in Kuntisuyu and Qollasuyu (the southwestern and southern quadrants of the empire, respectively; see pages 230–33 for a discussion of these discoveries).

Processions, networks, and order

The empire-wide *qhapaq hucha* processions and offerings mirror the rituals and sacrifices offered to the network of shrines that defined Cusco's ritual and economic organization. Forty-two imaginary lines, known as *ceques*, defined by the shrines located along them, crossed the Cusco valley, radiating out from or near the Qorikancha. Royal *ayllus*, known as *panakas*, and non-royal lineages were responsible for particular *ceques*, maintaining them and making offerings to their *wakas*. Chinchaysuyu, Antisuyu, and Qollasuyu contained nine *ceques* each, while Kuntisuyu included fifteen. Accounts of the system, taken from a *khipu*, list the *ceques* in groups of three; these, in turn, were ranked *kollana*, *payan*, and *kayao*. The terms apparently reflect kinship hierarchies, with *kollana* designated as the most prestigious line in each group of *ceques*.[38]

45 The "tired stone" near Saqsawaman, Cusco, one of several carved limestone outcrops dotting the hills surrounding the Inca capital. Many stones were viewed as sacred; according to legend, this stone refused to budge and wept blood.

The Cusco *ceques* are not necessarily straight, as scholars once thought, but zigzag across the landscape from shrine to shrine.[39] Altogether, some 328 *wakas* lay along the *ceques*. As we saw earlier, some *ceque* shrines commemorated mythical events and the lives and deeds of particular rulers. More than half of the *wakas* mark water sources, and they also included hills and passes, palaces and temples, springs and canals, tombs, ravines, caves, quarries, trees, and roads. Because so many *ceque wakas* signaled water sources or the origins of irrigation canals, seashells featured among the most common offerings. Mamacocha (Mother Sea) was "the mother of all waters," and seashells, the "daughters of the sea," were offered to springs, rivers, and lakes.[40]

Ceques were not limited to the immediate Cusco area. Every year at the winter solstice, priests commemorated Wiraqocha's mythical journey from Lake Titicaca to Cusco (a passage mirrored by that of the sun from solstice to solstice) by walking along a 90-mile-long (150 km) *ceque* that linked Cusco with the temple of Vilcanota, near the watershed between Cusco and Lake Titicaca. This long-distance *ceque* featured nine ritual stops including the temple of Wiraqocha at Raqchi (see pages 216–18). From Cusco the sun traveled northwest toward the ocean, where it disappeared into the sea, a passage also honored by a long-distance *ceque* linking Cusco with Chincha and Pachacamac on the coast and featuring important settlements and shrines (see Chapter 8).

45

Wiraqocha's sinking into the sea is variously described as having occurred at Acarí, Pachacamac, or Manta in Ecuador, probably reflecting the path of an expanding empire.[41] The shrines of Titicaca and Pachacamac ranked second and third in importance, respectively, after the Qorikancha, and this may reflect their links to Wiraqocha's emergence in Lake Titicaca and his disappearance in the Pacific Ocean.

Local and long-distance *ceques* as well as the *qhapaq hucha* processions connected Cusco, the center, with the outermost confines of the empire, embracing volcanoes, Pacific islands, and sanctuaries across Tawantinsuyu. "In this manner [the processions] went walking throughout the land the Inca had conquered…making the said sacrifices until…the road reached the farthest…boundary marker the Inca had placed."[42]

The end of imperial religion

Inca state religion declined in importance in the aftermath of the Spanish invasion, partly because it was indeed imperial religion and relied on state infrastructure to exist, and partly because it bore the first brunt of efforts by the Spanish clergy to stamp out "idolatry." Local beliefs, on the other hand, proved more resilient to Spanish efforts to destroy them, often surviving into the seventeenth century and beyond to become the targets of new campaigns against "idolatry."

In 1535, a young Spanish priest witnessed one of the last Inca ceremonies in Cusco. His words evoke the solemnity of the rituals and the reverence paid to the sun: "All the effigies of the shrines of Cusco [were brought out] on to a plain at the edge of the city in the direction of the sun's rise at daybreak. The most important effigies were placed under very fine, beautifully worked feather awnings… All the lords and chiefs of Cusco [participated,] wearing rich silver cloaks and tunics… They formed up in pairs…in a sort of procession…and waited in deep silence for the sun to rise. As soon as the sunrise began, they started to chant in splendid harmony and unison…as the sun continued to rise, they chanted louder… They all stayed there, chanting from the time the sun rose until it had completely set."[43]

6 · Technology and the Arts: Architects, Potters, Weavers, and Smiths

As the Inca empire expanded, it imposed its distinctive style on architecture, pottery, weaving, and metalwork. Architects built the backdrops, rich in symbols, through which an elaborate ceremonial life helped to create the new imperial order. Textiles, imbued with age-old Andean social and ideological symbolism, continued to be the most effective medium, the most valued commodity, and the most prestigious gift. Precious metals, especially gold and silver—associated with the divine sun and moon, the Inca ruler and his wife-consort, as well as the origin myths of Tawantinsuyu—conveyed status, wealth, and political power in life as well as in death. Pottery, though important, had less impact than cloth or metals, but the standardized forms and uncluttered geometric designs made it instantly recognizable.

The visual strength and clarity of Inca art and architecture, as well as the tendency to repeat a fairly limited repertoire of motifs (which made them easy to copy), can best be understood in terms of their role as the official media of communication. Artisans working for the state produced most of the bold architecture, metalwork, textiles, and ceramics. The state controlled production not just to guarantee substantial quantities of necessary and valuable goods, but also because it wanted to stamp those objects and buildings with its own identity. Yet this uniformity of style was not apparent everywhere. The diversity of objects whose production escaped imperial control reflects the patchwork nature of Tawantinsuyu. Sometimes local artisans combined elements of the imperial style, and in other cases they ignored it almost completely. Not surprisingly, some of these stylistic relationships reflect the extent of local resistance to Inca rule.

As the most visible and effective symbol of Inca power, the architectural remains of the Inca empire, scattered across the Andes from Ecuador to Argentina, are its most lasting legacy, echoing Cieza's words: "[They] were of beautiful stone and finely constructed [and] will endure for time and ages without…disappearing."[1] The nineteenth-century naturalist Alexander von Humboldt summed up the essence of the style, noting its "simplicity, symmetry and solidity."[2] Remarking on the similarity of the constructions he saw in the northern part of the empire, Humboldt observed that they appeared to have been designed by "a single architect." The forms of Inca buildings and stylistic elements, such as trapezoidal doorways, windows, and niches, show considerable standardization, and served as hallmarks of the style.

46, 47, PL. 129

77

46 ABOVE The main gateway at Machu Picchu. Barholds on either side of the doorway probably served to secure a wooden door.

47 OPPOSITE, LEFT Trapezoidal niches, windows, and doorways are one of the hallmarks of the Inca architectural style.

48 OPPOSITE, RIGHT A carved stone monolith, embellished with a stepped diamond pattern, at Ollantaytambo.

Although Inca stoneworking technology does not appear to have derived from Tiwanaku as several chroniclers claimed,[3] the Incas did borrow decorative elements of Tiwanaku stonework (such as a distinctive zigzag step motif), while the great Inca plazas designed for massive ceremonies recall Tiwanaku and its mastery of glittering spectacle. The large enclosures and gridlike plan of Pikillaqta, a Wari settlement south of Cusco, and the fieldstone (unworked stone collected from the surface of fields) enclosures and niched halls of Chokepukio, in Cusco's Lucre basin, also influenced the imperial style.

The basic unit of Inca architecture, a rectangular structure lacking interior divisions, formed the style's building block.[4] The structures served a variety of functions, from dwellings to palaces and temples. A *kancha*, for example, consisted of several rectangular structures set around a courtyard and enclosed by a high wall with a single entryway. These varied in size from a large city block, such as Cusco's Qorikancha, to Ollantaytambo's smaller blocks of two *kanchas* (each *kancha* composed of four buildings around a small courtyard). One or more *kallankas* (large rectangular halls) often fronted large plazas. These halls, some of the largest structures ever built in the ancient Americas, served as temporary lodgings or as public places for feasting.

The classic imperial style, which some scholars associate with the legendary ruler Pachakuti, is evident in Cusco's Qorikancha and at Pisaq, Machu Picchu, and parts of Ollantaytambo—settlements that are all attributed to Pachakuti's *panaka*, or lineage group. This style features largely rectangular buildings with symmetrically arranged doors and niches, all distinctly trapezoidal and accomplished in well-fitted, coursed masonry (regular rows of rectangular masonry).

48

9
10

50

49

56

49 ABOVE Large halls with multiple doorways facing plazas, such as this one at Huánuco Pampa, are a typical feature of Inca provincial settlements.

50 OPPOSITE Reconstruction of an Inca-style *kancha* at Ollantaytambo, where a city block typically contained two *kanchas*, each composed of four buildings surrounding a central courtyard. The house in the center had a common wall but the *kanchas* were not connected. Double-jambed doorways led into the compounds.

Settlements, especially in the Cusco region, tend to be located on mountain tops or ridges, oriented toward mountains or other landscape features. The later imperial style, perhaps beginning during the reign of Wayna Qhapaq, featured oversized doorways, high rooms, and tall, double-jambed niches.[5]

Key to the spread of the Inca style was the empire's access to labor and its ability to organize a huge workforce. Many of the masons were part-time workers, who provided their labor in rotation, while others were full-time specialists. The workforce quarried, shaped, and moved stone to building sites, constructed roads, bridges, irrigation canals, and agricultural terraces, and tamed rivers with retaining walls. Many Inca sites reflect local building traditions and styles, the ethnic origins of the laborers who built the sites, or the relationship between the state and local groups.

Building temples, palaces, terraces, and storehouses

As elsewhere in the ancient world, the placement of Inca settlements, as well as the alignments of certain buildings within them, often reflected concepts of sacred geography and cosmology. Views of sacred mountains or passes and the heavens and horizons, as well as the proximity of water (springs, lakes, the sea), all played a role in the location of Inca settlements. Frequently, the individuality of Inca settlements reflects the way that Inca architects took advantage of a site's natural setting. Machu Picchu is only the most famous example of the Incas' sense of harmony between setting and architecture.

At times, rock outcrops and boulders, carved or uncarved, dictated the location and layout of settlements and sometimes became the focal points of certain buildings, such as the Torreón at Machu Picchu and the temples at Pisaq and Tipón. Aside from sacred considerations, practical ones also influenced the location of settlements, such as proximity to an Inca road, population density, and the availability of resources, both human and natural.[6]

Generally, the Incas founded highland administrative centers on flat or gently inclined terrain, and coastal settlements on valley edges. While there is no fixed distance between administrative centers, they are more regularly spaced in central and northern Tawantinsuyu than in Qollasuyu, probably reflecting more scattered populations in the south, as well as proximity to water

and other resources. In contrast, royal estates (founded by rulers and maintained, after their deaths, by their descent groups) were often built on mountain tops or ridges and involved leveling sloping terrain with retaining walls and terraces. At Chinchero, Tipón, and Huaytará, where terracing is one of the most   51 obvious features, the Incas tamed the natural curves of nature into geometrical shapes. Terraces destined exclusively for agriculture, on the other hand, generally followed the natural contours.

As common as buildings of finely fitted stonework may appear to be to the casual observer, this building style was reserved for the most prestigious structures in and around Cusco, the Urubamba valley, and at select administrative or ceremonial centers throughout the realm. Most Inca structures, in fact, were built of rough fieldstones set in mud mortar or, especially along the coast, of adobe.

In some cases even prestigious structures, such as the temple at Huaytará in the Pisco valley (see pages 140–42), had lower courses of masonry and upper ones of adobe, including the gables. Interiors of buildings were plastered and painted, and even some of the finely built stone walls we see today were covered in a thin layer of plaster. Adobe walls were frequently painted in hues of red and yellow ochre and white, such as Tambo Colorado in the Pisco valley, or   115 Pachacamac, painted with a deep red ochre.

Some Inca centers far from Cusco replicated the capital's "mythical space."[7] Not only did the names of rivers and mountains often recall those of Cusco, but specific architectural features such as plazas, *ushnu* platforms, and sun temples echoed the capital's social, political, and religious concepts. The native chronicler Felipe Guaman Poma de Ayala mentions several "new Cuscos," including Quito and Tumibamba in Ecuador, Huánuco Pampa and Hatun Qolla in Peru, and Charcas in Bolivia. As discussed in Chapter 2, *cozco* may mean "stone of possession" or "boundary marker," and these "new" Cuscos may have been located at or near frontiers at varying stages of Inca expansion. At the same time, the sovereign's presence at a center far from Cusco converted that city into a de facto Cusco.

Although Cusco served as the conceptual model for Inca administrative centers and many distant settlements scattered across the realm, no two Inca sites are alike. Despite their differences, however, all Inca sites emphasized ceremony. Careful planning is evident and most sites share a number of features, including the great halls known as *kallankas*, and plazas with *ushnus* either within or adjacent to the plaza. *Ushnus* range from ceremonial stones, often flanked by carved stone seats and basins for receiving libations, to large, finely built stepped platforms such as the ones at Vilcaswaman or Huánuco Pampa.   52, PL. 135 A large stone outcrop once covered in gold and fine cloth flanking the plaza on the Island of the Sun in Lake Titicaca may also have formed part of an *ushnu*.

51 The royal estate of Tipón, south of Cusco. Fine architecture, waterworks, and terracing that carved the terrain into geometric shapes are features of royal estates.

52 The *ushnu* or ceremonial platform at Huánuco Pampa. These platforms, which symbolized the sun, were commonly located in or flanking plazas. Dignitaries presided over administrative, religious, and military ceremonies from the *ushnus*.

Kallankas generally had numerous doorways facing plazas, and some had a wide entryway at one of the end walls. Chinchaysuyu's centers often boast two or more *kallankas*, while in the south sites generally contain only one *kallanka*. The great hall at Incallaqta in Bolivia was 256 ft (78 m) long and 82 ft (25 m) wide[8] and could have accommodated as many as 600 people. Although little remains of Cajamarca's Inca glory, Spanish eyewitnesses reported that the great halls fronting the town's plaza measured 200 paces in length. The temple of Wira-qocha in Raqchi featured a great hall 302 ft (92 m) long and 82 ft (25 m) wide.

Hip or gable roofs, composed of frameworks of poles and rafters covered by matting and a thick layer of thatch, crowned most Inca structures. Roofing structures as large as the ones at Raqchi or Incallaqta must have been a great challenge. As Cobo noted, "The roof and covering of all these buildings was of large beams without nails. The beams were attached with cords."[9] Inca thatched roofs were quite sophisticated. In his description of the original domed roof covering a structure known as the Sondor Huasi near Huancané in the Lake Titicaca region, the nineteenth-century American traveler George Squier noted vertical and horizontal supports bound with finely braided grass. Over the skeleton of the dome he observed a fine mat of braided cane and another coarser mat to which was "fastened a fleece of finest *ichu* [grass],"

176

174

covered by another layer of coarser grass or reeds, followed again by *ichu* "and so on."[10] One can see why the roof survived for 300 years. As Cieza noted, Inca thatched roofs are "so artfully laid on, that unless destroyed by fire, they will last many ages."[11] The curious stone pegs and eye bonders projecting from gables at Machu Picchu and Choquequirau were used to tie down the thatch and matting rather than the pole and rafter framework.[12] While most Inca buildings were single-story constructions, builders sometimes created two-story buildings by setting wooden beams to support the second floor on projecting stone cornices.

Most Inca walls are straight and slightly battered, although they occasionally built curved walls. These seem to have been reserved for special structures, such as part of the Qorikancha's enclosing wall in Cusco and the Torreón at Machu Picchu, although in the latter case, the large boulder on which the temple rests dictated the shape of the temple's wall. Circular storehouses are found throughout the empire, as are round funerary structures. Though rare in Cusco, circular houses are common in areas where round dwellings existed before Inca expansion, such as the Mantaro valley or Chachapoyas.

Storehouses for the realm

The highlands' marked rainy and dry seasons and frequent droughts required an effective storage system to insure a reliable food supply over time. In such an environment, the state's ability to build and manage a large-scale storage system became a major requirement.

The Incas dotted their realm with thousands of storehouses. These store- 38 houses appeared in many contexts, but, aside from Cusco, they were most commonly part of administrative centers and way-stations, and they are mostly found along the great highland road from Cusco to Quito, underscoring the need for an assured food supply at these important centers far from bountiful cultivation zones. The cool temperature and high altitude of most of these installations made them ideal for storage, and the storehouses were typically located on hills above the centers to take maximum advantage of cooling breezes.

Valuable and easily portable maize filled many of the storehouses. Excava- tions of circular storehouses at Huánuco Pampa found shelled maize stored 22, 37 in large jars. Curiously, excavations in state administrative centers have not uncovered significant quantities of the exceedingly storable *chuño*, made by alternately freezing and drying potatoes during the sunny days and frigid nights of the Andean high plains. Perhaps this very important, but rather bland, food was not sufficiently prestigious to figure in the diet of imperial centers. Many varieties of tubers, however, were carefully stored between layers of straw in storehouses not surpassed in technological sophistication until the development of electro-mechanical refrigeration in the twentieth century. By closing windows and floor vents in well-insulated storage cham- bers during warm days and opening them during cold nights, the Incas maintained an average storage environment close to the temperature most advantageous for tubers. In this manner tubers, including those needed for seed, could be effectively stored for almost a year.[13]

Quarrying and working sacred stones

A number of Inca settlements and shrines in the Cusco region and select places far from Cusco feature carved stones and bedrock outcrops, as well as natural boulders integrated into architecture. Often linked to water—natural streams or intakes of irrigation canals—some stones and outcrops apparently served as boundary markers, while others commemorated ancestors, the feats of legendary rulers or mythical warriors, or served as protectors of agricultural fields or symbols of identity.[14]

Some special stones were unmodified natural boulders, such as the one that graced the shrine of Wanakawri or the sandstone outcrop of Titikala on the Island of the Sun. In other sites, smaller carved boulders feature geometric or abstract designs with the occasional animal figure (generally a puma). While the carved stones include common elements, they lack the rigid standardization so characteristic of official architecture, ceramics, and textiles; many carved stones exhibit a high level of individual artistic creativity.

53　　The imagery carved on the upper Saywite stone, a 2.35-m-high (7¾ ft) limestone boulder, is unique. Located west of Cusco, the boulder may have celebrated the Inca victories in the Chanka wars and marked the frontier between the two rivals. The boulder dominates a terraced platform overlooking a large plaza, an *ushnu*, and other carved stones at Rumiwasi. The upper Saywite stone appears to represent an imaginary landscape, incorporating hills, canals, plants, humans, and, especially, animals. The carving emphasizes figurative representation over the usual geometric style that dominates both Inca architecture and sculpture.[15]

Near the top of the stone are three circular reservoirs supplying a series of canals that irrigate the carved boulder. Several springs bubble forth in the vicinity, but none are connected to the monolith. Water, maize beer, sacrificial blood, or other liquids appropriate for a particular ceremony would have been carried to the stone in vessels and poured into the reservoirs. The flow of water or other liquids may have featured in divination rituals.

The puma, frequently used to symbolize the dominating power of the Incas and their ruler, features prominently on the Saywite stone. It is sculpted lying on its side and occasionally standing, with a human or a trophy head held between its paws. Large pumas seem to delimit the four main sections of the artificial landscape, and another on the lower section may portray "the puma as the carrier of the world,"[16] not unlike the Incas' image of themselves as balancing the world of Tawantinsuyu.

Inca reverence for stone extended to the quarries, such as the limestone outcrops dotting the hills around Saqsawaman, near Cusco, where quarrymen extracted the huge blocks that form Saqsawaman's zigzagging ramparts. At Rumiqolqa, the quarries southeast of Cusco that furnished much of the ancient city's andesite blocks, workers followed natural fractures to extract the stone, using bronze pry bars or thick wooden clubs.

Another, even more impressive source of Inca building stone was the rock-falls of Kachiqata in the Urubamba valley. Much of Ollantaytambo, located 3 miles (5 km) upstream on the opposite bank of the Urubamba, is built of

54

53 OPPOSITE A carved limestone boulder at Saywite, west of Cusco. One of the most intricate examples of Inca stone-carving, it appears to represent an imaginary landscape.

54 ABOVE A partially worked stone at the rockfalls of Kachiqata, ready to be shipped to the building site at Ollantaytambo on the opposite bank of the Urubamba river.

rhyolite extracted from Kachiqata.[17] Kachiqata's highest rockfall rises almost 3,000 ft (900 m) above the valley floor, and the entire area is crisscrossed by a 5½-mile (9 km) network of ramps and roads, along which the quarrymen dragged the stones—some weighing close to 100 tons—from the rockfalls to a chute overlooking the Urubamba, where one block is still wedged. Suddenly, perhaps during the 1536 siege of Ollantaytambo, the quarrymen, rock-dragging crews, and masons stopped work, abandoning some forty blocks in different stages of transport on both sides of the river.

Achieving the fit

57, PL. 131   The Incas developed two remarkable types of tightly fitting masonry: "polygonal" (produced by pounding irregularly shaped stones until they interlocked 56   precisely) and "coursed" (in which rectangular stones were laid in regular courses). How did the Incas achieve the accurate fit between the stones? The most plausible theories of Inca stoneworking are based on evidence from the chronicles, archaeology, and studies of Inca stoneworking technology. Inca masons used hammerstones (fashioned from river cobbles) to form blocks, shaping and reshaping them by pecking and grinding many times until they achieved the desired fit, a technique documented by chroniclers who observed indigenous laborers building fine masonry constructions for their new Spanish 55   masters. In an experiment, it took architect Jean-Pierre Protzen ninety minutes to dress three sides and cut five edges of an andesite block measuring about 10 by 10 by 11¾ inches (25 by 25 by 30 cm).[18] This trial-and-error method recalls José de Acosta's description of 1589: "All this [fitting] was done with much manpower and much endurance…for to adjust one stone to another until they fit together, it was necessary to try the fit many times."[19]

55 OPPOSITE Architect Jean-Pierre Protzen uses a hammerstone to shape a stone block in much the same way as Inca masons.

56 TOP Detail of the enclosure wall of the Qorikancha in Cusco, built in the coursed masonry style.   57 ABOVE A wall at Tarawasi (Limatambo) in the polygonal masonry style.

58, PL. 161

Although this technique demonstrates how the Incas shaped blocks and created walls composed of medium-sized coursed masonry, it does not explain how builders worked and lowered into position massive, monolithic blocks such as the ones at Saqsawaman. How did they fit them to neighboring stones so accurately? One theory posits that the Incas used a compass or scribe made of string, wood, and a stone plumb bob (a method employed by builders of traditional log cabins).[20] It enabled them to transfer the precut shape of an upper stone onto the stone already in place below by following the contour of the upper stone and marking the fit on the stone below. Earthen ramps and log scaffolds supported the stones, in much the same way as Cobo observed: "They transported the stones to where they were needed by pulling them. Having no hoists, wheels, or lifting devices, they made a sloping ramp up against the buildings and lifted the stones by rolling them up this. As the building rose, they raised the ramp proportionately."[21]

As with so much Inca technology, quarrying, transporting, and fitting stone was based on well-honed human skills, energy, and organization. The Spaniards saw indigenous laborers move large stones during the construction of Cusco's cathedral, using "much human labor and great ropes of vine and hemp" as "thick as a leg." Another eyewitness remarked that the stones "were in fact heaved by main force with the aid of thick cables. The roads by which they were brought were not flat, but rough mountainsides with steep slopes, up and down which the rocks were dragged by human effort alone."[22]

58 LEFT Gouges in this limestone block at Saqsawaman may have been used to raise the stone into position.

59 OPPOSITE The Inca road near Huari in Ancash, Peru; here the road is almost 42 ft (13 m) wide.

Linking the empire: roads and bridges

The Inca road and bridge network was one of the New World's greatest engi- 59
neering feats, rivaling that of the Romans in the Old World. The 25,000-mile
(40,000 km) network linked Cusco to its far-flung domains. "In the memory
of people," wrote Cieza, who traveled over the Qhapaq Ñan, the principal
highland road, in the late 1540s, "I doubt there is record of another highway
comparable to this, running through deep valleys and over high mountains,
through piles of snow, quagmires, living rock, along turbulent rivers."[23]

Bridges formed an integral part of the system. Indeed, they played a strategic role in Inca expansion and control of territories that were once isolated by
natural barriers.[24]

Although the Incas reused or re-engineered pre-Inca roads, the imperial roads
and installations built along them were probably conceived as a whole, and
together they display state planning on a scale never before seen in the Andes.

PL. 31,
60

Two roads formed the system's backbone: the Qhapaq Ñan, which linked Cusco and Quito, and a parallel coastal road. Dozens of lateral roads connected the two, and spurs extended from Bolivia as far south as modern Santiago, in Chile, and into northwestern Argentina. The Qhapaq Ñan ran north to a point just shy of the modern Ecuadorian–Colombian border, and a so-called conquest road ran from the great administrative center of Huánuco Pampa in north-central Peru to Chachapoyas, on the forested eastern slopes.

The Qhapaq Ñan certainly impressed early Spanish travelers, and its importance may reflect Wayna Qhapaq's focus in late Inca times on conquests in Ecuador. No other road featured more Inca centers, or boasted longer stretches of formal construction, embellished with stove paving, culverts, drainage canals, and causeways that raised the roadbed above swampy ground.

Road widths varied according to the terrain and their importance. In the high jungle or cloud forest, the Incas built daring, cobbled roads that clung to cliff-sides, with steps and tunnels often cut into the living rock, such as the 65-ft-long (20 m) tunnel cut through solid granite on the road between Puyu Pata Marka and Sayaq Marka, en route to Machu Picchu. There, the steep and rugged terrain forced engineers to design narrow roads between 3 and 10 ft (1–3 m) in width. On the desert coast, where it seldom rains, the road was never paved, and generally was a less formal construction than its highland counterpart.

60 OPPOSITE The Inca coastal road near Guadalupe on Peru's north coast. Desert roads were rarely paved and often flanked by low walls.

61 RIGHT A *chaski* messenger blows a conch shell trumpet. Running in relay, *chaski* messengers could deliver messages between Cusco and Quito in five days.

Some sections of coastal road, however, included flights of steps as the road made its way across low-lying hills. Widths varied from 10 ft to over 30 ft (3–10 m) and, as the road ran through the desert, stones or wooden posts served as markers. When the road reached irrigated valleys, walls of adobe or *tapia* (tamped earth) prevented people and llama caravans from trampling adjacent fields. In these coastal oases, noted Cieza, the road "ran beneath trees, and in many spots the fruit-laden boughs hung over the road."[25]   PL. 30

Travel along the roads was apparently restricted to those occupied in state business: the Inca emperor, accompanied by his court, inspecting his far-flung domains; soldiers engaged in conquest or in countering frequent rebellions; great caravans of llamas carrying produce and goods to stockpile in the store-houses scattered throughout the realm; inspectors and *khipu* masters on state missions; *mitmaq* dispatched as colonists to distant regions; or *chaskis*, the runners who carried messages from one end of the empire to the other. Several chroniclers claim that *chaskis* running in relay could cover 155 miles (250 km) in a day, delivering messages from Quito to Cusco in five days, and that "neither horses nor mules could travel more swiftly."[26]   61

Peoples living in areas traversed by the roads and bridges were responsible for maintenance and repair. Several chroniclers lamented the lack of road upkeep in the wake of the Spanish invasion. The roads "are deteriorating more and more...because of our carelessness and neglect," observed Cobo.[27] At the same time, the pedestrian and llama traffic of Inca times caused less deterioration than the horses and mules introduced by the Spaniards.

Vital to the network were roadside installations, ranging from large administrative centers such as Huánuco Pampa to medium- and small-sized *tampus*, or

62 ABOVE The suspension bridge near Quehue, south of Cusco, is made of braided grass rope. 63 RIGHT The bridge spans a 120-ft-wide (36 m) gorge over the Apurímac river and is small compared to some of the great suspension bridges that crossed rivers in Inca times.

way-stations, which often contained large halls for lodging travelers as well as communal kitchens, storehouses, and llama corrals. The Incas maintained some 2,000 *tampus* along the road system, and generally travelers encountered *tampus* every 3–5 leagues, or 10–15 miles (15–25 km), roughly a day's journey.[28] Scattered along the road were posts for the *chaskis*, control posts at strategic locations, and gatehouses at bridge crossings. At the entrance to Caxas, north of Cajamarca, a Spanish scouting mission led by Hernando de Soto reported "a house by a bridge" where a "guard resided who receives the loads from those who came from Cusco to Quito... No traveler could enter or leave by another road carrying a load, only where the guard is, under penalty of death."[29]

62, 63   The Incas devised ingenious suspension bridges for crossing wide spans, constructed of stout, braided ropes that sagged in the middle and pulled at stone abutments. "The bridge sags with its long span," noted Pedro Sancho, Pizarro's secretary, "so that one is continually going down until the middle is reached and from there one climbs until the far bank... The bridge...trembles very much; all of which goes to the head of someone unaccustomed to it."[30] The suspension bridges had to be replaced annually, and rebuilding one of

the larger bridges took twenty days according to Spanish eyewitnesses, who observed workers replacing a bridge under the direction of a *chakakamayuq*, or bridge master.

The most famed suspension bridge of all crossed the gorge of the Apurímac, west of Cusco on the Chinchaysuyu road. This bridge, near the shrine of Markawasi, achieved fame and literary renown for the beauty of its setting and the fear it struck in the hearts of early European travelers.[31] The approach to the bridge is an extremely steep zigzagging trail, where Cieza noted that several horses laden with gold and silver had slipped and plunged into the river. On the opposite bank the trail passed through a tunnel carved into the rock and pierced by light shafts.[32] Because the bridge had been destroyed by the time that he passed through, Cieza crossed the chasm in a basket, pulling himself along with a rope tied to the stone abutments on either side of the river. Of this terrifying experience, he wrote, "It is a fearful thing to see the risks the men who go out to the Indies undergo."[33]

The bridge was later rebuilt, and Squier, who crossed it in 1865, noted that it measured 148 ft (45 m) in length and at its lowest point loomed 115 ft (35 m)

64 Detail of Inca road construction showing a culvert on the Qhapaq Ñan, the royal road that connected Cusco to Quito. The road system has survived for more than 500 years thanks to sophisticated engineering and drainage.

above the roaring river. It was built of five, 10-cm-thick (4-inch) cables of braided *cabuya* (a fiber extracted from the agave plant) and had a floor of small sticks and canes fastened with rawhide. The braided ropes were anchored to two pairs of stone abutments—which have since collapsed—on either side of the gorge.

The Inca road system did more than facilitate travel. It moved goods, people, and information, and served as a physical and conceptual link between Cusco and its subject peoples in the hinterland. Sometimes the road appears almost over-engineered—as in the case of the Qhapaq Ñan, the Cusco–Quito route. Even in remote sections Inca engineers paved and embellished some stretches 64 with stairs, drains, and culverts—and in this sense the road and bridges were probably as much symbolic as they were practical. The network served as a visible reminder to subject peoples of Inca might and sovereignty and as a symbol of Tawantinsuyu itself.

Imperial tableware

In ceramics, as with almost everything they produced, the Incas built on millennia of technological and artistic achievements. Potters maintained high technical standards, and decorated vessels with clean, geometric polychrome designs. Though rather limited in range, the motifs are vibrant and attractive. Standardized forms and geometric designs are easy to reproduce and lend themselves to mass production. Inca-style ceramics featured prominently at state-sponsored banquets, including vessels for brewing and decanting *chicha*, as well as serving plates and bowls. The so-called *aryballo*, with its distinctive flaring neck and conical bottom, is the most common form found outside Cusco.

PLS 83, 84

PL. 82

Inca-style pottery has been found mainly in Cusco and the centers built by the Incas along their road system. The Incas established specialized pottery manufacturing enclaves, dispatching skilled potters from one part of the realm and resettling them in others, where they produced ceramics for regional consumption. In some cases, Inca-style ceramics overshadowed local wares, while in others potters produced hybrid styles.

66

In Cajamarca, for instance, the Incas set up a pottery workshop staffed by a *pachaka*, who was responsible for 100 potters and their families from the north coast.[34] Milliraya, northeast of Lake Titicaca, included two settlements, one of which housed several hundred potters[35] who produced Inca polychrome and local wares.[36] The Incas admired pottery produced by the Chimú, and blackware Chimú–Inca-style vessels enjoyed widespread distribution, as did ceramics from Pacajes, south of Lake Titicaca. Throughout the empire, the Incas' mass-produced, easily recognizable pottery served as yet another reminder of imperial power.

65

65 BELOW Chimú–Inca blackware ceramics were produced in Inca times by north coast potters and distributed throughout the empire; these were found at Laguna de los Cóndores in the cloud forest of northern Peru.

66 RIGHT A typical Inca-style pedestal jar with a strap handle, used for cooking.

Fine garments and emblems of rank

The Incas, as Andean peoples before them, regarded cloth as the most valued of all goods. By Inca times, weaving had become the second most important economic activity after agriculture. The state invested heavily in cloth production, storing cotton and camelid fiber in state storehouses for distribution to families to manufacture their annual quota of cloth, and for the specialized weavers who produced textiles for the state and for the religion.

Many chroniclers describe storehouses containing camelid fiber, cotton, cloth, garments, and feathers. "The woolen clothing in the storehouses was so numerous and so fine that if it had been kept and not lost, it would be worth a fortune."[37] One of the early eyewitnesses to Atawallpa's capture by the Spaniards in Cajamarca (see pages 235–36) noted storehouses filled with "so much cloth of wool and cotton that it seemed to me that many ships could have been filled with them."[38]

In Inca society, as indeed throughout the ancient Andes, textiles served as ethnic markers and, in some cases, imbued wearers with status and power. In provinces where the Incas had consolidated their rule, local weavers incorporated aspects of the Inca style into their repertoire, creating classic Inca-style garments as well as hybrid styles. Nonetheless, other areas continued to enjoy considerable autonomy, producing cloth much as they had before the Inca conquest. At the same time, the state distributed standardized garments, especially tunics (*unkus*) and small bags used to carry coca leaves, among select subject peoples. Specialized weavers produced these garments at state workshops and *aqllawasi* in Cusco and provincial capitals.

An enclave of state-sponsored weavers has also been documented at Milliraya, where 1,000 specialized weavers produced *qompi* (the finest cloth, usually tapestry) and feather cloth. State-sponsored weavers could be divided into three categories: *aqlla*, or "chosen women," who wove fine cloth for the priests and shrines, as offerings, and for the Inca; the wives of provincial administrators; and *qumpikamayuqs*, male weavers.[39] Cobo noted that weavers produced a variety of textile types: *awaska* ("coarse and ordinary"), *qompi* ("fine and valuable"), a kind of *qompi* "made with colored feathers" or "cloth of silver and gold embroidered in *chaquira* [sequins]," and, finally, a "very thick and coarse [cloth]...used for various rugs and blankets."[40]

Only Inca nobles or those who had received *qompi* as a gift from the ruler could wear fine cloth, especially garments woven from the silky fiber of the vicuña, the wild ancestor of the domesticated alpaca. The sovereign wore garments made of even more exotic materials, as this exchange between Atawallpa and Francisco Pizarro's cousin, Pedro, illustrates: "I felt his cloak, which was softer than silk, and I said 'Inca, what is this soft garment made of?' And he said, 'It is made of some birds that fly at night in Puerto Viejo and in Tumbes, which bite the Indians...' He said it was made of bat skins."[41]

The Incas required vast amounts of feathers to embellish cloth, fashion headdresses, dress their armies, and decorate gateways, litters, and awnings. Indeed, the chroniclers describe storehouses in Cusco filled with feathers and hundreds of desiccated birds, "because from their feathers, which are of many colors, clothing is made, and there are many houses for this."[42] Pedro Pizarro

67,
PLS 88–90,
PL. 92

67 Inca-style *unku* or tunic with red yoke and black-and-white checkerboard motif. Such tunics were apparently worn by warriors.

was astounded by "deposits of iridescent feathers that looked like fine gold and others of a shining golden green color... Quantities of them were threaded together on cotton thread and were skillfully attached to agave stalks... They were all stored in leather chests."[43] On the Island of the Sun in Lake Titicaca, one gateway leading to the sanctuary was covered in hummingbird feathers, while another was festooned with the green and red plumes of the *pilco*, a bird (probably a member of the trogon family) found in the tropical lands of the Chunchos to the east of the lake.

As the empire expanded northward, the number of tropical regions supplying feathers grew accordingly. The cloud forest east of Huánuco Pampa was an important source of feathers. A Spanish inspection of the Huánuco region in 1562 lists the goods and services supplied to Huánuco Pampa by subject communities living in the tropical lowlands to the east, including feather workers (*ttikakamayuq*) and feathers.

Inca garments show considerable standardization of design, especially the *unkus*, or tunics, worn by men. The designs displayed on the *unkus* were proba- PL. 89 bly related to the status of the wearers. Standard attire for women included wrap-around dresses pinned at the shoulders and cinched at the waist with a belt, and a shawl or *llikla* worn around the shoulders, also pinned. Men wore *unkus*, loincloths, and cloaks, and both sexes wore sandals or moccasins. Bright colors and bold designs told knowledgeable observers at a glance the ethnic identity and other essential social and political facts about the wearer. Such

PL. 91 ethnic markers extended to headdresses. As Cieza remarked, "If they were Yungas, they went muffled like gypsies; if Collas, they wore caps shaped like mortars, of wool; if Canas, they wore larger caps and much broader. The Cañari wore a kind of narrow wooden crown like the rim of a sieve; the Huancas, strands that fell below their chin, and their hair braided; the Canchis, broad black or red bands over their forehead. Thus all of them could be recognized by their insignia."[44]

The state devoted much of its cloth production to dressing the army, often reserving some of the finest garments, especially feather cloth, for its soldiers. Provincial storehouses contained "ample supplies of food, clothing, tents, weapons and all the implements of war,"[45] and Estete observed that the storehouses in Cajamarca contained "new clothes" earmarked for the soldiers when Atawallpa formally donned the royal fringe, the Inca equivalent of being crowned.[46] (Inca rulers wore a crimson fringe attached to a golden helmet-like headpiece, held in place by a headband wrapped around the head several times.) Cloth, in fact, played an important role in all aspects of warfare. "[Soldiers] used mantles of thin cotton wrapped many times around the body. Some wore doublets or tunics reinforced also with cotton, with helmets of the same material or wooden helmets. Other helmets were made of plaited cane... All of the men carried small round shields of woven palm slats and cotton on their backs, and they carried other larger shields...sheathed with deerskin and covered on the outer side with a piece of fine cotton, wool or feather-cloth, embroidered in several colors... They fought with slings made of wool or cabuya."[47]

Sadly, such garments and "the defensive weapons that they used...were so light that none could withstand either a blow from a sword or from an iron-headed weapon."[48]

Metalworking: glitter of the sun, glow of the moon

69,
PLS 86, 87

For Andean peoples, the importance of metals was symbolic. Precious metals, especially gold—associated with the divine sun—and silver, linked to the moon, conveyed status, wealth, and political power in life as well as in death. The symbolism of gold and silver reached new heights under the Incas. Sumptuary laws restricted the use of precious metals to the nobility, and by extension, the Inca theoretically held sovereign rights over mines and a monopoly on their output. The symbolic associations of gold with the sun and silver with the moon extended to the use of metal adornments by men and women. Noble men generally wore and used gold, while silver fastened the garments of noble women. Non-nobles mainly used copper and bronze.

As in weaving and pottery-making, the Incas introduced few technological innovations in metallurgy, instead borrowing technologies and deploying skilled artisans around the empire. Their contribution, as in so many other Andean technologies, lay in the scale of production and the widespread distribution of tin bronze, making it the "imperial alloy par excellence" of the Andes.[49] The Incas organized and increased mining on a scale never before seen in the Andes. Some 60 miles (100 km) east of Samaipata in Bolivia, for instance, the Incas established 1,000 miners and 5,000 *mitmaq* to support them.[50]

Along with the laborers assigned to the mines, the Incas set up enclaves of accomplished metalworkers throughout the realm. Chimú smiths from the north coast and workers from the central coast produced much of Tawantinsuyu's metal output. The Chimú mastery of metalworking, especially the production of alloys, underscored a north coast tradition dating back several thousand years, and the Incas exploited their proficiency. "Many of them were taken to Cusco and the capitals of the provinces, where they wrought jewelry, vessels and goblets of gold and silver."[51] At Hatun Xauxa (modern Jauja), in the Mantaro valley east of Lima, Cieza noted that there were "many silversmiths who made goblets and vessels of silver and gold for the service of the Inca and the adorning of the temple."[52]

Inca expansion into Qollasuyu signals keen interest in the region's metallic ores. They adopted tin bronze from the Andean high plains south of Lake Titicaca and exploited the rich cassiterite (a tin ore) mines of Bolivia and northwestern Argentina. Once they had gained control of the tin fields, they could manage the source and the production of tin bronze objects. Unlike gold and silver, which the Incas distributed as objects, primarily as gifts from the ruler, they supplied tin or tin bronze ingots as raw metal to metalworkers far from tin sources. Tin bronze soon replaced arsenic bronze in the former Chimú heartland and was used by the Incas to disseminate certain standard imperial items issued by the state, especially T-shaped axes, star-shaped mace heads, and ceremonial *tumi* knives.[53]

Precious metals, specifically gold, were of primary interest to the invading Spaniards, and the chronicles are filled with breathless descriptions of Tawantinsuyu's wealth. "There is no kingdom in the world so rich in precious ores," the usually level-headed Cieza remarked. "It amazed me that the whole of the city of Cusco and its temples were not of solid gold."[54] Despite Cieza's emphasis on Tawantinsuyu's mineral wealth, the empire's architecture, pottery, and weaving were just as important in promoting and reflecting imperial power. The pinnacle of these creative endeavors lay in Cusco, the heart of the empire, to which we dedicate the next chapter.

68

68 LEFT Cast bronze ceremonial knife. Tin bronze was the "stainless steel" of the Incas.

69 RIGHT A hammered gold female figurine. Similar figurines, dressed in Inca-style garb and topped with plumed headdresses, were common offerings at human sacrifices.

7 · Cusco: Capital of the Realm

Early Spanish descriptions of Cusco abound in superlatives: "Nowhere in this kingdom of Peru was there a city with the air of nobility that Cusco possessed," or "the richest city in all the Indies." Yet it is hard to envision Cusco at the time of the Incas, for today this UNESCO World Heritage Site is a city of modern concrete structures, Spanish colonial churches, and residences topped by tiled roofs. Nevertheless, scattered among colonial and modern structures, bold Inca walls have survived the ravages of almost 500 years of wars, earthquakes, demolition, and remodeling.

70

The confusing and contradictory descriptions of the earliest eyewitnesses to see the city before the 1536 siege, when Wayna Qhapaq's son Manco Inca—who was crowned Inca by the Spaniards—rebelled against the Spanish invaders, hamper attempts to reconstruct Inca Cusco. In 1534 the Spaniards

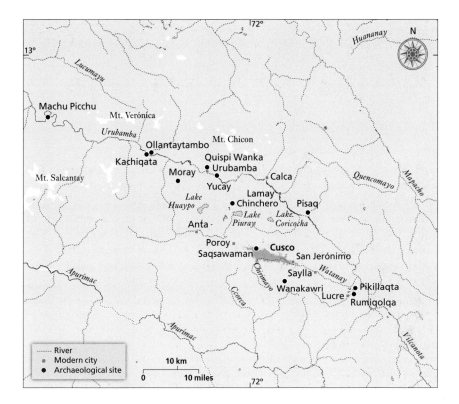

began dividing Inca city blocks into house lots, altering the original plan. 94 Cusco's surviving Inca walls are generally retaining walls or the enclosure walls of compounds, few of which contain their original buildings.[1] In addition, Inca walls served as convenient quarries for the Spanish settlers, who pilfered the stones to build their churches and residences. So, let us turn to one eyewitness, Pedro Sancho, Francisco Pizarro's scribe and secretary, who entered Cusco on November 15, 1533. Spread out before him he saw a city nestled against low hills, tucked into the end of a long, forested valley: "The city...[is] full of palaces of the nobles... The plaza is mostly flat...around it there are four houses of nobles who are the illustrious people of the city, painted and carved in stone... There are many other buildings and much grandness; on both sides flow two rivers...[which] are paved so that the water runs clean and clear and, although it may rise, it does not overflow; there are bridges to enter the city."[2]

70 OPPOSITE Aerial view of Cusco's main square, photographed in the 1930s. The plaza was once the Inca Haukaypata, surrounded by the town palaces of the reigning monarch and deceased kings.

71 ABOVE Map of Cusco and the Urubamba valley.

The conceptual plan

As with so many Inca settlements, Cusco's plan focused on a large open space, a dual plaza, rather than on a tall structure, in marked contrast to the bell towers that dominate the skyline today. The plaza functioned as the axis of the empire's territorial *suyu* divisions and, by extension, the roads to the four *suyus*: Chinchaysuyu to the northwest, Antisuyu to the northeast, Qollasuyu to the southeast, and Kuntisuyu to the southwest. In turn, the dual divisions of *hanan*, upper, and *hurin*, lower, separated the city into two parts. *Hanan* Cusco included Chinchaysuyu and Antisuyu, while *hurin* Cusco incorporated Qollasuyu and Kuntisuyu. Scholars, however, disagree over whether the southeast side of the plaza, the Saphi river, or the Qorikancha marked the division between *hanan* and *hurin*.

The system of forty-two lines known as *ceques*, most of which radiated from the Qorikancha, the sun temple, circumscribed Cusco's ritual organization: "From the temple of the sun...there went out certain lines which the Indians called ceques; they formed four parts corresponding to the four royal roads which went out from Cusco. On each one of these ceques was arranged in order the guacas [*wakas*] and shrines which there were in Cusco and its districts, like stations of holy places, the veneration of which was common to all."[3]

These ritual pathways, whose orientations were dictated by some 328 natural and artificial shrines, snaked their way across the landscape. They included palaces, shrines, water sources, mountains and mountain passes, astronomical sighting points, and places that marked legendary battles and the heroic exploits and mythical deeds of Inca rulers and ancestors.

The system organized ritual space and land tenure among Cusco's kin groups, the royal *panakas* and non-royal *ayllus*, responsible for making offerings to the *wakas* along designated *ceques*. The *ceques* played an important part in the organization and planning of the city, and since about a third of the *ceque* shrines were water sources or marked the origins of important canals, they were linked to Cusco's economic base: water and productive farmland.[4]

Pachakuti the architect?

Some chroniclers credit Cusco's design to the legendary Inca emperor Pachakuti. They wrote that he had built the imperial capital from the ground up, an effort that took twenty years. "He had decided to rebuild the city of Cusco in such a way that it would be permanently constructed of certain structures that he had in mind... [He] outlined the city and had clay models made just as he planned to have it built."[5]

93, 94 According to Betanzos, "[Pachakuti] named the whole city [puma's] body, saying that the residents of it were limbs of that [puma]."[6] Some scholars read a puma shape into the ceremonial core of Inca Cusco. They view the temple-fortress of Saqsawaman as the puma's head, the Tullumayu river as its back, and the confluence of the Tullumayu and Saphi as the puma's tail (an area called *puma chupan* or "puma's tail"). Others interpret the puma as a metaphor for the "body politic" of Cusco, the Inca, and the city's inhabitants, and not the town plan or shape of the city.[7]

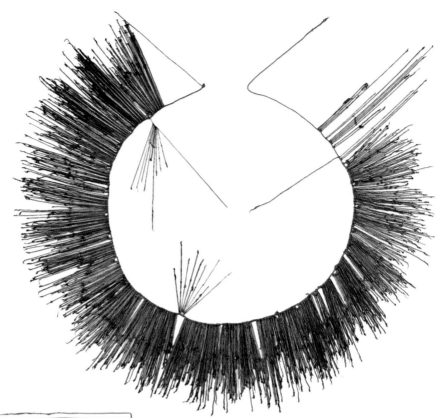

72 ABOVE This *khipu*, from Laguna de los Cóndores in northern Peru, may have recorded information spanning two years.

73 LEFT A *khipukamayuq* (*khipu* reader/maker) holds out a *khipu*. A *yupana*, a device used to tally sums with kernels of maize or small stones, can be seen in the lower left-hand corner.

74 BELOW A cotton *khipu* found on the coast of Peru.

75, 76 ABOVE Female figurines of gold (*left*) and of *Spondylus* shell (*right*) found on Ampato volcano in southern Peru. Both are clothed in Inca-style female attire and feather headdresses.

77 RIGHT This female figurine, topped by an elaborate feather headdress, was discovered on Llullaillaco volcano in Argentina.

78 OPPOSITE, ABOVE The mummies of a boy and a young woman found on Llullaillaco in Argentina, surrounded by some of their burial offerings.

79, 80 OPPOSITE, BELOW The same two mummies with their outer wrappings removed. The boy, some eight years old, wears a tunic, a *Spondylus* shell necklace, and sandals. The young woman, perhaps fourteen years old, had a plumed headdress, ceramics, and figurines among her burial offerings.

81 ABOVE, LEFT A carved and painted wooden *kero*, probably one of a pair used to drink *chicha* (maize beer). This *kero* dates to colonial times. 82 CENTER An Inca-style jar used for pouring *chicha*. 83 BELOW, LEFT A provincial Inca-style face neck jar found at Laguna de los Cóndores in the northern Peruvian cloud forest. 84 BELOW, RIGHT One of a pair of bird-headed miniature plates found buried on the summit of Ampato in southern Peru.

85 ABOVE This cache of offerings, found on Llullaillaco in Argentina, accompanied the young boy shown on page 107 and includes gold and silver male figurines wearing Inca attire and headdresses, a *Spondylus* shell necklace, *Spondylus* shell llamas, and two sets of matching miniature plates.

86 BELOW, LEFT A long-haired llama or alpaca made of crimped silver sheet metal.

87 BELOW, RIGHT This llama, found on the Island of the Sun in Bolivia, is made of silver sheet metal joined by soldering and wears a blanket of cinnabar with gold inlay.

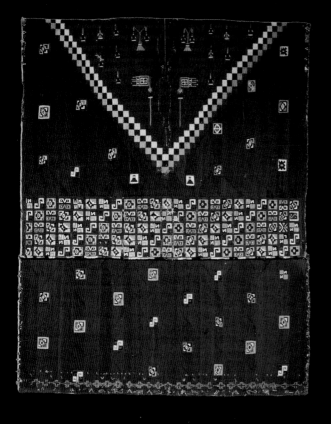

88 LEFT, ABOVE Inca-colonial style tunic found on the Island of the Sun, Bolivia. Dating to the late sixteenth–early seventeenth century, it retains many aspects of classic Inca-style tunics.

89 LEFT, BELOW This Inca men's tunic, featuring the Inca key design, was folded and draped over the shoulder of the young woman sacrificed on Llullaillaco in Argentina, illustrated on page 107.

90 OPPOSITE This tunic, said to have been found at Pachacamac on Peru's central coast, is Inca in style but was probably woven in early colonial times.

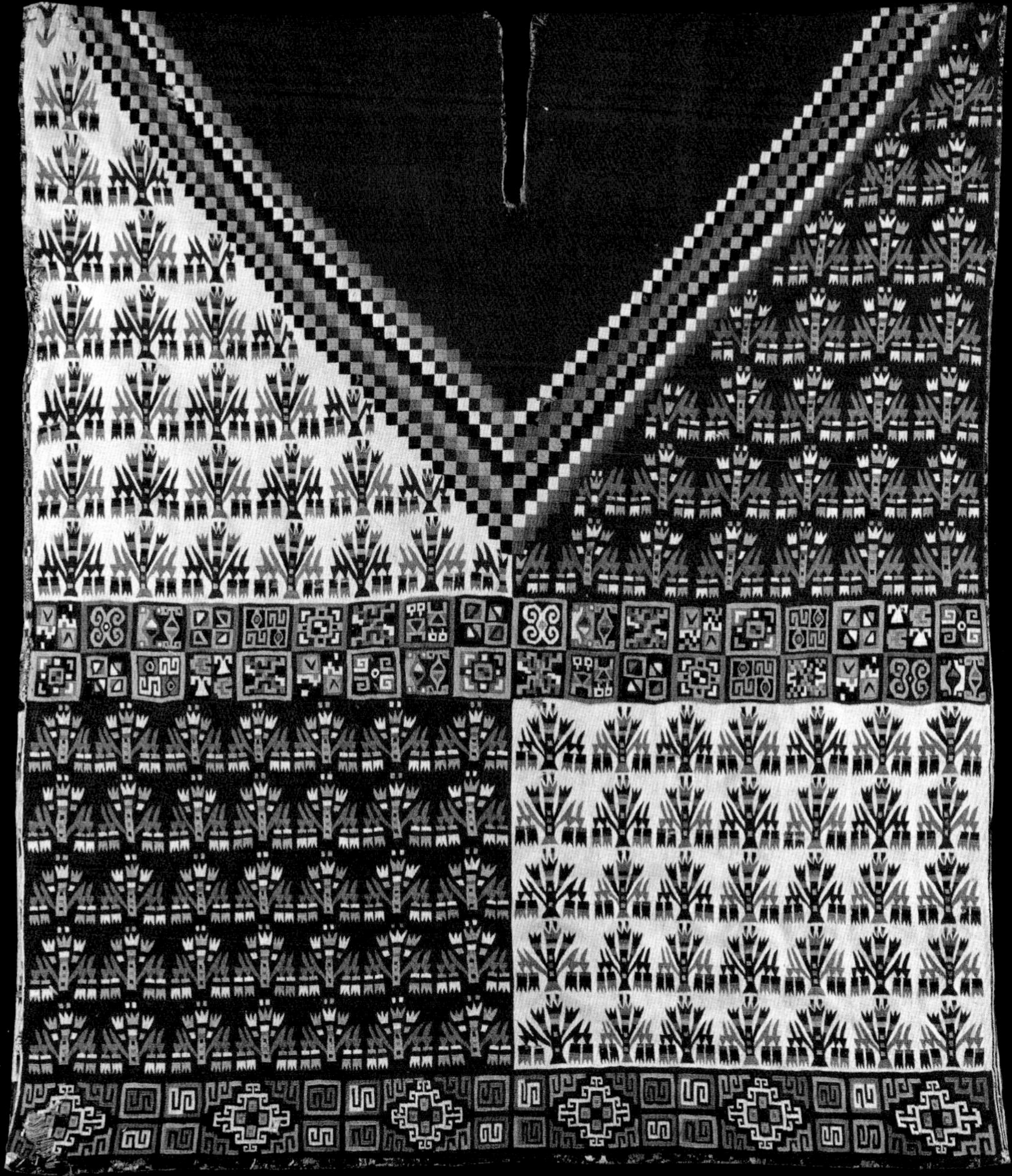

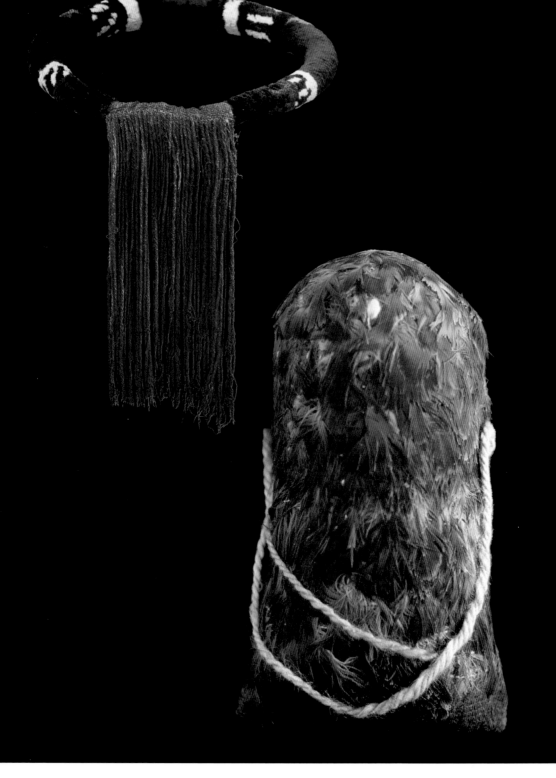

91 ABOVE, LEFT This headband of camelid fiber with cut pile and red fringe recalls the headdress said to have been worn by the Inca ruler.

92 ABOVE, RIGHT Found on Llullaillaco in Argentina, this feathered bag contains coca leaves.

It is hard to imagine that a single ruler-architect designed and built the entire city in a mere twenty years, given that different building phases and imperial styles are evident. Whether Inca Cusco was the creation of one inspired ruler or the result of decades of pre-imperial and imperial building episodes—as pre-imperial Killke wall remains scattered throughout the city suggest— careful planning is evident.

The scheme not only embraced the ceremonial core of the city, which covered some 100 acres (40 hectares), but extended many kilometers beyond Cusco. It included small agricultural estates such as Callachaca, a low-status Inca settlement composed of rectangular buildings of fieldstones topped by adobe walls, as well as small hamlets, irrigation canals, terracing complexes, and storage centers.[8] Although the city contained warehousing facilities, including maize stored in the *aqllawasi* and the Qorikancha, most storehouses were probably located at Colcampata ("storage terrace") on the hill below Saq-sawaman, at Saqsawaman itself, and at larger storage complexes located throughout the Cusco valley.[9]

In addition, the Incas improved the valley's road system and canalized the city's rivers. "For more than twenty leagues down that valley, where there are many settlements, [the river is] paved on the bottom and the vertical sides of its bed are faced with dressed stone, something never [before] seen nor heard."[10] By the time Cieza reached Cusco in 1549, however, there were "great rubbish heaps alongside the banks of [the] river."[11] Several bridges spanned the city's rivers. An illustration by Squier, the nineteenth-century traveler, shows a cantilevered stone bridge, which has since disappeared. Its construction technology suggests that it pre-dated the Spaniards.

A sacred city

Cusco, especially its ceremonial core, was not a city that ordinary subject peoples could move to and reside in at their whim. The center of Cusco itself was sacred: no one could go in or leave the city at night, and all those who entered had to carry a burden as a sign of humility and respect.[12] Above all, the capital as a whole was a city of the ruling Inca elite: the emperor, his wives, his court, and retainers; the Willaq Umu, high priest of the sun; the *panakas* or lineages of past rulers and their attendant personnel; the non-royal *ayllus* or descent groups; Incas-by-privilege; specialized artisans: weavers, potters, silversmiths, woodworkers, and masons; imperial officials and *khipukamayuqs*, who recorded the vital data of the empire on *khipus*, and the sons and daughters of conquered provincial lords.

The priest Cristóbal de Molina observed that Cusco "was probably a town of more than forty thousand citizens in the city-center alone—with suburbs and outlying settlements around Cusco to 10 or 12 leagues, I believe there must have been 200,000 Indians."[13] Though difficult to calculate, greater Cusco's resident population probably numbered around 100,000 people, making it Tawantinsuyu's largest settlement.[14] The numbers fluctuated as construction projects, religious rites, and political ceremonies took place, or when non-Incas were required to leave the city during the Citua rite (see page 73).

City planners earmarked some twelve outlying residential districts for the non-Inca groups known as Incas-by-privilege. These extended for about 7 miles (11 km) below and on some of the hillsides above the ceremonial core.[15] Provincial lords and their families also lived in these outlying settlements. "Anyone who contemplated the wards and the dwellings of the numerous and varied tribes who had settled in them beheld the whole empire at once, as if in a looking glass or a cosmographic plan."[16] Provincial non-Incas lived in the directions of their respective *suyus*. The Chachapoya and Cañari, for instance, resided in the Karmenka district, in the Chinchaysuyu quarter of Cusco. "This city was full of strange and foreign peoples, for there were Indians from Chile, Pasto and Cañari, Chachapoyas, Huancas, Collas, and all the other tribes to be found in the provinces."[17]

The ceremonial core

In ancient times, Haukaypata, the plaza that made up the center of the sacred city, formed a dual plaza with Kusipata, the modern Plaza Regocijo. Though divided by the Saphi river, "In Inca times the two squares were one: the whole stream was covered with broad beams, and great flags were laid over them to make a floor."[18] Together, the two plazas created a grand, imposing space open to the southwest; indeed, Kusipata may have extended as far as the modern Plaza San Francisco. In addition to this main, dual plaza, two other plazas embellished the ceremonial core: Inti Pampa facing the famed Qorikancha, or golden enclosure, and Rimaq Pampa, also located near the Qorikancha.

A layer "two and a half palms" (around 20 inches or 50 cm) deep of sand from the Pacific coast covered the main plaza. Inquiries by Cusco's chief magistrate, Polo de Ondegardo, revealed that the sand had been brought "out of reverence for [Tiqsi Wiraqocha]," the creator god linked to the sun's daily journey from Lake Titicaca to the Pacific Ocean.[19] In 1559 Polo ordered that the sand be removed after he discovered gold and silver "goblets" and figurines representing humans and camelids buried in the plaza.

Excavations in the mid-1990s in the square not only uncovered part of the layer of sand (much of it used in Spanish construction projects), but also an alignment of stones that may have formed part of a retaining wall. Alongside the wall, archaeologists unearthed Inca ceramics and four camelid figurines in gold, silver, and *Spondylus*, arranged in a row facing southeast.[20]

A "stone made like a sugarloaf pointed on top and covered with a strip of gold"[21] served as the plaza's ceremonial focus. The 5-ft-high (1.5 m) stone, "where they drank to the sun in the plaza,"[22] symbolized the sun. The stone topped a low, stepped stone platform flanked by a basin for receiving liquid offerings. At night, attendants covered the stone with a rounded wooden roof.

93 OPPOSITE, ABOVE Cusco in the 1930s, looking north.

94 OPPOSITE, BELOW Central Cusco at the time of the Spanish conquest, with Saqsawaman (1), the large dual plazas of Haukaypata (2) and Kusipata (3), the *aqllawasi* (4) and the Qorikancha (5).

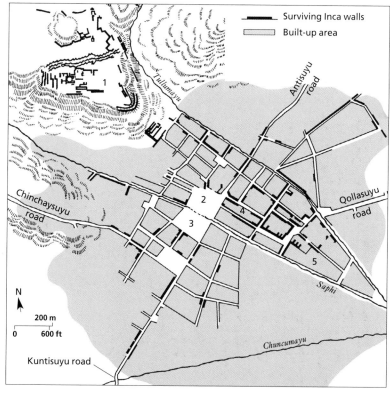

PL. 135 Known as *ushnus*, these ceremonial platforms, stones, and basins ranged from the simple stone and basin gracing Cusco's plaza to large, beautifully built platforms such as the one at Vilcaswaman, which combines a terraced platform with a stone seat, a basin, and a canal. Large provincial *ushnus* were often located in or beside plazas, where dignitaries presided over military and religious ceremonies. "Thus [Wayna Qhapaq] entered the most important town, where they had in the plaza a certain seat that resembled a high platform and in the middle of the platform, a basin full of stones... The Inca climbed up on that platform and sat there on his chair... They then poured out much chicha into the basin."[23]

The dual plaza served as the setting for the many public ceremonies that marked Cusco's ritual calendar, festivities that ranged from the daily excursions of the sun image and the mummies of the dead rulers from the Qorikancha (see page 120) to monthly ceremonies that drew thousands of pilgrims bearing offerings of precious metals, cloth, and sacrificial animals. Thousands gathered in the plaza for the June and December solstice festivals, as well as for the May ceremonies honoring the harvest and the August sowing festival.

The plazas, especially Kusipata, also functioned as a backdrop for ritual and mock battles, such as those enacted as part of a sovereign's mourning rituals. "Two squadrons of warriors came out, one with people from Hanan Cusco and the other from Hurin Cusco. One squadron came out from one side of the plaza, and the other from the other side, and did battle. The people from Hurin Cusco acted like losers and those from Hanan Cusco, representing the wars the lord had in his life, like winners."[24]

95 Generally, Cusco's buildings stood no taller than one story but appeared higher because of their pitched thatched roofs. "Most of the buildings are built of stone and the rest have half their façade of stone. There are also many adobe houses, very efficiently made, which are arranged along straight streets on a cruciform plan."[25] Each city block contained one or more *kanchas*: walled compounds with one entrance, comprising three to four rectangular buildings surrounding central courtyards.

The size and shape of the city blocks varied, ranging from 100 to 150 ft (30–45 m) in width and 150 to 230 ft (45–70 m) in length.[26] The slopes of Cusco's hills were terraced, with straight streets; some stepped, following the contours. Apparently, the Incas did not name the streets, but rather the blocks or compounds.[27] Streets ranged from 14 ft 5 inches to 18 ft 4 inches (4.4–5.6 m) in width, while passageways measured 5 ft 3 inches to 10½ ft (1.6–3.2 m) wide. Sancho noted, "The streets are all paved, and a stone-lined water channel runs down the middle of each street. Their only fault is to be narrow: only one mounted man can ride on either side of the channel."[28]

95 Enclosure wall of Cusco's *aqllawasi*, which housed the "chosen women," built in the coursed masonry style.

Town palaces

The Haukaypata contained the palace compounds, those "splendid buildings" in Cieza's words, of the reigning monarch and the *panakas*. Inca queens (*Qoyas*) had separate palaces: "The palace of the queen…was almost as large as the Inca's… She had shrines, baths and gardens, both for herself and for her ñustas, who were her ladies-in-waiting."[29] It is difficult to assign the town residences to individual Inca rulers, *Qoyas*, or *panakas*, although one, the Qasana, has been reliably linked to Wayna Qhapaq.

A large terrace containing one or two impressively large halls dominated the plaza's northeast side. It was destroyed when construction began on the cathedral in 1559. There are conflicting accounts about the type of structure or structures that stood on this side of the plaza; some say it contained a temple called Quishwarkancha, dedicated to the creator god Wiraqocha, while others assign the hall or halls to Wiraqocha Inca's palace.

On the plaza's southeast corner stood the Hatunkancha, the "great" or "large enclosure," seat of the former *aqllawasi* (part of it later converted, fittingly, into the convent of Santa Catalina). The Hatunkancha-*aqllawasi* lodged the *aqlla*, or "chosen women," who attended Cusco's religious shrines, served as custodians of the royal mummies, wove fine cloth, brewed *chicha* beer for the state religion, and were given in marriage to *kurakas* to seal alliances and to soldiers who had shown prowess in battle. The building's single entryway faced the plaza and, according to Garcilaso, was as "luxurious" as the Qorikancha. The women worked in "many cells" located off a narrow alleyway that ran down the compound's center, which also contained storage bins for the maize that the *aqlla* used to brew *chicha*.

Next to it stood the Amarukancha, "enclosure of the serpent," today occupied by the Jesuit Compañía church. Some chroniclers portray this compound as the residence of Waskar, Atawallpa's brother. It was apparently fronted by a vast, rectangular hall roofed with beams and thatch. (These large halls functioned as temporary shelters, perhaps for celebrants attending Cusco's ceremonies or, as archaeology has demonstrated in other places, as a public place for feasting.) Only portions of the Amarukancha's enclosure wall remain.

On the northwest side of the plaza loomed Wayna Qhapaq's town palace, the Qasana. It too boasted a large hall with an open front, and it was apparently so big that Garcilaso said it could hold 3,000 people (although this is probably an exaggeration) and "sixty mounted men could easily joust with canes in it."[30] Sancho described Wayna Qhapaq's palace as Cusco's "best," and it is probably no coincidence that Francisco Pizarro occupied it as his residence when he entered Cusco in late 1533.

The compound, noted an early eyewitness, contained a small lake, Ticci-cocha, which Cobo said was worshipped as a shrine in the *ceque* system, and is remembered today in a street name behind the plaza. The compound was flanked at its two outer corners by round masonry towers roofed with thatch. According to Sancho, its entryway was of white marble and red stone, although it was probably only painted white and red. Other structures facing the plaza were apparently also painted. Segments of the Qasana's enclosure wall survive in shops and restaurants on the side of the plaza known as the Portal de Panes.

One description, written in the late sixteenth or early seventeenth century, speaks of a complex of buildings divided into two parts, perhaps Wayna Qhapaq's town palace. Elaborate doors or gateways provided access into each sector, both of which contained spacious courtyards. "This great palace," wrote Martín de Murúa, "has two large principal doors, one at the entrance of the complex and the other, farther inside, from which the most meritorious of the famous stonework could be seen; at the entrance of this [first] door there were two thousand soldiers, on guard with their captain; and they guarded [for] one day, and later came another [captain] with another two thousand; and these were from the multitudes of Cañaris and Chachapoyas who...were certain warriors who guarded the person of the Inca... Between this door and the other farther in was a great and wide plaza, into which all of those who accompanied the Inca entered, and the Inca and the principal *orejones*, the four of his council, who were the most privileged, passed to the second door; at the second door there were also guards; they were men of this city of Cusco and relatives of the Inca, those in whom he had greatest trust, and it was those who had the charge of raising and teaching the sons of the principal leaders of all this realm, who went to serve the Inca and be with him in his court when they were boys... By this [second] door was the weaponry and arrows of the royal palace of the Inca, and at the door of the palace were 100 captains proven in war; and a little farther on was another great plaza or patio for the officials of the palace and the regular service, and then going farther in, were the salons and rooms where the Inca lived. And this was all full of delights, since various areas were planted with trees and gardens, and the royal lodgings were spacious and built with marvelous artistry."[31]

The golden enclosure

The Qorikancha, or sun temple, features one of the most superb constructions in Tawantinsuyu: a curved wall of shimmering gray andesite. "In all Spain," wrote Cieza, "I have seen nothing that can compare with these walls."[32] The complex housed the "hall of the sun"—*the* Qorikancha (the original Dominican church of Santo Domingo was apparently built over it)—and several "chapels," and its enclosing wall probably had a single entryway. Careful mapping and observation by John Rowe in the early 1940s, as well as more recent research and restoration, suggest that the Qorikancha may have contained as few as four and as many as seven rectangular halls surrounding a central courtyard. 96, 97

Because of its wealth and grandeur, every chronicler devoted long passages to the Qorikancha, or golden enclosure, for "it was one of the richest temples in the whole world."[33] Only three Spaniards, dispatched to Cusco in early 1533 to hasten the shipment of gold to secure Atawallpa's release, however, saw it before its ransacking. Moreover, only four chroniclers read their long-lost report.[34] Although later chroniclers would have us believe that gold sheet covered the entire compound, the earliest account states that only the façade of the hall of the sun was "sheathed with gold, in large plates, on the side where the sun rises, but on the side that was more shaded from the sun the gold in them was more debased."[35] In "another house" in the complex, probably the temple of Quilla, the moon, the Spaniards observed "very debased" sheathing, which may in fact have been silver. Impervious to the sanctity of the Qorikancha and the taboos required of devotees, the three Spaniards used crowbars to remove 700 gold plates from the hall of the sun.

The Qorikancha was perhaps more than a temple dedicated to the sun god Inti, for some chroniclers say it housed shrines to thunder and stars as well as Quilla. Other chronicles, however, note that the creator, the sun, and weather gods shared the Qorikancha's main "altar." Some 500 female and 200 male attendants "served" the temple, presided over by the Willaq Umu, the high priest of the sun.

In the Qorikancha's central courtyard, eyewitnesses observed a stone carved in the shape of a seat and covered in gold—a "fountain" or basin—and next to it, an image shaped like a young boy, all of gold. Dressed in a tunic of fine cloth and wearing the *mascaypacha*, the Inca "crown" and symbol of kingship, this image was known as Inti Punchao. Its hollow stomach contained the ashes of deceased rulers' internal organs. The fountain and seat, in fact, formed an *ushnu*, a ceremonial platform associated with the sun that contained an opening for liquid offerings. An eyewitness observed a noon ceremony during which women uncovered the seat and offered the image maize, meat, and *chicha*; they burned the meat and maize and poured the *chicha* into the basin.

A similar, more public ritual took place in the Haukaypata plaza. Attendants carried the sun image to the middle of the square and placed it on a carved seat adorned with feathers, where it received food and *chicha*. Again, attendants burned the food and poured the *chicha* into a basin, connected to the Qorikancha by an underground canal. At night, the sun image's female attendants set it in a small room in the Qorikancha, where it "slept" on a seat covered in iridescent feathers.

A ceremonial garden faced the hall of the sun, linking the sun and the reigning Inca ruler with maize, the empire's most important ritual crop and source of *chicha*, imbibed in great quantities at every ceremony. Three times a year—at sowing, harvest, and when Inca noble youths were initiated into adulthood—the Inca emperor ritually cultivated the garden. On those occasions, the garden was "cunningly planted with stalks of corn that were of gold,"[36] "with their cobs and leaves made just as maize is in nature."[37]

Not only did the Qorikancha serve as the ritual center of the realm, but it also housed the mummies of the deceased rulers and their queens, attended by a woman who fanned "away dust and flies."[38] The royal mummies apparently only attended Cusco's most solemn occasions, and their body doubles or substitutes—statues of gold, silver, wood, or stone—were brought out for the less solemn ones. (See box overleaf.)

The mummies shared power with the ruling, living Incas, and by late Inca times they had become so controlling—and plentiful—that Waskar, who ruled briefly in Cusco, threatened to take away their authority. With their *panakas* acting as mediums, the mummies of the dead kings and queens squabbled amongst themselves and meddled in state affairs, voicing their opinions on successions and marriages.

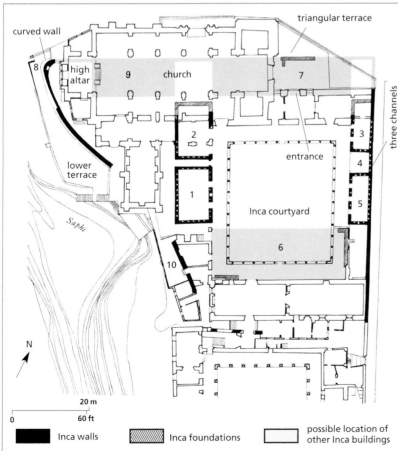

curved wall

triangular terrace

8

high altar

9   church

7

three channels

2

3

entrance

4

lower terrace

1

5

Saphi

Inca courtyard

6

10

N

20 m

0   60 ft

Inca walls   Inca foundations   possible location of other Inca buildings

96 ABOVE The Dominican church of Santo Domingo was built over the Qorikancha.

97 LEFT Plan of the Qorikancha.

1, 2, 3, 5 side chambers.

4 alcove with three channels.

6 largest chamber.

7 main temple.

8 curved wall.

9 supposed building beneath the colonial church.

10 continuation of the curved wall.

The Royal Mummies

Although ancestor worship in the Andes has been traced back several millennia, it is best known from the Inca cult of the royal mummies. During the early years of the invasion, many Spanish eyewitnesses in Cusco actually observed royal mummies playing a dynamic role in the lives of the living. As we have seen, rulers established *panakas* (royal *ayllus*) during their lifetimes. When a ruler died, the *panakas* were responsible for "the cult of his body and the sustenance of his family," according to Cobo, and they "adored the body as a god." The mummies were viewed as oracles, and mediated and meddled—through their mediums—in affairs of state. When they weren't holding court at the Qorikancha or engaged in attending Cusco's many festivities, they retreated to their country estates.

In the early years of the Spanish invasion the mummies were worshipped openly, attending public ceremonies in Cusco's main square. After Manco's failed siege in 1536, however, ancestor worship became more clandestine because the Spaniards viewed it as idolatrous. In addition, the mummies were accompanied by goblets of gold and other "treasure," making them especially profitable targets for Spanish treasure-hunters. In 1559 Cusco's chief magistrate, Juan Polo de Ondegardo, was instructed by the Viceroy to put an end to "idolatry" and search for the hiding places of the mummies. So successful was Polo that he managed to find the mummies of the Inca kings (or their substitute statues) as well as several queens (*Qoyas*). He had some secretly buried, and dispatched four mummies (apparently those of Wayna Qhapaq, Pachakuti, and two

women, one of whom was Wayna Qhapaq's mother) to Lima, where they were put on public display and eventually buried ignominiously in the hospital of San Andrés (where attempts to find them have been unsuccessful).

On the eve of the chronicler Garcilaso's departure for Spain in 1560, Polo showed him some of the mummies. "The bodies," Garcilaso remarked, "were perfectly preserved without the loss of a hair of the head or brow or an eyelash. They were dressed as they had been in life, with llautus on their heads...in a sitting position... Their hands were crossed across their breast...and their eyes lowered." When Garcilaso touched the finger of Wayna Qhapaq, he noted that it "seemed like that of a wooden statue, it was so hard and stiff." Another eyewitness, Father Acosta, observed that the mummy of Pachakuti was "so complete and well-preserved with a certain rosin, that it seemed to be alive." Even so, his "close investigations" failed to reveal how he had been embalmed. Garcilaso ventured a guess: "My own opinion is that the main operation in embalming was to take the bodies above the snow line and keep them there until the flesh dried, after which they would cover them with the bitumen Padre Acosta mentions." Another, more telling, clue is provided by Betanzos, who noted that when Wayna Qhapaq died in Ecuador, "the nobles who were with him had him opened and took out all his entrails, preparing him so that no damage would be done to him and without breaking any bone. They prepared and dried him in the Sun and the air. After he was dried and cured, they dressed him in costly clothes and placed him on

On especially important ritual occasions, the mummies' attendants carried them to the main square, where they seated the five kings of *hanan* (upper) Cusco on the right side of the plaza and the five rulers of *hurin* (lower) Cusco on the left side. There, the attendants offered them food and *chicha*, "and the dead toasted each other and the living, and the living toasted the dead."[39] Since

an ornate litter well adorned with feathers and gold. When the body was prepared, they sent it to Cuzco."

While no royal Inca mummies have survived, Inca-period mummies found in tombs overlooking Laguna de los Cóndores in Chachapoyas provide hints of how the Inca royals may have been embalmed. The dry and cold microclimate of the tombs and the many layers of cloth in which the bodies were wrapped certainly enhanced preservation, but the bodies were also embalmed. Embalmers controlled decomposition by emptying the abdominal cavity through the anus, sealing the orifice with a cloth plug. Fly casings found in the mummy bundles suggest that the mummification procedure may have taken some time. The skin appears leathery, and has apparently been treated with some as yet unidentified substance or substances, perhaps the "balsam" or "rosin" mentioned by Garcilaso and Acosta, respectively. Unspun cotton placed under the cheeks, in the mouth, and in the nostrils preserved facial features. The Chachapoya-Inca mummies were placed in a seated position, with the knees pulled up to the torso and the arms crossed over the breast, much as Garcilaso had observed. The mummies from Laguna de los Cóndores have their hands tucked under their chins or placed across their faces, which prevents the jaw from slacking open.

Just like the royal mummies seen by Garcilaso in Cusco, the Chachapoya-Inca ones weigh barely anything "so that any Indian could carry them in his arms."

We suspect that the *purucaya* ceremony, the mourning ritual that took place a year after a ruler's death and celebrated the feats of the deceased, may have also marked the completion of the mummification process. Nevertheless, the procedure does not appear to have been entirely successful: one of the first Spaniards to enter Cusco observed a woman wearing a golden mask whose sole duty was to fan flies from the mummy of Wayna Qhapaq.

98 In this drawing by Poma de Ayala the mummified bodies of Wayna Qhapaq, his principal wife, and son are shown being carried to Cusco on a litter.

each attendant had to drink for two, these drinking binges became drunken affairs and the plaza's "two wide drains over half a vara [18 inches or 46 cm] in diameter...ran with urine throughout the day...as abundantly as a flowing spring."[40] The mummies made one of their last public appearances in late 1533 for the swearing-in of Manco Inca, one of Wayna Qhapaq's sons.

The temple-fortress

High above Cusco perches Saqsawaman, the temple-fortress. "Upon the hill which, towards the city, is rounded and very steep, there is a very beautiful fortress of earth and stone," recalled Sancho. "Its large windows, which look over the city, make it appear still more beautiful."[41]

Saqsawaman includes three sectors. To the north lies a large, circular reservoir surrounded by the foundations of sophisticated architecture. It may have been the spring of Calispuquio ("spring of good health"), a shrine on the *ceque* system. An outcrop that features the so-called Throne of the Inca (another *ceque* shrine, carved into a series of steps) divides the reservoir area from the second sector—the plaza—while the third sector includes the zigzag terrace walls, and the summit structures, which overlooked Cusco and featured at least two towers, one round and one rectangular.

Saqsawaman's most notable feature is three retaining walls (called "ramparts" by some) which flank one side of the hill overlooking the plaza. They stretch for some 1,300 ft (400 m), punctuated by around fifty zigzagging angles. The lowest wall contains the megalithic, perfectly fitted stones that so astounded the Spaniards: "The most beautiful thing which can be seen in the edifices of that land are these walls, because they are of stones so large that anyone who sees them would not say they had been put there by human hands, for they are as large as chunks of mountains and huge rocks."[42] Spaniards and modern observers alike are baffled as to "how the stones were conveyed to the site...since [the Incas] had no oxen and could not make wagons; nor would oxen have sufficed to carry them."[43]

Building Saqsawaman was an enormous undertaking, involving "twenty thousand men from the provinces... Four thousand of them quarried and cut the stones; six thousand hauled them with great cables of leather and hemp; the others dug the ditch and laid the foundations, while still others cut poles and beams for the timbers."[44] Cieza observed that the workers' houses "can still be seen...near the site where the building was to be erected." Again, the reliable Cieza has been borne out by archaeology: a survey revealed an extensive, 12-acre (5-hectare) settlement known as Muyu Cocha spread across a hill not far from Saqsawaman. Much of the pottery found on the surface was imported from the Titicaca region, suggesting that Saqsawaman's builders came from that area.[45]

"This work was conceived on such a vast scale that even if the monarchy had lasted until now, it would not have been completed," remarked Cieza.[46] In fact, Saqsawaman's impressive walls were never finished. Studies indicate that the lowest rampart was built first and the second and third walls added later. The first rampart shows signs of work in progress, including incomplete fitting of stones, tops of stones left uncut, and unfilled gaps between stones.[47]

The great boulders that formed Saqsawaman's zigzagging ramparts are of limestone, quarried at the building site itself and from the many outcrops dotting the surrounding hills. Other stones, such as the smaller andesite blocks used to construct Saqsawaman's towers, came from Rumiqolqa, a quarry 22 miles (35 km) southeast of Cusco. Still worked today, Rumiqolqa is littered with Inca stones in varying stages of production. Quarrymen dispatched finished stones

PL. 160

PL. 159

99,
PL. 161

100

99 Saqsawaman's set of three zigzagging walls, overlooking Cusco. The site served as a setting for ritual battles, included a sun temple, and housed a large storage depot.

from Rumiqolqa to construction sites in Cusco, where in addition to Saqsawaman they grace the Hatunkancha and the Qorikancha. The Spaniards viewed Saqsawaman as a convenient quarry, and only the sheer size of its megalithic blocks saved the ramparts from being completely dismantled; in fact, a 1559 ecclesiastical council edict ordered that Saqsawaman's stones be used to build the cathedral.

To the Spaniards Saqsawaman resembled a fortress, which is how most modern observers tend to refer to it as well. There is no evidence, however, that it ever functioned as a fortress except during Manco Inca's 1536 siege of Cusco (see pages 240–41). Cieza called it a "house of the sun," which suggests that it played a role in the Inca solar cult. Its military function may have been primarily symbolic, and the wide plaza or esplanade that lies between the terrace walls and the carved stone outcrop might have served as a setting for ritual battles or re-enactments. Pedro Pizarro describes one such ritual staged by Topa Inca to commemorate his victories in the north. On that occasion, festivities included a feigned attack on Saqsawaman led by the then young Wayna Qhapaq.

100 Abandoned blocks of andesite in the quarry of Rumiqolqa, south of Cusco. The quarry supplied much of Cusco's building stone.

In addition, almost all the early chroniclers stress that Saqsawaman served as an enormous storage depot. Recent clearing and excavations just west of one of the summit towers unearthed a maze of small rooms, perhaps the remains of storage chambers.[48] According to one early eyewitness, "There were so many rooms that ten thousand soldiers could get in them."[49] All these rooms, wrote Sancho, were filled with "arms, clubs, lances, bows, arrows, axes, shields, heavy jackets of quilted cotton, and other weapons of different types. And there was clothing for soldiers, all collected here from all areas of the land subject to the lords of Cusco."[50] Cieza, too, noted that Saqsawaman "should house everything imaginable, such as gold and silver, precious stones, fine garments, arms of all types they used, materials of war, sandals, shields, feathers, skins of animals and birds, coca, bags of wool, a thousand kinds of jewels; in a word, everything anyone had ever heard of was in it."[51]

Royal country estates

Aside from their town palaces in Cusco, the Inca royals founded estates, mainly in the Cusco basin and in the Urubamba valley. There, the rulers and especially the *panakas* (royal descent groups) occupied some of the best lands in the Cusco region. Produce from the estates sustained the royal families and the mummy cults, and some chroniclers claim that the mummies resided at their estates when not in Cusco. Waskar complained "that he should order [the ancestors] buried and should take all their belongings from them. [He said that] the goods should belong to the living, rather than the dead, and that the dead had all the property in the kingdom."[52]

Not only did the royal estates serve as retreats, but in some cases they may have commemorated military victories. Almost all were established in awe-inspiring natural settings and distinguished by elaborate architecture, terracing, and waterworks, as well as carved stones and outcrops. In such places, notes a document unearthed by John Rowe, "they established hereditary estates, live-stock pastures, gold and silver mines, woodlands, and other properties."[53]

Garcilaso de la Vega, referring to the Urubamba valley, which was a favorite setting for royal estates, wrote that it "excels all others in Peru so that all the…kings…made it their garden and haunt of pleasure and recreation… The site is very pleasant with soft and fresh air, sweet waters [and] a climate of great moderation."[54] The valley's temperate climate is well suited to maize, a prestige crop and essential ingredient of *chicha* beer. The Incas settled the valley with experienced maize farmers from other parts of the realm, especially Qollasuyu and Chinchaysuyu.

Wayna Qhapaq's estate at Quispi Wanka, which stretched for some 6 miles (10 km) between the towns of Urubamba and Yucay, was maintained by some 2,400 workers and their families. The lands included gardens, pastures, groves, water tanks, lagoons, a salt mine, and a hunting lodge. Its finely built agricultural terraces were mainly devoted to maize, although farmers also cultivated tropical crops such as hot peppers, coca, cotton, and peanuts.[55]

The estate boasted some of the most striking architecture and ambitious land reclamation projects in Tawantinsuyu, many of which still sculpt the valley today. Wayna Qhapaq had the meander plain of the Urubamba canalized, ordering "that one hundred thousand Indians…come from all the land… He had the river moved along the side facing Cusco, making it stronger and making a bed where it went. Along the path of the river the Inca had hills leveled. Thus he made the valley flat so that it could be planted and harvested."[56] In some parts, the retaining walls built by Wayna Qhapaq still confine the Urubamba to its banks; in others, his agricultural terraces sustain the crops of modern farmers.

Topa Inca, on the other hand, chose to build his main royal estate at Chinchero, on a cold and wind-swept plain high above the Urubamba valley that was more suited to crops such as potatoes than maize. He imagined it as a monument to himself, "so that he would be better remembered."[57] After choosing the building site, his "technicians and master builders took their cords and measured the town…with the houses and streets outlined… [Topa Inca]…had this town made of stone and very well-constructed buildings."[58]

101

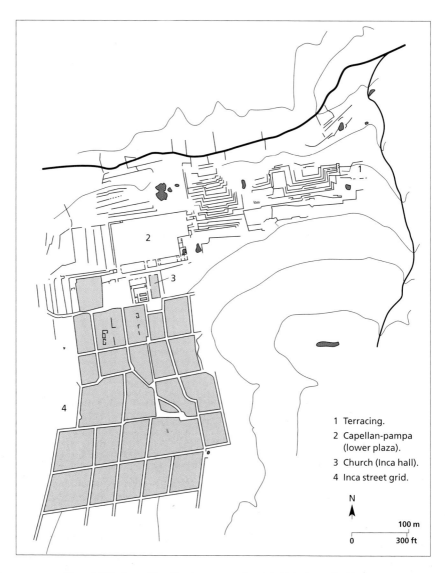

1 Terracing.
2 Capellan-pampa (lower plaza).
3 Church (Inca hall).
4 Inca street grid.

N

100 m
0   300 ft

101 ABOVE Plan of Chinchero, Topa Inca's estate on the plain high above the Urubamba valley.

102 OPPOSITE Overlooking the Urubamba river, Pisaq was a royal estate belonging to the lineage of Pachakuti. The Pisaqllaqta sector is to the left, and the Intiwatana group, right.

Building Chinchero involved earth-moving and terracing on a large scale, and the estate included two plazas, fine terraces, gardens, a royal residence, storage facilities, carved stone outcrops, and fountains. Topa Inca's death apparently cut short his elaborate plans for Chinchero, and much of the estate was never completed.[59]

The chroniclers are unusually silent about Pisaq, a royal estate attributed to Pachakuti's lineage. Located on a spur high above the Urubamba valley, parts of Pisaq are encircled by an imposing wall pierced by gateways, with flights of finely built agricultural terraces sweeping down toward the valley. Pisaq boasts some of the finest stonework in the valley, including a rock outcrop known as the intiwatana that is embellished with two bosses and surrounded by a D-shaped wall, probably the remains of a sun temple. An elaborate canal system —fed by one of Pisaq's many springs—once brought water to the Intiwatana sector, culminating in a suite of fountains on the east side.

At Ollantaytambo, downriver from Pisaq, Pachakuti's *panaka* maintained yet another estate. The Patakancha river, a tributary of the Urubamba, divides Ollantaytambo into a residential area to the east and a temple complex on a terraced hill to the west. Beneath the temple hill are a series of sculpted bedrock shrines, the foundations of walls either never built or dismantled, and a lovely fountain carved into the living rock, sculpted with a step motif.

Ollantaytambo's residential sector is the only Inca settlement with a surviving trapezoidal grid plan whose dwellings are still occupied today. The town plan included four long streets crossed by seven shorter ones; each of the resulting blocks contains two *kanchas*, or walled compounds, with each *kancha* composed of four buildings around a central courtyard. Impressive double-

102, PL. 32

PL. 130

103

104

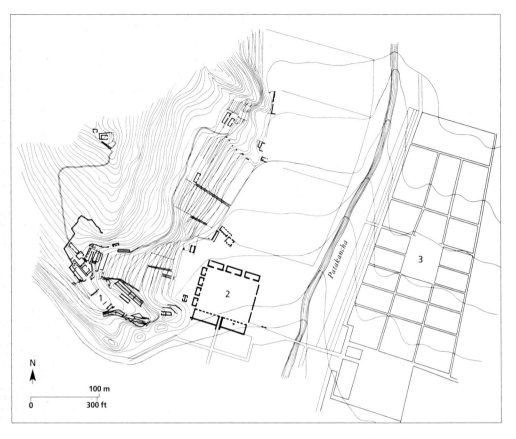

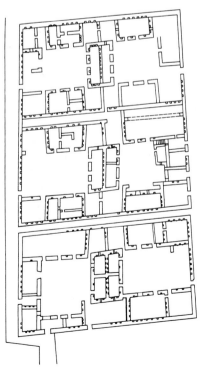

103 ABOVE Plan of Ollantaytambo, a royal estate that formed part of the lineage of Pachakuti. The town, laid out in a grid (*right*), has been continuously inhabited since Inca times.

1 Temple complex.

2 Square of Mañay Raqay.

3 Inca town.

104 LEFT Plan of *kanchas* at Ollantaytambo.

105 OPPOSITE Terraces at Ollantaytambo.

jambed doorways led into the compounds. Such features, reserved for only the most prestigious Inca buildings, suggest that Ollantaytambo's residents were members of the Inca nobility. Sadly, few of the double-jambed entryways have survived because over the centuries residents have modified the doorways to accommodate the girth of farm animals first introduced by the Spaniards.

On Ollantaytambo's temple hill is a religious precinct surrounded by a wall, which is reached by a steep stairway flanked by finely built terraces. The temple hill is often called a fortress, but the surrounding walls probably served to limit access to a restricted ceremonial area. Manco Inca, in fact, may have built the walls during his 1536 rebellion against the Spaniards, when he made Ollantaytambo his headquarters. The area around the so-called Wall of the Six Monoliths (probably the remains of a retaining wall for an unfinished sun temple) is strewn with massive blocks of andesite and rhyolite, ranging from partially worked to finished stones removed from earlier constructions—the Spanish invasion apparently cut short an ambitious remodeling project.[60] Behind the temple lies the staging area for a 1,150-ft-long (350 m) ramp, used to drag stones up to the construction site from the valley floor. Many of Ollantaytambo's stones came from the rock falls of Kachiqata across the river (see pages 87–88).

105

At Ollantaytambo, the valley begins to narrow and steep canyon walls flank the Urubamba as it tumbles down to the tropical forest and its confluence with the Apurímac river. A document of 1568[61] indicates that all the lands, from Torontoy downriver to Chaullay, once formed part of a densely populated area of Inca towns and agricultural complexes, noted as properties of Pachakuti's *panaka*. These included a constellation of settlements near the valley bottom, notably Patallaqta, and others clinging to the high road to Machu Picchu, poised hundreds of meters above the Urubamba. The document mentions a place named "Picho" and notes that "Indians" from Picho paid tribute to Spanish officials in coca leaves. Although some believe that Picho is none other than the Urubamba valley's most famed site, Machu Picchu, *picho* or *picchu* means "peak" in Quechua, and could refer to any number of places.

• • •

The next three chapters survey Cusco's hinterland through the *suyus* that formed Tawantinsuyu, "the four parts together." The available information on the boundaries of the *suyus* is limited and contradictory, and thus the borders are subject to revision. As we saw at the beginning of this chapter, the Incas also divided greater Cusco into *suyus*, but the borders of these did not extend outward to coincide with the *suyu* divisions of broader Tawantinsuyu.[62]

In the early years of Inca expansion, before extensive conquests to the north and south, the four *suyus* may have been roughly equivalent in size. Eventually, Chinchaysuyu and Qollasuyu grew to become the largest *suyus*, while geographical factors—the Pacific Ocean to the west and the tropical Amazonian lowlands to the east (a region often beyond the reach of imperial control)—constrained Kuntisuyu's and Antisuyu's growth, respectively. In the Inca dual system, as we have seen, the *suyus* were paired into an upper half (Chinchaysuyu with Antisuyu) and a lower half (Qollasuyu with Kuntisuyu), with Chinchaysuyu and Qollasuyu occupying superior positions within the halves.

We now leave Cusco and its royal estates to embark on a survey of the empire, beginning with Chinchaysuyu, the most prestigious half of the upper empire, followed by Antisuyu, the forested quarter that embraced the cloud forest and the fringes of the rainforest. We end with Qollasuyu, the largest *suyu* and superior half of the lower empire, followed by Kuntisuyu, the smallest of the *suyu* divisions.

8 · Chinchaysuyu: Land of the Setting Sun and the Sacred Shell

According to the legend of the Chanka war, the Incas' defeat of their rivals set the stage for imperial expansion to the north and west of Cusco, into what would become Chinchaysuyu. By the time the European invasion cut short imperial growth, Chinchaysuyu had expanded northward to embrace a series 106 of small and large coastal and highland polities, as well as lands bordering the tropical eastern flanks of the Andes and a great swathe of what is today highland Ecuador. Although smaller than Qollasuyu in the south, Chinchaysuyu's wealth and population exceeded all the other *suyus* combined.

The route of the setting sun

The Chinchaysuyu road runs west from Cusco, and at the important junction of Vilcaswaman connects the capital with the principal highland road north to Quito and a lateral road leading to the coast. Given the importance of the sun in Inca religion and the almost due-west direction of the road, it is not surprising that the route assumed unusual religious significance. Scholars believe that many of the sites on or near the road constituted shrines on a long-distance *ceque* some 250 miles (400 km) long, a continuation of the better documented one that is associated with Wiraqocha's mythical journey from Lake Titicaca to Cusco (see page 75).[1] The Incas incorporated scores of natural and carved rocks as well as *ushnu* platforms into the cities, shrines, and way-stations along this westward route.

The first of many important settlements and shrines along the road lies 22 miles (35 km) west of the capital at **Quillarumi**, a large limestone boulder into 107 which the Incas carved a semi-oval shape flanked on either side by carved steps. At the northern end of the shrine is a fine masonry structure with an interior niche and a small bench. It is tucked under a large boulder known as Salaqaqa, and nearby are a cave, a waterfall, and flights of finely built terraces.[2]

Tambokancha, on the Pampa de Anta near Zúrite, probably features some of the most unusual site plans and architecture ever recorded in Tawantinsuyu. Covering approximately 20 acres (8 hectares), overall the site assumes the shape of a *tumi*, or ceremonial knife, and includes two step-shaped patios facing the main plaza, as well as several buildings with curved walls. It may have been a royal estate of Topa Inca, perhaps the remains of the "sumptuous, rich palaces where the rulers of Cuzco used to come to take their pleasure and recreation."[3]

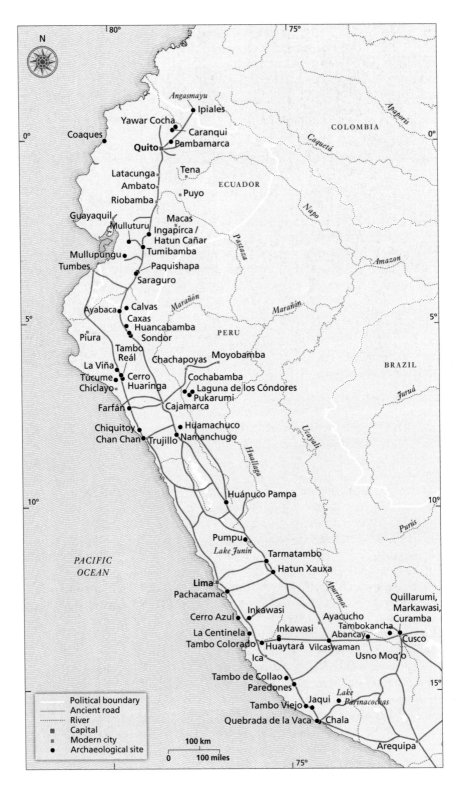

106 OPPOSITE A map of Chinchaysuyu, showing the road system and principal sites.

107 ABOVE This carved rock, known as Quillarumi, formed part of the first important shrine on the westward-leading route that connected Cusco with the Pacific Ocean.

In the lower Limatambo valley, only a few kilometers east of the Apurímac river, a series of sites cluster near Tilka mountain, the likely destination of some of the non-Inca residents of Cusco who had to retreat temporarily during the Citua cleansing ritual (see page 73). The Tilka shrine of **Markawasi** covers about 15 acres (6 hectares) and includes elaborate masonry and extensive agricultural terraces. Markawasi is perhaps the place Cieza noted after he had crossed the Apurímac river, "where the lodgings of the Incas were, and where 108 they had an oracle."[4] Pedro Pizarro provides us with the richest description: an elaborately painted hall in which stood a sacred shaft of wood "covered in the blood of sacrifices... It was completely encircled by a band of gold...welded to it in the form of inlay. In front it had two golden breasts the size of a woman's, fixed to the same band. [The Indians] had this pole clothed in very delicate women's clothing, with many gold [*tupus*], which are the form of a pin that the women of this land used... [They] said that the devil spoke to them from this large idol, and they called it Apu-rimac. The guardian of this was a lady called Asarpay."[5] Asarpay is said to have thrown herself into the Apurímac in protest against the Spanish desecration of the oracle.[6] Apurímac ("lord who speaks") probably alludes to the river's loud roar and its oracular significance.

One of the most remarkable sites on the Chinchay-suyu road is **Saywite** at the edge of the Curahuasi valley, around 30 miles (50 km) west of Cusco. The name Saywite derives from a Quechua word meaning "marker of lands," and the Incas placed this settlement and its famed sculpted boulder (see pages 86–87) in the territory of the Chankas. Some scholars believe the Incas may have been inspired by the myths of the war that was so crucial to their expansion, and the site may have signaled the boundary between the Chankas and the Incas of Cusco.[7]

In the heart of Chanka territory, 120 miles (190 km) directly west of Cusco, lies an *ushnu* known as **Usno Moq'o**, the sole remains of what was once an important Inca settlement, perhaps the Tambo of Amancay. Located in the modern city of Abancay, the 25-ft-high (7.5 m) *ushnu* is composed of three superimposed platforms, lending it the appearance of a solid, truncated pyramid, and heralding the *ushnu* at Vilcaswaman, farther west, although the stonework of Usno Moq'o is rustic in comparison.[8]

Farther west, **Curamba**, located halfway between Abancay and Andahuaylas, reputedly served as a center for smelting silver ores.[9] It too has a terraced *ushnu*, recently restored, which is oriented east and situated on the edge of a large rectangular plaza surrounded by the remains of some sixty structures, including three large halls or *kallankas*.

Vilcaswaman: city at a pivotal junction

At **Vilcaswaman**, as in Cusco, a modern town covers most of the Inca settlement. Though small in comparison to Huánuco Pampa, Pumpu, and several other Inca cities, comments in the Spanish chronicles and the high quality of the surviving structures indicate that it was politically, economically, and, above all, religiously significant.[10]

Archaeological research suggests an estimated 1,500 to 2,000 permanent residents, among them 500 *aqlla* or chosen women, noted by Cieza, as well as a few hundred administrative personnel.[11] Cieza saw some 700 storehouses filled with "arms and fine clothing"[12] and the food supply of the city's residents and

109

108 OPPOSITE, ABOVE The Incas dedicated an oracle to the "lord who speaks," alluding to the roar of the Apurímac river, seen here.

109 OPPOSITE, BELOW A detail of the carved boulder of Saywite (see page 86), located on the road that linked Cusco with the coast.

visitors. On the south side of the plaza, on the summit of three tiers of terraces, rose the sun temple, "large and finely built."[13] On another side of the plaza, "toward the rising sun,"[14] are the remains of one of the most impressive terraced *ushnus* in the whole empire, entered through a magnificent trapezoidal, double-jambed gateway with a stairway leading to the summit. Pedro de Carvajal, writing in the sixteenth century, noted that "this is where the Inca used to go in person to be seen, and on top of it were two large stone seats, covered in gold at that time, where the Inca and his wife used to sit, as if on a tribune, and from where they worshipped the sun... He would sit there under a great canopy of plumage of a thousand colors, and the posts on which this awning rested were of gold."[15] The *ushnu* stands about 28 ft (8.5 m) high, but unlike other *ushnus* it was surrounded by a walled compound, and entered by two or three double-jambed gateways, of which only the central one survives.[16] Topa Inca and Wayna Qhapaq are said to have had palaces near the *ushnu*.[17]

Vilcaswaman shows several marked similarities with the sacred core of Cusco itself, implying that it too may have been a sacred city. These include a plaza divided by a canal and many natural or carved rock outcrops in both the city and the nearby landscape. Vilcaswaman's importance as a sacred religious center thus seems to outweigh its role as a regional administrative or economic center for the relatively sparsely populated region that surrounded it.

Indeed, Vilcaswaman's spectacular architecture contrasts with the unimpressive archaeological sites from the immediately pre-Inca period that dot the surrounding region, home to the Chankas. Their small settlements of mainly circular structures give little indication of their legendary role in Inca imperial expansion.[18] Did the Incas deliberately embellish the power of the Chankas to enhance their own reputation, in part by memorializing the Chanka myth in art and architecture at Vilcaswaman and elsewhere?

In Chapter 10, we will see clearer examples of this at the impressive ritual centers of Paqariqtampu (Maukallaqta) and the Islands of the Sun and Moon, where the Incas converted mythic places of creation into pilgrimage shrines. The extraordinary buildings and sculpted rock shrines along the route west from Cusco center on the solar religion, but the importance of the Chanka wars may also have played a part. The incorporation of coastal centers into the empire's religion and politics probably featured as well; indeed, it has been suggested that the adoption of the stepped pyramid form of the Vilcaswaman *ushnu* may have been inspired by the great religious structures at Pachacamac and Chincha.

110, PL. 135

111

110 OPPOSITE, ABOVE The *ushnu* at Vilcaswaman was one of the most elaborate ceremonial platforms ever built. It sits at the junction of the westward-leading route to the Pacific Ocean and the Qhapaq Ñan, the royal road between Cusco and Quito.

111 OPPOSITE, BELOW The Inca ruler and his wife may have sat on this carved stone bench—once covered in gold—that rests on the summit of the *ushnu* at Vilcaswaman.

Lodgings before the descent

West of Vilcaswaman, before the road to the coast begins to descend through the rather narrow Pisco valley, Inca architects designed a small but extraordinary settlement that is now called, as so many others, **Inkawasi** ("house of the Inca"). The beauty of Inkawasi derives in large part from its location at the edge of a stream. Water flows around majestic rocks in the midst of the stream, forming a natural centerpiece for the site's plan. Double-jambed doorways, numerous niches, and fine, dressed (worked) stone masonry in parts of the complex testify to its importance. The site appears to have been a religious and, possibly, a palace complex that did not house a significant population.

112

Some 9 miles (15 km) farther west along the road, the Incas built yet another installation of special religious significance. Huaytará has largely been covered by a modern town, but the Spaniards saved, perhaps unintentionally, a unique building through their policy of countering the indigenous religion by building a church on the walls of Inca temples. One of the great masterpieces of Inca architecture, Huaytará's church of San Juan Bautista incorporates the greater part of a long, slightly trapezoidal structure that probably served as an important temple.

Built of fine, dressed stone masonry, the temple at Huaytará is famous for the niches in its interior and exterior walls. The exterior walls on the south and west sides have grand double-jambed trapezoidal niches, the size of a doorway. On the long south wall eight of these niches alternate with nine small niches.

113
114

112 OPPOSITE The remains of a finely built masonry structure at Inkawasi in the Pisco valley, Peru.

113 ABOVE Unusual triangular niches in the interior of the church of San Juan Bautista in Huaytará, Peru, once an Inca temple.

114 RIGHT Double-jambed exterior niches at the temple of Huaytará.

A small trapezoidal window in the back of each of the tall niches furnishes light and ventilation to the interior of the building, where the windows perforating the walls alternate, at a slightly lower level, with small trapezoidal niches. In the interior north wall, Inca architects fashioned a unique set of nine tall niches, alternating with ten small ones. These niches are trapezoidal in elevation and triangular in plan, giving a prismatic effect to the back part of the double niches. The building's east wall was partially destroyed in the construction of the church, but it apparently contained a wide entryway.[19] Below and west of Huaytará the Inca road continues to drop rapidly.

A city coded in brilliant colors

The spectacular stone architecture of Huaytará's temple contrasts markedly with the adobe or fieldstone and mortar, both plastered with mud, that form the buildings of **Tambo Colorado**, one of the best-preserved Inca coastal constructions. While Tambo Colorado contains many of the distinctive hallmarks of Inca architecture, it also includes some unusual decorative features such as a frieze (of which only a trace remains) composed of stepped triangles with plumed appendages, and "latticework" made of *tapia* (tamped earth). Although archaeologists documented the remains of a similar stepped frieze in the nearby Chincha valley, the motif of the frieze and the latticework are reminiscent of decorative elements found on the north coast, particularly at Chan Chan, the Chimú capital.[20]

115, PL. 133

The main road entered the city's semi-trapezoidal plaza on the eastern side through an unusual double double-jambed gateway (that is, double jambs on both sides of the gateway); the western gateway is no longer standing. An administrative palace lies on the north side of the plaza, adjoined to the east by an apparently pre-Inca complex of structures built of *tapia*. An Inca wall, with trapezoidal doors and niches, extends from the palace, almost hiding the pre-Inca constructions from viewers in the main plaza and seemingly commemorating the earlier structures. Regular, but much less fine, compounds of rooms and patios are on the north side of the city, east and west of the palace, while other patio and room complexes lie alongside the southern and eastern sides of the main plaza. An *ushnu* platform overlooks the valley from the plaza's western end.

PL. 134

As with some other Inca administrative centers, Tambo Colorado may be subdivided into three ranked zones, each containing public ceremonial spaces and more private rooms and patios.[21] Two of these zones constituted an elaborate administrative palace complex. Martín de Murúa's account of such a palace in Cusco (see page 119) suggests that Cusco officials and their entourage used the innermost zone of this palace, while intermediate elites, in this case

(see page 119)

115 Traces of red, yellow, and white paint still cling to the walls of Tambo Colorado in the lower Pisco valley. This coastal Inca installation is built of adobe.

probably local leaders, used the outer zone. Commoners gathered in the third zone, featuring the city's great central plaza.

Tambo Colorado takes its modern name from the red, yellow, and white colors painted in bands on its walls and around its windows, doors, and wall niches. Ongoing research has revealed that the painted bands were not simple decoration, but instead constituted a complex color code that probably served as signs to guide the people and groups who once used the imperial center.[22] Yellow and white occur most frequently in the inner sector of the palace, especially in the innermost part corresponding to the "royal quarters" referred to by Murúa in the previous chapter, while red predominates in the outer zone. As one moved progressively into the palace, away from the main plaza, spaces became more restricted, marked with more yellow and white bands, increasingly identified with the Cusco elite and their representatives, whether male or female.

Tambo Colorado's main plaza is the largest and most important of the public areas. Roofed platforms built against the palace and other buildings once surrounded the plaza, probably serving similar functions to the *kallankas* in highland cities that housed transients. One hundred and fifty-six double niches lined the north and south walls of the buildings behind the roofed platforms, providing a color-coded setting for the ceremonies that took place in the plaza.

An oracle by the sea

At Lima la Vieja ("old Lima"), an Inca site that served briefly as a Spanish settlement in the lower Pisco valley, the main road turns north toward the great settlements that flanked the bountiful sea and the irrigated coastal valleys. The road is not the only change of direction, however, for here the Incas took a new approach and set a different agenda for their rule. Long before the Incas, many coastal societies had developed centralized rule, which the Incas modified and incorporated into their vision of Tawantinsuyu.

The road crosses the desert between the Pisco and Chincha valleys, heading 116 for the Chincha capital—now the archaeological complex of **La Centinela**— near the valley's northern edge. Centuries before the Incas, the people of Chincha built irrigation canals across this broad valley, turning it into one of the most fertile and richest regions in all Tawantinsuyu. An archaeological survey located substantial pre-Inca centers featuring large stepped mounds with extensive platforms, executed in *tapia*. The Incas sometimes modified such structures by adding elements of their own in adobe. La Centinela served as the principal seat of power and consequently saw the most modifications.

The Spaniards, drawn to the Chincha valley because of its wealth, left us especially rich accounts of this area. The most remarkable of these sources refers to three specialized groups of people: farmers who cultivated maize and other crops in extensive, irrigated fields; fishermen who went to sea in reed rafts; and "merchants" who engaged in long-distance exchange, perhaps obtaining metals in the south which they traded for *Spondylus* shell from the north.[23] The merchant scenario, however, is far from conclusive. Archaeologists have uncovered only small amounts of *Spondylus* and no metal objects to suggest a standard of exchange.[24]

Chincha's fishermen and their reed rafts provide another clue to the possible source of the area's wealth: guano islands off the coast of Chincha. There is compelling evidence that coastal people harvested the vast heaps of guano— bird droppings that had accumulated over the millennia on offshore islands —and that coastal and highland peoples used it to fertilize their fields, especially maize. In Inca times the "merchants" of Chincha may have facilitated guano distribution in the highlands.[25]

Although largely eroded, La Centinela's great stepped mounds were once 117 painted gleaming white and often decorated with mudbrick friezes. Little is known of its founding and early growth, but it was not an Inca settlement built on virgin terrain. A major oracle made it a pilgrimage center, and most of the people connected with the city were either permanent residents or lived in the smaller sites throughout the valley.

116 OPPOSITE, ABOVE Aerial view of La Centinela in the Chincha valley, Peru, which had been an important oracle before the Inca conquest.

117 OPPOSITE, BELOW A mudbrick frieze of stylized birds graces a wall on the summit of La Centinela's highest mound.

118   The compounds at La Centinela do not appear to have had a residential function, except perhaps for a small elite. Instead, they served as settings for ceremonies, probably related to local descent groups. A large permanent population lived in modest dwellings between La Centinela and the neighboring site of **Tambo de Mora,** forming a large urban complex,[26] where archaeologists have uncovered extensive evidence for the production of shell, gourd, and metal objects.[27]

The shrine of Chinchaycamac, a branch oracle of the great Pachacamac, appears to have been a sacred rock (from which the oracle was thought to speak) located in La Centinela's tallest stepped platform, some 130 ft (40 m) high.[28] In transforming the Chincha capital, the Incas co-opted the oracle shrine and reoriented access to it through a new imperial compound built in the Incas' signature adobe bricks, contrasting with the earlier *tapia* construction. The Incas also built a sun temple in Chincha,[29] but it seems that almost token respect was paid to the official sun cult, and major efforts focused on converting the shrine of the local oracle into a vehicle for Inca dominance.

Research in La Centinela's elite areas is revealing some of the intricate details of a complex form of parallel rule involving the Lord of Chincha, who enjoyed a close alliance with the Incas. A double-jambed doorway led into a new Inca palace from a small plaza that also served as an entrance to the reoriented Chin-

118 The Inca sector at La Centinela in the Chincha valley. The Lord of Chincha, who lived in a nearby palace, enjoyed an especially close alliance with the Incas.

chaycamac oracle complex. That doorway led into another small plaza or court-yard, analogous to Tambo Colorado's much larger plaza, where the local elite gathered. At Chincha, a stairway linked the plaza to the more restricted "inner" zone of the palace with its "royal lodgings," again recalling Tambo Colorado. The striking difference between Chincha's two-part palace and its apparent equivalent at Tambo Colorado is the drastically reduced public space. In Chincha, the critical local leadership could almost be reduced to a single person; thus, "royal hospitality" and other dealings between the two socio-political levels became more intimate, requiring relatively small spaces.

The most notable feature of the Inca addition to La Centinela is a residence built for the Lord of Chincha next to the Inca palace. It sat on a stepped plat-form, a reference to the traditional Chincha architectural style. The two palaces demonstrate a principle of Inca relationships with truly cooperative local leaders, as this remark by the chronicler Hernando de Santillán illustrates: "[The Incas] bestowed favors and gave gifts, both gold cups and clothing from Cusco, and in honor of their obedience [the Inca] ordered that in each of those provinces a house be built for the said lord beside that which he had built for himself, and those who did not obey of their own accord were forced into subju-gation with all vigor and cruelty."[30] This special relationship is also reflected in the pottery styles used in Chincha after its peaceful incorporation into Tawantinsuyu. The enduring effects of the Inca–Chincha alliance are apparent in the ceramics they made, using both Chincha and Inca design motifs. Inca-style pottery ceased to be produced in most of Tawantinsuyu shortly after the European invasion, but the Chincha–Inca ceramic style continued into the colonial period.[31]

Inkawasi: a new Cusco

Just north of Chincha, the Cañete river forms another broad, irrigated valley that witnessed centuries of impressive cultural development. Prior to its incor-poration into Tawantinsuyu, two relatively small but important polities dominated the valley: Lunahuaná in the eastern, upper valley, and Huarco in the lower valley.[32] Ethnohistorical and archaeological evidence indicates that Huarco's incorporation into Tawantinsuyu differed dramatically from that of the Chincha and Pisco valleys. Huarco's resistance to Inca expansion culmi-nated in a military campaign that lasted at least three years,[33] documented archaeologically by a special military installation, now called **Inkawasi**, built in the territory of Lunahuaná, up-valley from Huarco.

The contrasts among Inkawasi, Tambo Colorado, and La Centinela are striking. As we have seen, Tambo Colorado and the Inca additions to the Chincha capital comprised grand public plazas and administrative palaces, designed to assemble and tie people together. Although Inkawasi contains several residential areas and many of its compounds have religious references, the overall character of the settlement is consistent with passages in the chron-icles that refer to a "new Cusco" built to conquer the unwilling people of Huarco. Nearly half of all the rooms are systematically arranged storage bins. Inkawasi represents a serious and successful effort to use military tactics to add

119

119 Inkawasi in the Cañete valley was a specially built installation that played a key role in the Inca conquest of this lush, coastal valley on Peru's south coast.

a very reluctant area to the empire. The Incas sealed important doorways at Inkawasi, suggesting that it had been closed down, perhaps marking the end of hostilities, as implied by Cieza.[34]

Near the fishing village of **Cerro Azul**, at the northern end of the valley, the Incas built a compound in adobe brick and a two-tiered, 13-ft-tall (4 m) oval platform clinging to a cliff overlooking the Pacific. Given the platform's location, it may have related to worship of the sea and the setting sun. The platform is probably the one described by Cieza: "To celebrate his victory, [the Inca] ordered built on a high hill of the valley the most beautiful and ornate citadel to be found in the whole kingdom of Peru, set upon great square blocks of stone... From the top of this royal edifice a stone stairway descends to the sea."[35]

Southern coastal Chinchaysuyu

South of the Pisco valley the road headed across the desert for the Ica valley, where **Tacaraca** served as the main Inca settlement and the German archaeologist Max Uhle excavated rich Inca-period burials. Farther south in the Río Grande de Nasca watershed, the Incas built two installations, **Tambo de Collao** at the northern end, and **Paredones** on the south side of the Nasca valley.

120

Paredones, along with Cerro Azul and Pachacamac, is one of the few Inca coastal settlements to feature dressed stone. Part of the site was destroyed to make way for the modern road heading east for the highlands; in antiquity an important lateral road also connected Nasca to the highlands. Traces of white paint as well as red and yellow ochre on the walls and remains of a double-jambed doorway suggest that this small settlement was of some note and probably served as a regional center.

Some 60 miles (100 km) south of Nasca in the Acarí valley, the Incas founded **Tambo Viejo**, built over an older settlement using the local construction style of river cobbles set in mud mortar. The ancient road leads directly into a plaza and a sunken room in a platform mound, probably an *ushnu*.[36]

In Yauca, the next valley to the south, a *tampu* known as **Jaqui** functioned as a way-station on the coastal road.[37] The road then loses itself among the dunes and the windswept beach of Tanaka, to appear again on the massif of Atiquipa, where the Andean foothills, covered in the largest fog meadows (*lomas*) in Peru,

120 Paredones in the Nasca valley, Peru, is one of the few Inca coastal centers with walls built of finely worked stone. It lay at the junction of a road leading to the highlands and the coastal road.

121 Detail of a house wall at Quebrada de la Vaca in southern coastal Peru. The trapezoidal niches are a telltale sign of Inca construction.

meet the sea. In antiquity the entire area—some 6,400 acres (2,600 hectares)—was covered in field systems including small, stone-faced terraces and irrigation canals. The fragile *lomas* ecosystem began to collapse in the sixteenth century as a result of deforestation and overgrazing by European livestock, and today the fields are abandoned.[38]

Between Atiquipa and Chala, the Inca road is a much more formal construction than other sections of coastal road, perhaps to protect the cultivated fields. The road averages nearly 23 ft (7 m) in width and is bordered by stones, with occasional flights of stone stairways skirting the low hills. A branch road led to the settlement of **Quebrada de la Vaca**, passing abandoned llama corrals. Its residents lived in high-gabled stone houses surrounding small patios, a style more reminiscent of the highlands than the coast. They interred their dead in above-ground stone tombs with corbeled roofs, a practice that also recalls highland burial ones. Harvesting and storing dried fish, shellfish, and seaweed (and possibly gathering guano) appear to have been the settlement's major economic focus. Quebrada de la Vaca contains scores of bottle-shaped subterranean storage chambers and more formal above-ground storerooms. As recently as a few decades ago, highlanders descended to Atiquipa with their llamas between July and August to collect seaweed and shellfish, returning to their homes between November and December,[39] suggesting that in antiquity not all the ruined settlements scattered along Atiquipa's coves and inlets were occupied year-round.

121

From Chala, a large bay to the south, a lateral road set off for the highlands, skirting the shores of Parinacochas ("flamingo lake"). Although Cusco is 280 miles (450 km) distant, this road provided the shortest route between the coast and the capital, and the fresh fish that Cobo claims took two days to reach the Inca ruler may have been carried, wrapped in seaweed, along this road. In the following pages we rejoin the coastal road north of Chincha as it heads for the Lurín valley near Lima.

Pachacamac: the lord of earthquakes

Pachacamac ranked among the most powerful, influential, and feared Andean oracles. People believed that his wrath could unleash earthquakes: "When he gets angry, earth trembles / When he turns his face sideways, it quakes / Lest that happen he holds his face still / The world would end if he ever rolled over."[40] Ethnohistorical accounts pinpoint Pachacamac as the center of a vast pan-regional ceremonial network that included branch oracles (viewed as wives, sons, and daughters of Pachacamac) at Mala (Sulcavilca, described as a "mountain by the seashore"), Chinchaycamac in Chincha, Andahuaylas in the southern highlands, and a fourth "son" taken to Cusco by Topa Inca (probably a "hostage" *waka*). Tribute to Pachacamac came from as far away as Esmeraldas in Ecuador and included cotton, maize, coca leaves, dried fish, llamas, and guinea pigs, as well as finely woven cloth, ceramic drinking vessels, and raw materials such as gold, all stockpiled in the temple's storehouses.[41]

Under the Incas, the pilgrimage center of Pachacamac also functioned as an administrative and storage center for the Lurín, neighboring Rímac, and possibly Chillón valleys. Just prior to Inca incorporation, these coastal valleys formed part of a loosely organized polity known as Ychma. "[Pachacamac] is very large," wrote Estete. "Adjoining [the temple of Pachacamac] there is a house of the Sun, well built... The town appears to be old, judging from the ruined houses it contains; and the greater part of the outer wall has fallen."[42] East–west and north–south cross streets divided the city into four sectors. In the southernmost, highest, and holiest sector, the Incas built their sun temple next to the older Pachacamac temple. Walls delimited parts of the city, including the temple sector.

A zigzagging stairway of "rough stones" led to the summit of the sun temple, topped by a portico and vestibule. The Incas painted and repainted the entire temple in red ochre, traces of which still cling to some of the walls, although just over a century ago Uhle also noted a layer of yellow ochre in some of the niches. Excavations of storehouses on the temple summit revealed remains of hot peppers, maize, peanuts, and fine cloth. On a broad terrace on the southeastern side of the sun temple, Uhle, excavating in 1896, discovered the remains of forty-six women, who appear to have been strangled. Their Inca-style garb and grave offerings of weaving tools imply that they were weavers, perhaps *aqlla* dedicated to the sun temple.

To the north of the sun temple is a plaza measuring roughly 650 by 1,600 ft (200 by 500 m) with a central passageway bordered by column bases (suggesting that it may have been roofed). The plaza is flanked by an *ushnu* of adobe.

A restored building known as Mamacuna, north of the plaza, contains some walls of dressed stone and may have served as an *aqllawasi*, the house of the "chosen women." Hernando Pizarro, Francisco's half-brother, called them "the women of the devil" and noted that their residence included storerooms filled with gold.[43]

The route of the gods

From Pachacamac a lateral road linked the coast with the highland Qhapaq Ñan, running some 155 miles (250 km) from sea level over a 15,700-ft-high (4,800 m) pass before descending into the Mantaro valley. Cieza recalled that this road was built for Topa Inca after he had carried out sacrifices and festivals at Pachacamac. "It is no small thing to see and to note its grandness and how 122   many grand stairways it has."[44] The road also linked the coastal shrine to Pariacaca, a snow-covered, double-peaked mountain regarded as the abode of a mountain deity and his oracle, revered by many central Andean people. Some 1,800 steps took pilgrims to the foot of one of Pariacaca's open-air shrines, a small, roadside cave, whose entrance Catholic priests sealed with stones and mud in 1611.[45]

Travelers crossed into the Mantaro valley on a suspension bridge whose stone abutments still stand next to the ruined arches of a colonial bridge. Two leading ethnic groups inhabited the valley, the Wanka to the south and the Xauxa to the north. Their settlements—many located on easily defensible hill-tops—point to conflict and tension. Inca settlements, on the other hand, focused on the valley flanks and bottomlands, much of the latter devoted to maize cultivation on state farms.[46]

Following the valley's incorporation into Tawantinsuyu—accomplished by the usual combination of force and persuasion, as well as by gifts of "elegant shirts and blankets and some drinking cups which they call *aquilla*"[47]—the Incas divided the valley's inhabitants into three *sayas*, or groups, headed by indigenous elites, each of whom ideally controlled 10,000 heads of household.

According to Cieza, the valley contained "many storehouses filled with everything to be found."[48] Surveys reveal that nearly half of the valley's 3,000 or so storerooms are poised on hills west of **Hatun Xauxa** (modern Jauja), an important Inca administrative center along the Qhapaq Ñan, some 120 miles (200 km) northwest of Vilcaswaman.[49] Botanical analyses of storehouse contents noted maize, quinoa (a high-altitude grain), *tarwi* (a native Andean legume), potatoes, wood, and grasses; but the storehouses held much more. A lawsuit by the lords of Hatun Xauxa lists the labor and goods (transcribed from *khipu* accounts) provided to and pilfered by the Spaniards following their occupation of the valley. These included people (i.e., their labor), camelids, fine cloth, blankets, ceramics, sandals, maize, quinoa, potatoes, dried birds (perhaps for their feathers), dried fish, fruit, *chicha* beer, charcoal, firewood, straw and grass, and, finally, gold, silver, and copper.[50] Even more extraordinary, and despite the turmoil of the Spanish conquest, *mit'a* labor, storage, and *khipu* accounts still functioned after the invasion. Cieza too expressed his amazement, not only at the wealth of goods stored but at the

122 Flights of steps on the road that linked Pachacamac with the shrines of Pariacaca, an influential mountain deity. The road also connected the coast with the highland Mantaro valley.

accuracy of the *khipu* accounts, noting that everything had been recorded "without a single omission."[51]

It is difficult to determine the size of Hatun Xauxa because it served briefly as the first capital of Spanish Peru and is now buried beneath modern Jauja. Nevertheless, it was a "fine" city, with a plaza "one quarter league long"[52] or 0.6 to 0.9 miles (1–1.5 km) on a side, which makes it larger than Huánuco Pampa's square. The town, recalled Estete, "is built like those of Spain, with regular streets."[53] In the plaza rose an *ushnu*, which today stands 8 ft 10 inches (2.7 m) high. The small sections of remaining, original stonework indicate that it was not built of dressed stone. Cieza recalled an *aqllawasi*, a "very rich temple,"[54] as well as an enclave of metalworkers.

A junction on the Qhapaq Ñan

Some 30 miles (50 km) north of Hatun Xauxa the Qhapaq Ñan passed by Tarma, where "in bygone days there were great lodgings and storehouses of the lord-Incas."[55] At Tarma a road spun off from the main road and headed east for the tropical forest, a source of valued goods and commodities, especially

123 The provincial center of Pumpu, Peru, on the shores of Lake Junín, lay at the junction of the main highland road and a route leading to the Pacific coast.

coca leaves. The Qhapaq Ñan then climbed to meet the high, rolling *puna* grasslands surrounding Lake Chinchaycocha (today called Lake Junín), one of Peru's largest lakes, and on to the administrative center of Pumpu on its northern shores. Pumpu's seemingly bleak surroundings and high altitude (13,100 ft or 4,000 m) belie its rich resource base. Today flamingos pause in the shallow waters and the few llamas and alpacas that graze by the lakeshore are but a hint of the region's great camelid wealth in antiquity, which was based on "many flocks of llamas" and "great herds of...wild ones,"[56] probably vicuñas, whose fiber produced the finest cloth. In addition, the region provided the Incas with dehydrated foodstuffs derived from high-altitude tubers and root crops, fish and fowl from the lake, metallic ores, and salt.[57]

123   A bridge led into **Pumpu**, crossing the origin of the Mantaro river. Pumpu covers some 158 acres (64 hectares), with buildings surrounding three sides of an enormous trapezoidal plaza. Like Huánuco Pampa, the Incas founded Pumpu on virgin terrain, but unlike Huánuco Pampa, there are no fine masonry structures; Pumpu's buildings are all constructed of unworked stone, brought from a distant quarry. These include an *ushnu* and large *kallankas* bordering the plaza. A structure on the northern side of the plaza may have served as Pumpu's *aqllawasi*, the residence of women brewers and weavers.[58]

Surveys also recorded close to 325 rectangular and circular storerooms on a hillside to the east and within the site itself.[59] Excavations there unearthed remains of *maca* (cultivated for its edible root), *chuño* (freeze-dried potatoes), hot peppers, fragments of utilitarian ceramics, and great quantities of *ichu* grass, used either to roof the structures or to bale potatoes.

Pumpu also served as an important junction for two branches of the Qhapaq Ñan, which reconverged at Andamarca, a few hundred miles to the north. The easternmost of the two branches, the most direct route, led to the city of Huánuco Pampa, and may have been built by Wayna Qhapaq during the late campaigns into far northern Tawantinsuyu.

Huánuco Pampa

Cieza apparently never saw **Huánuco Pampa**, but he left us this description, drawn from an unknown informant: "In what is known as Huánuco [Pampa] there was an admirably built royal palace, made of very large stones artfully joined. This palace or lodging was the capital of the provinces bordering on the Antis [Andes; the eastern lowlands] and beside it there was a temple to the sun with many vestals and priests. It was so important in the times of the Incas that there were always over thirty thousand Indians to serve it."[60]

Huánuco Pampa lies on a gently rolling *pampa* (plain) at an altitude of about 12,500 ft (3,800 m). It covers an area of just over one square mile (almost 3 sq km) and is overlooked by some 500 storehouses built in neat rows on a hill to the south. Excavations of the stone chambers (once roofed with thatch) revealed

PL. 33

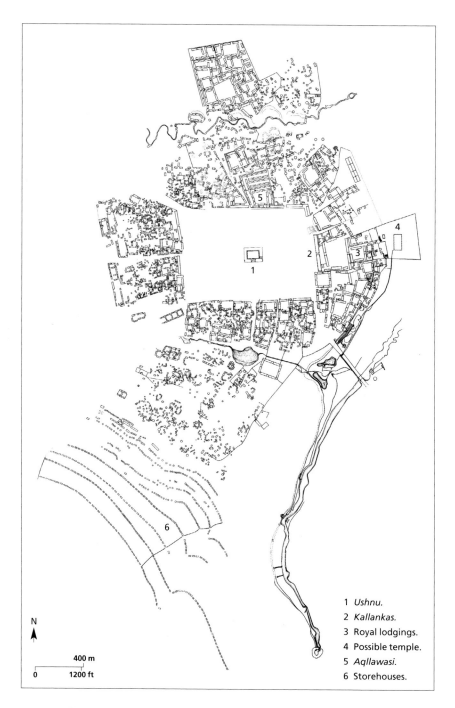

1 Ushnu.
2 Kallankas.
3 Royal lodgings.
4 Possible temple.
5 Aqllawasi.
6 Storehouses.

N

400 m
0   1200 ft

124 ABOVE Plan of the administrative center of Huánuco Pampa, Peru. The settlement had nearly 4,000 buildings arranged around a rectangular plaza and some 500 storehouses on a hill to the south.

125 OPPOSITE Craig Morris (right) and a visitor at Huánuco Pampa in the 1960s.

the remains of tubers, maize, and other foods. The storehouse hill affords a 22
view of the full sweep of Huánuco Pampa and its main feature: a plaza more
than a third of a mile long. The plaza is so much the centerpiece of the city plan 124
that the surrounding structures almost seem to cling to its edges. The Qhapaq
Ñan crossed the plaza, and the streets that separate many of the city's twelve
sectors open onto it.

Prior to the Inca conquest, the region surrounding Huánuco Pampa was
home to several ethnic groups, including the Chupaychu, Yacha, and Wamali.
The Incas reorganized the area, building the regional capital at Huánuco
Pampa. As many as 30,000 tributaries "served" the center, as Cieza noted. The
Incas organized the Chupaychu into four *waranqa*—units of 1,000 households.
A high-ranking Chupaychu was appointed as *kuraka* or leader of each *waranqa*,
and other decimal officials were named as well. In addition, the Incas brought
in *mitmaq* colonists from Cusco as herders and farmers to provide labor for
maintaining bridges, forts, and state temples, and also to extend Inca interests
into the tropical eastern lowlands. In turn, they dispatched Chupaychu to
Cusco as *mitmaq* where they worked as stonemasons, supervisors of state maize
lands, and retainers of the elite.

Stone blocks abandoned en route from a quarry and an unfinished structure,
perhaps a temple, indicate that the site was still under construction on the eve
of the Spanish invasion. The distribution of portable objects and the burning

157

126 ABOVE The *ushnu* or ceremonial platform at Huánuco Pampa before restoration.

127, 128 BELOW AND OPPOSITE One of the double-jambed puma gateways that led into the palace compound at Huánuco Pampa, before (*below*) and after (*opposite*) restoration.

of certain sectors imply a hasty abandonment. Because the Spaniards only occupied it fleetingly and it lies so far from modern roads and settlements, the site is unusually well preserved and the number of artifacts recovered by excavations is unprecedented. Archaeologists excavated almost 300 of the settlement's estimated 4,000 structures. Much of the city was not occupied year-round, and its population fluctuated throughout the year as tributary cycles and the ritual calendar brought the various political and ethnic units of the province to interact with one another and with Inca administrators.

Multi-door *kallankas* face the square. Evidence for large-scale cooking in most of them suggests that they served as transient housing, probably for commoners from the surrounding hinterland who came to Huánuco Pampa for rituals and ceremonies and to serve their short-term labor tribute. Near the center of the plaza rises a stepped, three-tiered *ushnu* reached by a wide stairway and adorned with carved images of crouching animals, probably pumas, flanking the entrances that led to the summit. Because of its impressive dressed stone construction (a rarity at Huánuco Pampa) and carved pumas (often interpreted as symbols of royalty), the *ushnu* probably served as an emblem of the Inca state and its rulers, while the various building sectors around it (with the exception of the administrative palace discussed overleaf) related to the incorporated groups. Excavations on the *ushnu* revealed hundreds of pottery fragments, many from very large vessels decorated with Cusco-style designs. This contrasts markedly with the pottery excavated in the *kallankas* fronting the plaza, where local and provincial designs predominated.

126

Why did the Incas build such an enormous plaza? Aside from the evidence of eating and drinking in the surrounding *kallankas* and the possibility that visiting Inca officials witnessed or officiated over the plaza's activities from the summit of the *ushnu*, it seems likely that the plaza was used for many of the political and religious rituals that punctuated the elaborate ceremonial calendar. It may even have served as a stage for ritual battles, as part of Inca provincial administrative procedures that established fighting not just as an act of conquest but as a fundamental instrument of rule. Given the Andean traditions of ritual warfare discussed in Chapter 3, Huánuco Pampa's plaza may have been a place where the many small groups from the surrounding hinterland could test their strengths and arrive at tentative positions in an emerging hierarchy.

Ethnographic references to Inca plazas suggest that the center's main plaza also witnessed tribute-collecting ceremonies and the distribution of imperial largesse; the initiation of elite youths; public judgments and punishments; the selection of human sacrificial offerings and *wakas* (shrines) for empire-wide distribution; and the public reception of Inca elites and administrators.

The city's most monumental sector lies to the east of the main plaza, where it is said that Topa Inca built a palace compound. The compound is linked to the main plaza by a series of finely built gateways graced with relief carvings of pumas, which led through two other spacious plazas surrounded by public buildings. Excavations uncovered the broken remains of hundreds of pottery vessels used for brewing, storing, and serving *chicha* beer. The final gateway led into a compound of six dressed stone structures—presumably the royal lodgings themselves—and five other, less ornate buildings.[61] Water from a spring about one mile (1.5 km) away fed a large pool and smaller dressed-stone basin or bath. At the eastern end a high platform overlooked a small, artificial pond. The northern end included a small, fine, incomplete building, probably intended as a religious structure.

Aqlla, the "chosen women" who brewed *chicha* and wove fine cloth, lived in a compound of fifty buildings bordering the north side of the city's main plaza. Archaeologists identified their residences and workshops by the spinning and weaving implements and the brewing jars they found in the compound. One of the principal roles of these women was as high-status brides to cement political ties with important local leaders, and this role along with their importance as brewers and weavers probably explains their presence at Huánuco Pampa. Given the size of the compound and the intensity of use, the number of *aqlla* could have easily exceeded 200.[62]

The Incas designed Huánuco Pampa as a place to facilitate social, political, and economic change and growth. It was "artificial" in ways not unlike Brasilia, a modern political creation. But it was not built primarily to house a relatively static and self-perpetuating bureaucracy. No *khipu* knot records are preserved, and while administrative bureaucrats must have been present, they were not the most visible feature of the Inca administration. Instead, what we see at Huánuco Pampa are the old traditions of reciprocity, including labor service, expanded to an urban scale. We also see a city with a mobile population. The city served, essentially, as an urban island in an archipelago of ecological complementarity.

127, 128

129 A gateway at Saqsawaman, the temple-fortess that overlooks Cusco.

130 The so-called Intiwatana sector at Pisaq above the Urubamba river features finely fitted masonry. The stone outcrop surrounded by a semi-circular wall (*center, right*) may have served as a sun temple.

131 ABOVE A retaining wall at Tarawasi (Limatambo) on the road that connected Cusco with the Pacific coast is composed of stones fitted in the polygonal style.

132 RIGHT Peg steps on a terrace at the royal estate of Tipón, south of Cusco.

133 LEFT Detail of *tapia* (tamped earth) latticework at Tambo Colorado in the Pisco valley on Peru's south coast.

134 RIGHT The palace sector at Tambo Colorado was painted in shades of red and yellow ochre as well as white.

135 BELOW The *ushnu* at Vilcaswaman, west of Cusco, was one of the most elaborate ever built.

136 RIGHT A carved stone at Rumiwasi, part of the Saywite complex west of Cusco.

137 A double-jambed doorway leads into a compound at Aypate, one of several Inca installations in the highlands of Piura, Peru.

138 The *ushnu* at Aypate in the highlands of Piura straddled the Qhapaq Ñan, the royal road that linked Cusco to Ecuador.

North to Huamachuco

The Qhapaq Ñan between Huánuco Pampa and **Huamachuco** boasts some of the best-preserved stretches of road in Tawantinsuyu. Little remains of Inca Huamachuco, buried beneath the colonial and modern town. Cieza spoke of two *kallankas* "22 feet wide and 100 feet long" (roughly 7 by 30 m) built of stone, with thatched roofs.[63] The town's unusually large trapezoidal plaza, the possible remains of an *ushnu* under a chapel, worked ashlars, and fragments of Inca-style ceramics scattered around the town, as well as remains of terracing and some 200 storehouses poised on three hills to the south and southwest, leave little doubt that modern Huamachuco covers the Inca settlement.[64] Huamachuco is strategically located along the Qhapaq Ñan and roads leading west to the Moche valley and east to the Marañón river.

The temple of Catequil, which served as the seat of an important oracle and shrine associated with local origin myths, water, and fertility, lies southwest of Huamachuco. Excavations uncovered the main temple compound at **Namanchugo**, at the foot of Mt. Icchal.[65] The complex comprised three compounds on top of a low mound with two lateral extensions, resulting in a U-shaped mound with a plaza in front and in between the wings. The shrine itself, on the central mound, measures 10 by 10 ft (3 by 3 m) on the exterior and contained three libation basins, two in the inner patio and one inside the shrine. Within the shrine, the remains of two canal systems were found: one carried libations away from the basins, and the other was linked to the pronouncement of oracular prophecies. The shrine's patio is paved with sling-stone-sized river cobbles—perhaps an allusion to Catequil, a weather god who was believed to punish offenders by hurling bolts of lightning with his sling.[66]

Cajamarca: strategic entrepôt

While Huamachuco functioned as a secondary center, **Cajamarca**, 70 miles (113 km) to the north, served as one of the most important administrative centers between Huánuco Pampa and Tumibamba in northern Tawantinsuyu; it was also the scene of the massacre of Atawallpa's soldiers and the ruler's imprisonment by Francisco Pizarro in 1532. It too lay at the junction of key roads: the Qhapaq Ñan and roads leading west to the Pacific coast and east to Chachapoyas and the tropical forest beyond. In addition, for many years it served as a staging area for campaigns into Chachapoyas, in the far north of Peru, and southern Ecuador. In many ways it mirrored Huánuco Pampa's function—more related to reciprocal administration and initiatives to incorporate new peoples into Tawantinsuyu than to administrative bureaucracy in the usual sense—serving as a depot for tribute from neighboring provinces. "It was here," noted Cieza, "that the accounts were rendered, and this was the capital of the neighboring provinces and of many of the valleys of the plains."[67] Cajamarca's storehouses must have numbered in the hundreds: an early Spanish eyewitness to the tragic events in Cajamarca noted "certain houses...full of cloth, packed in bales which reached to the roof... The Christians took what they required, and yet the houses remained so full that what was taken seemed hardly to be missed."[68]

Colonial and modern buildings cover the ancient settlement, and virtually nothing is left of Cajamarca's Inca past, except a solitary room built of finely fitted masonry. While some people claim (probably mistakenly) that it served as Atawallpa's prison and ransom chamber, there is no doubt that it was built by the Incas, and it probably formed part of a *kancha*. Cajamarca's plaza—apparently trapezoidal in shape—was "larger than any in Spain," and three *kallankas* (each measuring 200 paces in length, according to Francisco de Xerez) flanked the square. Near or in the center of the plaza rose "a seat of the Inca, high and fortress-like, which we call an *ushnu*."[69] A low earthen wall pierced by two small gateways "leading into the city streets" enclosed the plaza. Eyewitnesses reported a sun temple facing the entrance to the town "in an earthen-walled yard, in which there was a grove of trees." Cajamarca's *aqllawasi* flanked "another, smaller court, entirely surrounded by buildings, in which there were many women for the service of Atabaliba [Atawallpa]."[70]

Some 4 miles (6 km) to the east, a paved causeway 13–26 ft (4–8 m) wide led to the thermal baths at **Konoj** and Atawallpa's "pleasure house." There "he went…to enjoy himself and to bathe in a big pool…made of finely cut stone, and it was fed by two pipes of water, one hot and the other cold."[71] Modern visitors still take the waters in the town of Baños del Inca ("baths of the Inca"), near Atawallpa's lodgings. Xerez recalled that at the entrance "there were four hundred Indians in an open space, who appeared to be a body guard."[72] He remarked that although Atawallpa's lodgings were small, they were "the best that had been seen in the Indies"[73] and consisted of four rooms with a central court (probably a *kancha*). "The room in which [Atawallpa] stayed during the day was a corridor looking into an orchard, and near it there was a chamber where he slept."[74]

The kingdom of Chimor

Before proceeding north on the Qhapaq Ñan, we first turn west to the coast, home to the lords of Chimor, erstwhile allies of Cajamarca, and then head east into Chachapoyas. The dominions of Chimor—or Chimú—extended along the coast from the Casma valley in the south to Tumbes in the north. Chimor's sizable territory, power, wealth, and control over strategic resources made it a prize target for Inca expansion. Indeed, Chimor ranked as one of the richest and most powerful polities to rival the expanding Inca state.

Scholars have long puzzled over the paucity of Inca architectural remains on Peru's north coast. The lack of monumental structures, however, belies the impact and intensity of Inca control over the region's natural and human resources. Aside from the coastal road (the most obvious Inca engineering feat, although much of it incorporated Chimú and earlier roads), the Incas generally co-opted existing Chimú settlements rather than building new centers on virgin ground, as was often the case in the central and northern highlands.

In the Chimú heartland, archaeologists have excavated Inca remains at **Chan Chan** (the Chimú capital), **Chiquitoy Viejo** in the Chicama valley, Farfán in Jequetepeque, Túcume and Tambo Reál south of the Leche river, and La Viña north of the Leche river. At **Cerro Huaringa**, near Batán Grande, the Incas took over Chimú smelting and metalworking operations,[75] and in the Pampa de Chaparrí they expanded agricultural production in fields formerly tended by the Chimú.[76]

The chronicles relate that Topa Inca (either as sovereign or acting as his father's military commander) broke up the defensive alliance between Chimor and Cajamarca, dismantled Chimor's hold over its rich coastal domains, and sent the last independent Chimú ruler, Minchançaman, as a privileged hostage to Cusco, where he was married to one of Topa Inca's daughters.[77] The chronicler Cabello de Valboa said that the Incas found "incredible riches in gold and silver"[78] in the sumptuous palaces of the Chimú rulers at Chan Chan. With the booty amassed from the north coast conquests, Topa Inca ordered that statues be fashioned representing the sun, the god Tiqsi Wiraqocha, the goddess Mama Ocllo Inga Illo, and the gold band that graced Cusco's sun temple, the Qorikancha.

From Chimor the Incas dispatched large numbers of skilled metalsmiths, weavers, potters, and irrigation specialists around the empire. Cieza, for instance, noted that many north-coast metalworkers "were taken to Cusco and provincial capitals, where they worked silver and gold."[79] Unlike other conquered peoples, however, the Chimú were not permitted to bear arms or serve as soldiers, perhaps because of their tenacious opposition to Inca expansion and tendency to rebel. Under Inca domination, most of the valleys once controlled by Chimor "bore their tribute to Cajamarca"[80] and "the deputies of the Incas collected their tribute in the storehouses...from where they were taken to the capital of the provinces...where the temples of the sun were."[81] Agricultural produce from the region's fertile, irrigated valleys filled storage depots strategically located at junctions along the main coastal road and lateral roads to the highlands.

Farfán, like so many Inca administrative settlements, is situated strategically at a crossroads: the north–south coastal road and a lateral road heading east for the Cajamarca highlands. When Cieza passed through the valley all was "in ruins," but he noted that there were once "great storehouses."[82] Recent excavations at Farfán reveal that the Incas doubled the amount of space devoted to storage in two of the best-preserved Chimú compounds, and possibly in a third.[83] Rather than building new structures embellished with their trademark architectural features, they occupied the existing Chimú adobe compounds and built new or modified existing structures with large adobe bricks, the telltale sign of Inca construction. In keeping with their low-key presence, and perhaps to appease local elites, they built an *ushnu* in a restricted area linked to elite residences, rather than in a central plaza.

Some of Farfán's storage bins contained spinning and weaving implements, suggesting—much as Cieza observed—that production of cotton clothing in the valley was a primary occupation. The storage bins lie next to the remains of elite residences, suggesting that the Incas installed officials charged with managing warehoused goods destined for Cajamarca. This is reinforced by the discovery of a curious pattern of squares with central, circular indentations incised into a floor in one of the compounds, near a storage area. Perhaps the squares formed a *yupana*, a counting device used to tally numbers.[84]

Across the Pan-American highway, which slices Farfán in half, and at the foot of Cerro Facló, archaeologists excavated a stepped burial mound measuring 131 by 171 ft (40 by 52 m) that once stood 23 ft (7 m) high, containing the skeletal remains of some thirty-eight bodies, mostly females aged six to forty-five. The women may have been sacrificed, and burial offerings included Chimú–Inca ceramics, textiles, and weaving implements.[85]

Heading north, the coastal road reached **Túcume**, also a former seat of Chimú lords. The Incas occupied almost all of Túcume, which lay to the west of the Inca road, surrounded by lush fields watered by the Taymi canal. As in pre-Inca times, local lords continued to live on the tops of the adobe mounds that dot the settlement. Unlike the previous occupants, however, the Incas built in stone.[86] On Huaca Larga, one of Túcume's twenty-six flat-topped adobe mounds, the Incas destroyed parts of an earlier Chimú temple, filled it in, and built a structure of stone laid in mud mortar and a stone platform topped by ten columns. The structure contained four rooms. Buried in the fill beneath one of the rooms, excavators found the skeletons of nineteen women weavers, while another chamber housed the mummy bundles of three men. The structure on Huaca Larga may have served as an *aqllawasi* and the women, possibly sacrificed *aqlla* (similar to those found at Pachacamac and Farfán), were accompanied by weaving and spinning implements, fine cloth, and provincial Inca and Chimú–Inca-style ceramics.

The rich array of burial offerings accompanying the men suggests that they may have been Inca officials. The discovery of two wooden *keros* with one body indicates that one of the men may have served as a *pachaka kuraka*, or lord of 100 households, as these were often issued to such lords as gifts.[87] One of the other men, buried with prestige goods in local and Inca-influenced styles, may have been an even higher-ranking Inca functionary or perhaps a local lord.

139   Near the main entrance to the settlement the Incas co-opted an older shrine dubbed the Temple of the Sacred Stone, a U-shaped adobe structure graced by an uncarved upright stone. Three offering pits located in the temple's courtyard and on either side of the doorway contained *Spondylus* shell and silver figurines of males and females, dressed in finely woven Inca-style garments and some topped by elaborate feathered headgear. The figurines are like those found accompanying human sacrifices on mountaintop shrines in Qollasuyu and Kuntisuyu as part of the *qhapaq hucha* ceremony described in Chapters 5 and 10, suggesting that such an event may have taken place at Túcume.[88]

The Inca road, at times 46–49 ft (14–15 m) wide, continued north to the 16-acre (6.6-hectare) walled enclosure known as **Tambo Reál**, probably devoted to local administration and craft production. The road passed through Tambo Reál's large central plaza, which was surrounded by elite residences as well as a small storage area, workers' residences, and several pottery workshops. There, potters produced ceramics in the north coast tradition as well as hybrid styles. With the exception of one Inca vessel shape—the flared rim jar or *aryballo*—Inca influence is negligible.[89] From Tambo Reál the road continued to **La Viña**, which—at some 170 acres (70 hectares)—was one of the largest Inca settlements on the north coast road. Researchers recorded four pottery workshops that produced similar wares to those found at Tambo Reál. The Incas may have

139 The Temple of the Sacred Stone at Túcume, on Peru's north coast, was built before the Inca conquest. Offerings of *Spondylus* shell and silver figurines in Inca times point to interest in appeasing local religious beliefs.

encouraged the production of objects featuring local symbols to keep indigenous lords content.[90]

The coastal road carried on north some 155 miles (250 km) through desert and tropical scrub forest to **Tumbes**. Though often dismissed as an Inca outpost at the terminus of the coastal road, descriptions by the first Spaniards who disembarked at Tumbes sketch a very different picture. "Here," recalled the soldier Mena, "we heard of the grandeur of the land that lay ahead and the power and sovereignty of Atabalica [Atawallpa]."[91]

Mena's fellow countryman Juan Ruíz de Arce described a town (known today as **Cabeza de Vaca**) that "must have one thousand houses... [One house] had five doors...from door to door there were more than 100 paces. It had many lodgings, well-painted. In the middle there was a good-sized plaza...and other lodgings...with patios. In the middle of the patio there was a garden and next to it a bath... The Indians said [Wayna Qhapaq] made this house."[92] Cieza spoke of silversmiths and over 200 *aqlla*, "the most beautiful in the region, daughters of the local lords."[93] The sun temple "was painted inside and out with great paintings in a rich variety of colors."[94]

The elaborate constructions observed by the Spaniards at Tumbes may reflect its important role as a port of trade for balsa rafts laden with *Spondylus* and other warm-water shells from the north. Surface finds from marine shell workshops in Tumbes and, some 125 miles (200 km) farther south, Piura underscore the region's importance to the Incas. A workshop at Cabeza de Vaca yielded whole and cut shell, stone tools, works in progress, and finished figurines of camelids and humans that match those offered at *qhapaq hucha* ceremonies, leaving no doubt over the identity of the workshop's sponsors.[95] From Tumbes, figurines made of *Spondylus* and other shell made their way south along the coastal road on llama caravans. *Spondylus* also traveled east along roads to the highlands that connected northernmost coastal Peru to important Inca centers in the highlands of Piura and southern Ecuador.[96]

Chachapoyas: cloud forest crossroads

From Cajamarca a spur of the Qhapaq Ñan led eastward to Chachapoyas, a region that straddled the cloud forest juncture of the northeastern Peruvian Andes and the upper Amazon basin. Another road connected Chachapoyas to Huánuco Pampa, crossing the Marañón in the area of Huacrachucos or farther south. The Chachapoya people once held sway over a vast territory, today scattered with the distinctive remains of their trademark cliff tombs and hamlets of circular structures. There is mounting evidence to suggest that Chachapoyas (as the Incas called the province), often labeled as isolated and remote, in fact thrived at a cultural crossroads that once connected distant Andean and Amazonian societies—source of valued and vital tropical products and produce. It was this privileged position that allowed the Chachapoya to mediate Andean–Amazonian exchange and made them a target of Inca expansion.[97]

Despite the rebellions that plagued Inca rule in Chachapoyas, the region's human and natural resources must have been extremely desirable to the Incas. Early Spanish documents speak of rich gold mines, but the Incas probably valued the area more as a source of coca leaves and tropical forest produce and products, especially the feathers of tropical birds (which were used to decorate high-status textiles). To tackle the many rebellions, the Incas may have relocated as much as half of the population, resettling them around the empire.[98] Their diaspora is remembered by a town on the Copacabana peninsula in Bolivia called Chachapoyas.

The Inca presence in Chachapoyas amounted to a brief, yet intense, sixty or so years. Colonial documents state that the Incas divided the province into three *hunus*, or 30,000 heads of household, but this could be an ideal number (see page 33).[99] They built an administrative center at **Cochabamba** in central Chachapoyas (not to be confused with Cochabamba in Bolivia), perhaps the seat of a *hunu kuraka*, or lord of 10,000 households.[100] Cochabamba is one of the few Inca sites in the region to feature classic, imperial-style architecture, with double-jambed doorways leading into *kancha* enclosures, some of which contain baths built of finely fitted masonry.[101] Little, however, remains of

140
141

140 OPPOSITE, ABOVE A gateway into one of the compounds at Cochabamba in Chachapoyas, Peru. Built in the classic Inca style, the center probably administered the southern half of the Inca province of Chachapoyas.   141 OPPOSITE, BELOW Remains of a fountain or bath at the Inca administrative center of Cochabamba, Chachapoyas.

Cochabamba's "luxurious buildings,"[102] since they became convenient quarries for colonial constructions, particularly the church where an Inca lintel serves as the altar. Northern Chachapoyas may have been administered from a second center located in Levanto, near the modern regional capital of Chachapoyas.

Inca administrative centers along the Qhapaq Ñan often contained hundreds of storehouses. Archaeologists have documented very few in Cochabamba, which may reflect the region's location far from the main highland artery; much of the region's output was probably dispatched to Cajamarca. The lack of storerooms could also signal that the Incas preferred not to store goods in an unstable area and may also reflect the nature of the goods that Chachapoyas provided. As the sixteenth-century magistrate Polo de Ondegardo noted, specialized prestige and wealth goods were transported mainly to Cusco: "from the lands that were far away, little was brought...except gold and cloth, because they weighed little."[103]

Stone-paved roads—many based on Chachapoya foundations—ran eastward to the tropical lowlands. Near the forest's edge, the Incas colonized several Chachapoya settlements by adding their hallmark constructions. Many of these settlements controlled entryways into the tropical lowlands and may have functioned as staging areas for encounters between the Chachapoya and lowland tropical forest peoples to exchange goods. Indeed, such exchanges survived as late as the eighteenth century, when Huallaga tribes sold or traded salt fish, woven pouches, beeswax, manioc meal, feathered hats, and coca leaves to Chachapoyas.

One such road led to **Laguna de los Cóndores**, a lake southeast of Leymebamba, in the Huallaga watershed. There, in 1997, archaeologists salvaged a unique burial site on limestone cliffs overlooking the lake.[104] The finds, which include extraordinarily well-preserved mummies and burial offerings, including provincial Inca-style pottery and *khipus*, provide evidence of Inca administration near the easternmost edge of its domains.[105] Southeast of the lake, in the Huabayacu watershed, the Incas built another installation at **Pukarumi**, a walled site with a level plaza flanked by a 118-ft-long (36 m) *kallanka*.[106] The plaza also contains a sunken fountain, a *kancha* compound, and two platforms, one of which appears to have been an *ushnu*.

Strategic corridor into Ecuador

Between the provincial centers of Cajamarca and Tumibamba, in northern Tawantinsuyu, the Incas built a number of impressive settlements straddling the Qhapaq Ñan. These included Huancabamba and Sondor in the Huancabamba river drainage, and Ayabaca, Caxas, and Calvas in the Quiroz and Macará watersheds. The unusually large number of Inca installations in the highlands of Piura suggests that the area must have been an especially strategic corridor for Wayna Qhapaq as he focused on consolidating Inca rule in Ecuador.

Caxas, located in the highlands of Piura, covers almost one square mile (around 2 sq km) and sprawls across two sides of the Rey Inca river. Little remains of this impressive Inca installation as local people have pilfered the

142

143

142 Rich Inca-period tombs overlooking the Laguna de los Cóndores, pictured here, shed light on Inca policies in managing cloud forest peoples and resources in the rebellious province of Chachapoyas, Peru.

stones to build their farm walls. Caxas was the first highland Inca center seen by the Spaniards during a scouting expedition led by Hernando de Soto in May 1532, six months before Pizarro and his men entered Cajamarca. There, they first saw the Qhapaq Ñan, the impressive highland road that linked Cusco to Quito. Soto marveled at it when he "observed the way it had been built,"[107] and Xerez noted that it could easily accommodate six horsemen riding abreast.

Apart from the road, Caxas also provided the Spaniards with their first inkling of the empire's efficient storage system and the skill of its stoneworkers. Xerez recalled "large buildings…and three houses for the chosen women …there were more than 500 [women]…and the captain [Soto] gave many of them to the Spaniards." On witnessing such an act of sacrilege, the "captain of the Inca" threatened the Spaniards with reprisals.[108] Three *kallankas*, each 330 ft (100 m) long (the largest ever recorded in Tawantinsuyu), fronted a large rectangular plaza, which also contained an *ushnu*. The Spaniards described

143 Little remains of the Inca administrative center of Caxas in the highlands of Piura, Peru, where local farmers have pilfered stone to build farm walls. It was the first highland center seen by the invading Spaniards, who were impressed by the efficiency of Inca storage and road systems.

storehouses filled with maize and footwear for the soldiers.[109] **Huancabamba**, a day's march to the south, was larger than Caxas and "had better buildings."[110] It appears to have been a leading provincial center with a sun temple, but like so many Inca settlements occupied by colonial and modern towns, a few agricultural terraces and scattered stones are all that remain.

Far northern Tawantinsuyu: land of the sacred shell

Typically, both human and natural resources attracted the Incas to what is today Ecuador. Ecuador not only controlled the source of the coveted *Spondylus* sea shell, but two groups played a crucial role in its distribution: merchant seafarers in cargo-laden balsa rafts and a corps of far-ranging overland traders known as *mindaláes*, who dealt in luxury goods.

Nevertheless, military setbacks and rebellions overwhelmed the Incas, and gaining direct access to the sought-after shell proved challenging and, in the end, fruitless. Rather than a single, grand invasion, as some of the chroniclers suggest, the Incas appear to have carried out a series of incursions. Topa Inca may have been the first to venture into the region, probably from a base in Cajamarca or the highlands of Piura, where he orchestrated the Cañari conquests. Topa Inca's hold over the region appears tenuous, and his son, Wayna Qhapaq, who was born in Tumibamba in Cañari territory, set out to consolidate his father's conquests. The stark account of Francisco Vilca Cutipa, *kuraka* of *hanansaya* Ilave on the shores of Lake Titicaca, illustrates the enormous loss of human life caused by the Ecuadorian campaigns. He testified that he fought alongside Wayna Qhapaq against the "Indians of [Tumibamba]" and that his town alone provided 6,000 soldiers, of whom 5,000 died, and a further 2,000, of whom half died.[111]

Throughout Tawantinsuyu, the Incas sought to control the source, production, and, as completely as possible, distribution of status goods. But in the northern reaches of the empire they encountered hostilities and a very different scenario from the non-market economies of the central Andes. Sponsored by and subject to local lords, hereditary *mindalá* merchants supplied exotic status goods as tribute to their lords. They used polished gold buttons or shell and bone beads as a type of currency and traded the rest of their goods—coca leaves, hot peppers, metal goods, and *Spondylus*, among others—at marketplaces.[112] *Mindaláes* north of Quito in Pasto territory, where the Inca presence was fragile or nonexistent, operated largely independently, while the *mindaláes* of the Quito and Otavalo regions functioned under Inca supervision. The *mindaláes* proved vital to the lords of Cusco, procuring goods from areas beyond the reach of imperial control, such as the tropical Quijos area east of Quito, and northern coastal Ecuador, which boasts the richest *Spondylus* beds.[113] South of Quito in Cañari territory, however, there are no reports of *mindaláes*, suggesting that in regions that witnessed the longest Inca presence, the Incas had co-opted the traders and their networks. There, the evidence for Inca control—decimal organization, Quechua as a lingua franca, llama herding, and *mitmaq* colonists—is strongest.

The Cañari ranked among the most rebellious and recalcitrant of Inca subjects (by some estimates the Incas dispatched over 50 percent of the population as *mitmaq* around Tawantinsuyu), but as we saw in Chapter 3 many of the Cañari *mitmaq* also served, in late Inca times, as specialized soldiers and palace guards. Once the Incas had consolidated their hold over southern Ecuador, Tumibamba became the headquarters for Wayna Qhapaq's conquests farther north.

Tumibamba: a new Cusco

Tumibamba, in the heart of Cañari territory, must have been a splendid city, intended to rival Cusco. But unlike Cusco, not one Spaniard saw Tumibamba in its prime. "Today all is cast down and in ruins, but still it can be seen how great [it was]," lamented Cieza, who passed through in 1547.[114] Inca troops commanded by Waskar's generals destroyed much of Tumibamba during the war of succession following the death of Wayna Qhapaq, the father of Atawallpa

144, 145   and Waskar. Although Tumibamba is buried beneath the modern city of Cuenca, excavations by Max Uhle in 1919 and more recent excavations bear out the chroniclers' accounts of the fierce battle: building sites are littered with chunks of stone hacked off finely worked ashlars, as well as layers of ash from burnt thatch and wooden roofs.[115]

As one of the "new" Cuscos (see page 83), Tumibamba emulated Cusco in many ways: like the capital it featured a central sector embraced by two rivers, one of which is called Watanay, and a hill called Wanakawri, after Cusco's holiest shrine. It also had a trapezium-shaped plaza (flanked by a *kallanka* with eleven doorways), as well as the usual hallmarks of royal settlements: elaborate waterworks, terracing, and pools. Cieza speaks of an *aqllawasi* with more than 200 *aqlla*, storehouses filled with fine woolen clothing, "sumptuous palaces …among the richest to be found," and a sun temple "of stones put together with the subtlest skill."[116] "The fronts of many of the buildings are beautiful and highly decorative, some of them set with precious stones and emeralds, and, inside, the walls of the temple of the sun and the palaces of the lord-Incas were covered with sheets of the finest gold and incrusted with many statues, all of this metal."[117]

The chronicler Miguel Cabello de Valboa, who lived in Ecuador in the 1570s, describes an *ushnu* "where they sacrificed *chicha* to the sun" (probably the low platform excavated by Uhle), and a sun temple as well as temples to Wiraqocha and to thunder, "all modeled after and designed as Cusco." He also wrote of a structure known as Mullu Kancha ("enclosure of the *Spondylus* shell") that Wayna Qhapaq had built to commemorate the place of his birth. "To decorate it he had a statue made that portrayed his mother Mama Ocllo, of pure gold," and its inner walls were set with *Spondylus*, "which are some beads made from seashells similar in color to fine coral."[118]

Tumibamba's designation as a "new" Cusco, however, surpassed mere physical similarities and the conceptual replication of sacred space. A study suggests that the Incas may have actually transferred the essence of Cusco's political and sacred power to Tumibamba by transporting building stones to the northern city from the capital, a distance of over 1,100 miles (1,700 km).[119] This may explain, in part, the violent destruction of Tumibamba—seat of Waskar's rival, Atawallpa—by Waskar's warriors during the war of succession.

Several chroniclers comment on this remarkable feat of stone-moving. Cieza, for instance, wrote that "some Indians claimed the stones [of Tumibamba] came from Cusco,"[120] observing scattered building stones at a place called Las Piedras, south of Tumibamba. Martín de Murúa also tells of finely worked stones sent from Cusco to Ecuador, abandoned along the road near Saraguro, south of Tumibamba: "They carried all of those stones, and arriving with them near Quito in the land of the Cañares, in a settlement called Saraguru, a

144 OPPOSITE, ABOVE Inca Tumibamba, modern Cuenca in Ecuador, was designed to emulate Cusco. Only the foundations remain of its once luxurious buildings, which were mostly destroyed by rival Inca troops during the wars of succession.

145 OPPOSITE, BELOW This plan of Inca Tumibamba shows only a portion of the Inca city since modern Cuenca covers most of it.

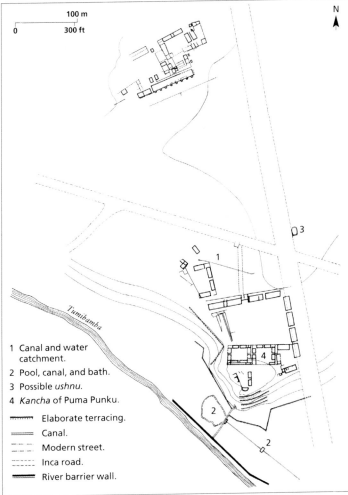

1 Canal and water
  catchment.
2 Pool, canal, and bath.
3 Possible *ushnu*.
4 *Kancha* of Puma Punku.

```
▭▭▭▭▭  Elaborate terracing.
══════  Canal.
─ ─ ─ ─  Modern street.
· · · · ·  Inca road.
▬▬▬▬▬  River barrier wall.
```

lightning bolt struck and broke the principal stone of the building...that was to lie over the primary doorway; and once they informed the [Inca] of this, he feared it and took it for a bad omen, and ordered that they leave there all of these stones, where they lie today...next to the royal road."[121]

A survey recorded over 450 worked blocks of andesite (weighing between 400 and 1,500 lbs, or roughly 200–700 kg) scattered in fields and serving as foundations of the church and post columns in and around the town of Paquishapa, near Saraguro.[122] Geochemical and X-ray fluorescence analysis of the stones suggest that they may have originated at the Rumiqolqa quarries near Cusco, but others argue that additional andesite quarries in Ecuador need to be analyzed for comparison with the Saraguro stones.[123]

Gateways to the sacred shell

Once established in Tumibamba, the Incas assumed control over ancient over-land *Spondylus* (*mullu* in Quechua) routes that led to the provincial center from coastal Ecuador[124] by way of at least two settlements, **Mullupungu** ("Mullu gateway") and **Mulluturu** (as its name implies, also related to *Spondylus*). Even so, they never managed to control the coastal chiefdoms that lived near the sources of *Spondylus*.

Cieza, for instance, remarked that Wayna Qhapaq's attempts to build a road along the Guayas river failed, and "even though these regions served Wayna Qhapaq with rich emeralds and gold and with the things they had most, there were no lodgings or storehouses as in the [highland] provinces."[125] Mullupungu is poised strategically along an Inca road on a hill 30 miles (50 km) west of Tumibamba, only 21 miles (33 km) from the Gulf of Guayaquil. Excavations and mapping revealed a 170-acre (70-hectare) settlement with a plaza, *ushnu*, bath, terraces, and structures of unknown function.[126] Nevertheless, although the Incas may have envisaged Mullupungu as a center from which they could control the coastal lowlands, it was neither completed nor occupied. Their grand scheme to control the elusive source of the coveted shell was frustrated, perhaps, by local rebellions and the Spanish invasion.

146, 147   Twenty-five miles (40 km) north of Tumibamba, the Incas founded **Ingapirca** ("Inca walls"), known in Inca times as Hatun Cañar. At this site, orig-inally a Cañari settlement, the Incas razed Cañari constructions to build one of the most unusual buildings ever recorded in Tawantinsuyu, an oval structure of fine masonry built over a rock outcrop that may have served as the Cañari *paqa-rina*, or origin place. Other features include a small plaza, storerooms, *kancha* enclosures, terracing, and waterworks. Ingapirca's proximity to Tumibamba means that it cannot have served as an administrative center, and its function probably focused more on enhancing local religious beliefs, part of a strategy designed to win over the hearts and minds of the recalcitrant Cañari.[127]

146 OPPOSITE, ABOVE The Incas razed Cañari constructions at Ingapirca, Ecuador, to build an unusual oval structure which may have served to honor local, pre-Inca beliefs.   147 OPPOSITE, BELOW Partial plan of Ingapirca, showing oval structure and nearby rectangular buildings.

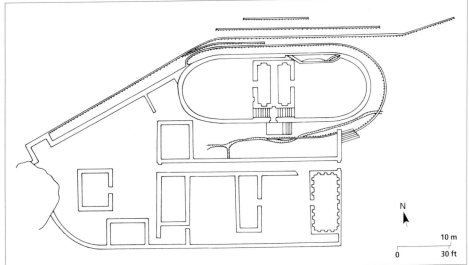

148 One of the forts at Pambamarca that formed a defensive chain near Quito, Ecuador, scene
of almost two decades of hostilities between the Incas and their rivals, the Cayambe.

Chains of forts

Quito, which grew to rival Tumibamba, was under construction on the eve of
the Spanish invasion, transforming from an enclave into a ceremonial and
administrative center. Although Cieza mentions that he saw storehouses, as is
so often the case, colonial and modern Quito—the Ecuadorian capital—has
eliminated any vestiges of Inca Quito. Its location reflects its strategic functions
as a marketplace and an important road junction: the north–south Qhapaq
Ñan, and roads leading to the territory of the Yumbos and the Pacific coast to
the west, and to the lands of the Quijos and the tropical forest to the east. The
early colonial market or *tianguez* (a term the Spaniards borrowed from Mexico)
teemed with foodstuffs, especially maize, as well as pearls, jewels from Esmeraldas in northwestern Ecuador, silver, gold, salt, hot peppers, coca leaves,
cinnamon, and possibly tobacco from Amazonia.[128]

The area north–northeast of Quito, settled by the Cayambe, witnessed some
of the most long-drawn-out military campaigns and bloodiest battles documented in Tawantinsuyu. The chronicles state that the Cayambe resisted the
Incas for seventeen years, a standoff documented by a series of fortified hills
148 overlooking the Quito basin.[129] **Pambamarca**, the largest complex of forts,
stretches for some 4 miles (6 km) along ridges and hilltops on the windswept
and rainy *páramo* grasslands. Defensive architecture includes concentric walls
and deep ditches outside the walls. Archaeological excavations and reconnais-
sance suggest that some of the Pambamarca forts were built by the Incas and
others by the Cayambe. Some forts may have been occupied and reoccupied by
both sides over almost two decades of hostilities.[130]

The chroniclers say that Wayna Qhapaq personally fought in the wars, and periodically retreated to Tumibamba to regroup. After one retreat, the Cayambe "sallied forth from their fortress"[131] and defeated a detachment of the Inca army, killing many soldiers. Wayna Qhapaq dispatched his brother Auqui Toma, who "attacked the fortress, captured four lines of defense and the outer wall." Auqui Toma died in action and Wayna Qhapaq attacked again, suffering heavy losses among his troops. Finally, the Cayambe "lost hope" and fled for a lake, headed by Pinto, the local *kuraka*, who escaped with 1,000 "brave Cañari" — who may have allied with the Cayambe. "Wayna Qhapaq, fighting most furiously in person, made such havoc and slaughter, that the lake was colored with the blood of the dead Cayambe. From that time forward the lake has been called Yahuar-cocha, which means 'lake of blood.'"[132]

Northernmost Tawantinsuyu

It has long been assumed—based on the chronicles—that the Angasmayu river, not far from the modern Ecuadorian–Colombian border, marked the northern frontier of Tawantinsuyu. Sarmiento notes that Wayna Qhapaq came to the Angasmayu river "between Pasto and Quito" and set up "boundary pillars at the limit of the country he had conquered…as a token of grandeur and as a memorial he placed golden staves in the pillars."[133] From his boundary markers, Wayna Qhapaq followed a river westward in search of the sea, to Coaques, where his troops "captured rich spoils, emeralds, turquoises, and a great store of fine [*Spondylus*]…more valued amongst them than gold or silver."[134]

But archaeological evidence and comments by Cieza suggest that Inca control beyond Otavalo, just north of Quito, was fragile and limited to a string of outposts. As we will see in Chapter 10, trying to pinpoint an actual border in what was a porous and dynamic state of affairs is an exercise in futility. The last Inca settlement of any consequence was **Caranqui**, 35 miles (56 km) north of Quito, which Cieza observed contained storerooms, a temple, and an *aqllawasi*.[135] Cieza, who traveled overland from Bogotá, Colombia, south into Tawantinsuyu in 1547, first mentions the Inca road near Huaca, south of the Angasmayu river. "From Ipiales, one comes to a small province called Huaca, and before reaching it, one sees the famous highway of the Incas, as famous as that which Hannibal built across the Alps."[136]

The Incas certainly made incursions well into Pasto territory. Cieza mentions a fort with "guards," close to Ipiales, where "they made war on the Pastos and sallied forth in their conquest of them"[137] and a bridge called Rumichaca ("stone bridge"), a natural crossing over the Carchi river that looked "artificial." Even farther north, near the Colombian border, additional outposts signal the Incas' ongoing effort to expand their territory northward.

Despite the Incas' ambitious efforts to conquer and settle the northern reaches of Tawantinsuyu, Chinchaysuyu was but half—albeit the larger and more important half—of the upper empire. We now turn to Antisuyu, the tropical, forested quarter of the empire, which served as an important source of highly valued tropical resources.

9 · Antisuyu: The Road to
Machu Picchu and Beyond

149   The Inca quarter of Antisuyu embraced the tropical forest north, northeast, and east of Cusco. It included the province of Vilcabamba, the last Inca stronghold, where the exiled Incas lived for thirty-three years stirring up rebellion and hounding the Spanish invaders (see Chapter 11). Antisuyu extended east of Cusco down to the Amaru Mayu, today the Madre de Diós river. Worked by thousands of *mitmaq* and crisscrossed by roads, these eastern provinces supplied much of Cusco's coca leaves.

"Anti" appears to have been a broad Inca name for tropical forest peoples. One chronicler, for instance, wrote that Wayna Qhapaq's son Manco Inca, after failing to trounce the Spaniards in Cusco, "retired to the wild forest of the Antis to a place called [Vilcabamba],"[1] while another located Antisuyu "to the east and north [of Cusco in the] dense forests and mountains of the Antis."[2] The Spaniards corrupted "Antis" to "Andes," referring to the *montaña*, or forested tropical slopes east of Cusco; eventually, the name came to include the entire mountain chain.

Antisuyu never became a region of great cities with large-scale plazas devoted to public ceremonies or spacious administrative palaces and storehouses. Instead, the Incas seem to have emphasized mechanisms for securing valuable tropical resources and establishing numerous private estates for the pleasure of the rulers and their kin groups. These estates, with their magnificent architecture and terraces, created a rather artificial setting, perhaps socially as well as physically. As a result, Antisuyu—much as Chinchaysuyu—emphasized order and centralized planning, and in that sense it was very much part of "upper" Tawantinsuyu.

Early tropical forest conquests

Following their legendary defeat of the Chankas, the Incas pushed beyond the Cusco valley and targeted parts of Antisuyu. They subjugated the Urubamba valley downstream from Ollantaytambo to the Chuquichaka bridge, modern-day Chaullay. From the Chuquichaka crossing, the Incas advanced up the Vilcabamba valley, founding Vitcos near its headwaters. They ventured over

149 Map showing part of the Antisuyu quarter of the Inca empire.

the Kolpacasa pass as far as Pampaconas, "which is before the woodland starts."[3] "The [*kurakas*], in order to please the Inca more and gain his good graces, told him that they wanted to give him a mountain filled with fine silver and some rich gold mines… With the silver and gold that they took out of [Vilcabamba] they accumulated in Cusco the wealth that the Spaniards found."[4]

Not only was the province of Vilcabamba a valued source of mineral wealth, but it and other parts of Antisuyu to the east and southeast of Vilcabamba supplied the Incas with highly sought-after tropical forest resources, especially coca, the mildly narcotic leaf on which the Incas held a quasi-monopoly (the Incas set up coca-growing enclaves in the Tono and Qosnipata areas and reportedly built a fort called Opatari in the Tono valley).[5] Antisuyu also provided other tropical crops such as cotton and hot peppers, as well as honey, resin, beeswax, dyestuffs, the hard wood of the chonta palm, medicinal and hallucinogenic plants, animal pelts, live animals for pets, and, especially, the feathers of brightly colored tropical birds to dress the nobles, the soldiers, and the *wakas*.

The Incas established contact with peoples who controlled river trade along the Amazon tributaries. Hampered by their lack of experience in canoe travel, in some cases they may have established *mitmaq* at small outposts near navigable rivers. There, at designated times of the year, the Incas exchanged salt, textiles, and bronze axes for tropical goods.[6] These encounters may also have been matched by yearly visits by tropical forest peoples such as the Campa and

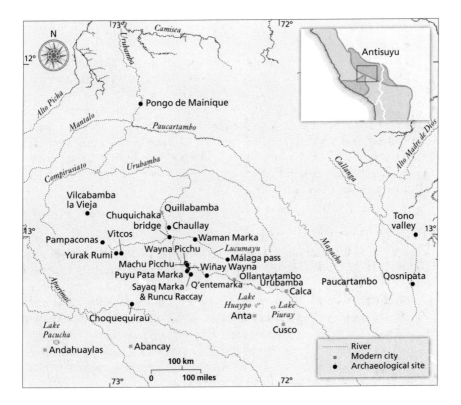

the Piro to Cusco itself, where they exchanged tropical products and produce for highland metalwork and other goods.[7] Downriver from the Urubamba's Chuquichaka bridge, the Incas befriended local indigenous tribes such as the Piro and the Chontaquiro near the Pongo de Mainique, a series of rapids on the lower Urubamba, where early colonial documents speak of an Inca "fortress" called Tonkini.[8]

150 Machu Picchu perches high above the Urubamba river surrounded by forested peaks. It may have been a royal estate managed by the lineage of legendary Inca ruler Pachakuti.

Ensuring access to tropical resources and trade networks along Amazon tributaries, perhaps by allying with local chiefs, may have prompted the Incas to mount expeditions into the tropical lowlands, such as the one Topa Inca is said to have led into the Madre de Diós area, east of Cusco.[9] In some cases, key alliances eventually allowed the Incas to exploit some exchange networks wholesale, a policy that may serve as a model for Inca strategies in "managing" the tropical lowlands, from the forested Andean slopes bordering Chinchaysuyu in the north to the Chaco plains flanking Qollasuyu in the south.[10]

The Urubamba river valley and the road clinging to its heights—the so-called Inca Trail—provided the initial entryway into the province of Vilcabamba. The Incas also used a second route, across the Panticalla (Málaga) pass and down the Lucumayu (Amaybamba) river, which joins the Urubamba after it loops around Machu Picchu. This second route overshadowed the roundabout approaches to the tropical lowlands along and above the Urubamba between Ollantaytambo and Chaullay.

The importance of the Panticalla pass lasted well into Spanish colonial times. Following Manco Inca's siege of Cusco in 1536–37 he withdrew to Ollantaytambo, where he again engaged the Spaniards before retreating over the Panticalla pass into the province of Vilcabamba. The Spaniards, intent on capturing Manco, also favored the Panticalla road, and, as a result, Inca settlements above and below the river between Q'entemarka and Chaullay, including Machu Picchu, escaped detection and destruction by the Spaniards.

A city of stairways

The daring, stone-paved road that is now the Inca Trail linked a series of settlements strung along the forested slopes of the high jungle, connecting Cusco to
150, PL. 166 Machu Picchu and beyond. In this spectacular setting, amid distant views of the sacred, snow-clad peaks of the Urubamba and Vilcabamba ranges, Machu Picchu's buildings and terraces spill over a ridge hundreds of meters above the turbulent Urubamba. Combining the remarkable landscape with brilliant site planning and architecture, the Incas created one of the world's most remarkable examples of harmony between architecture and sacred geography. They carved the ridge on which Machu Picchu is poised with terraces and, together with adjacent Wayna Picchu, turned the entire site into an enormous sculpture. Builders framed views of constellations and nearby mountains in doorways and windows, and linked the site vertically by a chain of sixteen spring-fed baths or fountains. The builders also sculpted living stone, even carving some stones to echo the shapes of the mountains.

The American explorer Hiram Bingham, searching for the lost city of Vilcabamba, the final Inca stronghold, may have been Machu Picchu's "scientific" discoverer in 1911, but earlier explorers had heard of its existence, or at least the names of the peaks known as Machu Picchu and Wayna Picchu. The earli-

151 One of the residential sectors at Machu Picchu, surrounded by a finely built enclosing wall. Recent fieldwork suggests that the site may have housed some 750 people.

est map to include Machu Picchu, for instance, is dated 1874, while the Italian explorer Antonio Raimondi also located Machu Picchu on his map, published in 1876. The Austrian traveler Charles Wiener noted "Matchopicchu" and "Huaynapicchu" (though they are not in the right place) on a map in his publication of 1880, and mentioned "rumors" of ruins.

On July 24, 1911, Melchor Arteaga, a farmer and tavern keeper in nearby Mandor Pampa, led Bingham on a tough slog up a steeply forested mountain. There, Bingham found local people living in and farming amid the ruins, and caught his first sight of Machu Picchu "in the midst of a tropical forest, beneath the shade of whose trees we could make out a maze of ancient walls, the ruins of buildings made of blocks of granite, some of which were beautifully fitted together."[11] In a journal entry of 1911[12] Bingham attributed Machu Picchu's discovery to one Agustín Lizárraga, a local farmer whose 1902 charcoal autographs Bingham's workmen spent two days "erasing from [Machu Picchu's] beautiful granite walls."[13]

We shall never be entirely certain of Machu Picchu's function. Nevertheless, the Incas may have built it and the other sites strung along the narrow, stone-paved Inca Trail (**Runcu Raccay**, **Sayaq Marka**, **Puyu Pata Marka**, and **Wiñay Wayna**, ritual stops along the route to Machu Picchu, graced with terraces, waterworks, and carved stones) to honor conquests and dominion over the region. But the overall quality of Machu Picchu's stonework, exemplified by finely wrought temples and shrines and compounds with double-jambed entryways, shows that it was more than an Inca outpost. Did its inaccessible location high above the river, surrounding walls, drawbridge, easily blocked approach roads, single, inner gateway, and dry moat restrict access to a highly religious site and demarcate the sacred from the profane? Alternatively, was it designed to deter incursions by hostile Antis? Machu Picchu may have evolved

152 One of many carved rocks at Machu Picchu, central to the site's design. This one appears to mimic the shape of the mountain in the distance.

from a defended outpost near a frontier in the early years of its founding[14] to flourish, in its heyday, as the showpiece of Pachakuti's royal estates. The site's relatively small plaza, few *kallankas*, and small number of storage structures imply that it was not an administrative center like Huánuco Pampa, where numerous storehouses provided foodstuffs to feed and entertain subject peoples and a vast plaza could accommodate thousands.

PLS 164, 165   Building Machu Picchu was an enormous undertaking, requiring workers to move great quantities of earth to create the terraced plaza, where archaeologists have recorded up to 7 ft 10 inches (2.4 m) of fill. An onsite quarry provided the white granite for its walls, and masons worked the stone with bronze crowbars and hammerstones fashioned from river cobbles. Like most Inca settlements, Machu Picchu is divided into *hanan* and *hurin*, a boundary probably marked by its terraced plaza. The *hanan* sector, northeast of the plaza, contained religious structures and royal residences, while the *hurin* sector, southwest of the plaza, included residential compounds, storerooms, and workshops.[15]

152   Carved stones, boulders, and outcrops, as well as fountains or baths, are especially prominent at Machu Picchu and central to the site's design. Sculpted stones flank burial caves, enhance structures or patios, or mimic the shapes of distant mountains. The so-called Intiwatana stone may have capped a

153, 154   terraced platform or *ushnu* that symbolized the sun.[16] The Intiwatana stone

153 A terraced hill at Machu Picchu may have served as an *ushnu*, a ceremonial platform.

154 A carved stone on the summit of the terraced hill is aligned with the cardinal directions and sacred mountains.

155 This sculpted cave beneath the Torreón, or sun temple (see page 72), at Machu Picchu may have served as a burial chamber.

(not a "sundial," as some have argued, but a beautifully carved stone) is aligned with sacred mountains and the cardinal directions[17] and also seems to replicate the shape of Wayna Picchu on the northern horizon. To the east, the highest summit of snow-capped Verónica (Wakay Willka in Quechua) may have pinpointed equinox sunrises, while to the west the sun set behind the highest summit of Pumasillo at the December solstice. Although Salcantay, one of the region's most sacred mountains in antiquity as well as today, is not visible to the south, it can be seen from the summits of Wayna Picchu and Machu Picchu mountains. Intimachay cave on Machu Picchu's eastern side may have been used to observe the December solstice sunrise.[18]

The first bath in the chain of sixteen fountains lies adjacent to the Torreón, which may have been a sun temple. Built over an outcrop, the Torreón—as we saw in Chapter 5—may also have served as an astronomical observatory. Beneath the Torreón is an elaborate, sculpted cave containing some of the site's finest stonework. The bath also adjoins one of the most elaborate compounds at the site, perhaps a royal residence, which contained a private garden.[19]   155

Residential remains at Machu Picchu indicate that it could have housed   151
some 750 people.[20] The agricultural terraces flanking much of the site, especially on the eastern side, protected it from erosion but did not provide enough land to sustain its residents, who probably also relied on crops grown at neighboring settlements. Pollen studies indicate that farmers grew maize on the terraces, as well as potatoes and a type of legume.[21] Some of Machu Picchu's inhabitants engaged in metalworking, revealed by the discovery of pure tin and copper sheet, which they alloyed to produce tin bronze, and cast to create tools and decorative items. Spindle whorls and bone weaving tools point to cloth production.

Bingham and his crew discovered over a hundred burial caves in and around Machu Picchu. A reappraisal of the 174 individuals and their burial offerings signal that they were mostly low-status *mitmaq* laborers. Distinct types of cranial deformation indicate that some came from the Titicaca area and others from Peru's central and north coast. Studies of pottery types reveal that still others came from Chachapoyas in the northern Andes.[22] Furthermore, and contrary to the report of 1916 by George Eaton, a member of Bingham's expedition, the majority of skeletal remains are not those of women. Rather, the bones reflect a balanced female–male sexual ratio.[23] The presence of infants and newborns, along with evidence that some of the women gave birth,[24] signals that Machu Picchu was not "the home of a considerable number of the Virgins of the Sun," as Bingham claimed.[25]

In the wake of Wayna Qhapaq's death in the 1520s and as the war of succession, followed by the Spanish invasion, enveloped Tawantinsuyu, Machu Picchu's residents found themselves cut off from Cusco. Life at this remote royal estate, so dependent on the capital, was no longer possible; the archaeological evidence indicates that Machu Picchu's abandonment was not sudden and that its inhabitants took most of their possessions with them.[26]

The gateway to Vilcabamba

Below the Panticalla pass, about halfway down the Lucumayu valley, Pachakuti reportedly founded another estate "for his recreation"[27] known as **Waman Marka**. Built on artificially leveled land overlooking a bend in the Lucumayu river, the site is composed of six structures with common walls surrounding a small plaza.[28] Its style is similar to the Urubamba valley sites, and its one surviving double-jambed doorway suggests that it may have housed Inca nobles.

Colonial documents indicate that the Incas cultivated maize in this part of the valley and that Topa Inca, his wife, and "the Sun" held properties as well.[29] Topa Inca settled the area with 1,500 *mitmaq*, including colonists from Chachapoyas, accompanied by their *kuraka*. Near the confluence of the Lucumayu and the Urubamba lies the famous Chuquichaka bridge, where a large boulder in the middle of the river once supported an Inca bridge. In 1998 a mudslide swept away the modern bridge, set on the Inca foundations, as well as the boulder. The Chuquichaka crossing is not far from the Urubamba's confluence with the Vilcabamba river, the traditional entryway into the province of Vilcabamba.

At the end of the Vilcabamba valley lies **Vitcos** or Rosaspata, perched on a hill at the end of a narrow spur and surrounded by steep bluffs on three sides. Vitcos, "whence the view commanded a great part of the province of Vilca-pampa,"[30] forms part of a sprawling complex of royal residences and carved rock shrines. Built of white granite, its architecture recalls Waman Marka's, and the two sites are probably contemporary.[31]

It too probably functioned as a royal estate run by Pachakuti's *panaka*, converted by Manco Inca in 1536 into his de facto capital. As there is only one approach, access to the spur is controlled, suggesting a restricted, royal site of ceremonial importance. The oldest, northern sector of Vitcos boasts the finest stonework in the province, with double-jambed doorways, probably the remains of a royal compound, opening onto a small plaza. No doubt, these were the "sumptuous and majestic buildings erected with great skill and art" described by a Spanish eyewitness.[32]

The central sector of Vitcos, most likely built by the "rebel" Inca Manco, is an area of fieldstone and mud mortar constructions that probably served multiple functions. The stonework is rough compared to the palace complex on the spur above. This sector has a *kallanka* and a small building fronting a courtyard that may have been Manco's residence.[33] Manco's son, Titu Cusi, reported that his father had had to build a new residence in Vitcos since "his forefathers" [i.e. their *panakas*], Pachakuti, Topa Inca Yupanki, and Wayna Qhapaq, "occupied the buildings already there."[34]

The southern sector, nestled at the end of a narrow valley watered by the Río de los Andenes, is the site of a famous carved stone, shrine, and oracle that is variously called Yurak Rumi ("white rock"), Chuquipalta, or Ñusta Ispanan ("where the princess urinated"). The waters of a small pool, now clogged with vegetation, once reflected the stone. Terraces surround the temple complex, and two sets of buildings with small courtyards, each boasting double-jambed entryways, once flanked the elaborately carved stone. Measuring 26 ft (8 m) in height, the granite boulder was sculpted with steps, channels carved on top to

157

156

156 ABOVE Detail of the carvings on the sacred rock of Yurak Rumi ("white rock") at Vitcos, Peru, showing steps, bosses, and pegs on the north side of the boulder.

157 BELOW A reconstruction of buildings with courtyards—entered by double-jambed doorways—surrounding the sacred rock of Yurak Rumi at Vitcos. This sculpted 26-ft-high (8 m) boulder served as the centerpiece of an oracular shrine.

receive liquid offerings , and rows of pegs and square bosses that project from the north side.

Bingham identified Yurak Rumi as the shrine described in the chronicle of Antonio de la Calancha, a seventeenth-century Augustinian cleric. Near Vitcos, wrote Calancha, "in a village called Chuquipalta is a temple to the sun, and inside it a white stone above a spring of water."[35] "The Devil," noted Calancha, "gave answers from a white rock…over a pool of water, which they worshipped as if it were divine."[36] Zealous Spanish clergy had the shrine complex destroyed and burned in 1570, tearing down the buildings, scattering the stones, and setting fire to Yurak Rumi, which may have been the centerpiece of a sun temple. Spanish destruction of the shrine appears to have been systematic. Bingham's excavations of 1912 revealed only "a handful of rough potsherds,"[37] while more recent excavations unearthed burnt thatch as well as Inca and colonial potsherds.

Four stone-paved roads converged on Vitcos. One led to Machu Picchu, a second to the Chuquichaka bridge, and a third over the Kolpacasa pass down to Pampaconas and Vilcabamba la Vieja. A fourth road headed for **Choque-quirau**, an Inca settlement poised on a ridge 5,900 ft (1,800 m) above the Apurímac and, until 1911, the only documented Inca site in the province of Vilcabamba. In fact, it was Bingham's visit to Choquequirau in 1909 that

158

encouraged him to search for the lost Inca cities of Vitcos and Vilcabamba, and led to the "discovery" of Machu Picchu. Choquequirau's elegant terraces (along with nearby terrace complexes), fountains (fed by a canal some 2 miles long), shrines, *kallanka*, storerooms, and small number of residences suggest that it may have served as an agricultural production enclave or as a royal estate, perhaps that of Topa Inca. Recent clearing west of the ceremonial plaza revealed a unique suite of terraces decorated with a mosaic of twenty-three llamas rendered in a lighter-colored stone than the darker stones of the terraces.

Despite the large number of double-jambed entryways and niches suggestive of the royal hallmark, Choquequirau's stonework is inferior to that of Machu Picchu, Vitcos, and other royal estates. This may reflect Inca masons' use of the local metamorphic stone, which is much harder to work than granite or andesite.[38] The local stone also frustrated recent restoration efforts, which resorted to using cement lintels when modern masons could not work the metamorphic rock. A road leading north connects Choquequirau to **Cerro Victoria–Qoriwayrachina**, a sprawling complex that may have housed farmers and camelid herders as well as *mitmaq* who mined nearby silver deposits.[39]

Empire in exile

In early 1539, with the Spaniards in pursuit, Manco and his court fled over the Kolpacasa pass to build a new capital at the place later known as **Vilcabamba la Vieja**, a two-day march from Vitcos. Over the decades, protracted negotiations between the Spaniards and exiled Incas resulted in frequent meetings between the two factions. An eyewitness account of 1565 reveals that little of the pageantry of Inca court life had been lost in the turmoil. "The Inca himself [Titu Cusi, Manco's son] came in front of all, wearing a headdress with plumes of many colors, a silver plate on his breast, a golden shield in one hand, and in the other a lance of gold… On his forehead was a crown of fringe and another was around his neck. He had a golden dagger and he wore a mask of several colors."[40]

Within a month of exploring Machu Picchu, Bingham had reached a place that his indigenous guides called Espíritu Pampa ("plain of the spirits"). Unaware of the chronicle of Martín de Murúa, which would have clinched Espíritu Pampa as the location of Vilcabamba la Vieja, *the* lost and last Inca city, he failed to realize the importance of his discovery.

As the years passed, Machu Picchu's impressive architecture and setting seduced Bingham, who regarded Vilcabamba la Vieja's inferior stonework and less spectacular location in the lowland tropical forest as a far less fitting site for the lost capital. By 1930, and despite overwhelming evidence to the contrary, he had not only proclaimed Machu Picchu to be Vilcabamba, but had also

167

158 Terraces that carve the terrain into geometric shapes, a chain of fountains, and double-jambed doorways suggest that Choquequirau, high above the Apurímac river, may have served as a royal estate.

described it as the cradle and grave of Inca civilization. Since Bingham's landmark discoveries, however, exploration and mapping in the region have shown that the Incas did indeed found their last capital at Espíritu Pampa.

Although built after the Spanish invasion, Vilcabamba's layout is typically Inca[41] and it contains many of the buildings and features commonly found at Inca sites: a *kallanka*, an uncarved boulder fronting a plaza, fountains, and plazas. Its setting in a lush, lowland rainforest valley, however, is unusual. The most striking difference between Vilcabamba la Vieja and Inca settlements built before the European invasion is the Spanish-style roof tiles that roofed the city's most important buildings; piles of these broken tiles lie scattered among the ruins. Although Bingham noted the "roughly made Spanish roofing tiles of various sizes,"[42] perhaps because of his ignorance of Murúa's chronicle, he did not grasp how this seemingly small but important detail identifies Vilcabamba la Vieja as the last Inca capital.

When the Spaniards marched into Vilcabamba la Vieja in 1572, they saw a large city "half a league wide...and a huge distance in length," but found it abandoned and smoldering from the fires set by the fleeing neo-Inca ruler Tupac Amaru, who had escaped downriver carrying the sun image (described on page 120), and the mummies of Manco, his father, and Titu Cusi, his brother. From the top of Vilcabamba's ceremonial entryway, a long, narrow stairway descended into the city. Sadly, years of mule traffic, heavily laden with molasses, sugarcane alcohol, and coffee, has all but obliterated this stairway.

Spanish eyewitnesses reported seeing 400 houses, as well as fields planted with coca, sugarcane, manioc, sweet potatoes, and cotton. In addition, the Incas cultivated "diverse fruits and wild trees" and harvested maize three times a year. "The houses," remarked Murúa, "were covered in good thatch... The house of the [Inca] was on different levels and covered with roof tiles. They had painted the entire palace in a great variety of colors, as was their fashion, and its doors were of very aromatic cedar... The town had a square large enough to hold many people, where they used to run horses and rejoice in merriments."[43] Mapping revealed a sunken fountain, double-jambed wall niches—the only ones at Vilcabamba—and the remains of a two-story building, remarkably well-preserved despite the large trees growing from its walls, as well as close to 300 of the 400 houses that eyewitnesses reported seeing at Vilcabamba.[44]

A long avenue crossing small streams leads into the center of Vilcabamba la Vieja. There, a 16½-ft-high (5 m) granite boulder flanks a large plaza, surrounded by a *kallanka*, a possible *ushnu*, and an *aqllawasi*. This was the "university of [the Incas'] idolatries" described by the Augustinian cleric Calancha, where they "spend their time...in the celebration of sacrifices and fasts and in pagan worship of their [*wakas*] and idols and in celebrating all the rest of the *fiestas* according to what was done in Cusco in the time of the ancient Incas."[45] In this setting, the Incas had "nearly the luxuries, greatness and splendor of Cusco in that distant, or rather, exiled land—and they enjoyed life there."[46]

The final chapter of our *suyu* survey explores the "lower" half of the empire, Qollasuyu and Kuntisuyu. In Chinchaysuyu and Antisuyu, the Incas built sun

159 These foundations at Saqsawaman are the remains of a circular tower, one of two towers overlooking Cusco.

160 A carved, stepped outcrop at Saqsawaman may have served as a shrine on Cusco's *ceque* system, a network of shrines worshipped by the city's lineages.

161 Saqsawaman's three zigzagging walls, formed of limestone blocks quarried from nearby outcrops; the city and valley of Cusco are visible to the left.

162, 163 Choquequirau, high above the roaring Apurímac river, may have formed
part of a royal estate.

164 ABOVE Machu Picchu's plaza and terraced hill, topped by the carved stone illustrated on page 193.

165 RIGHT Machu Picchu's builders moved great quantities of earth to create the leveled and terraced plaza that divides the cloud forest settlement into two sectors.

166 Wayna Picchu, the sugarloaf peak in the center, towers above Machu Picchu.
A stepped path leads to the summit, which is crowned by terraces and small structures.

167 Vilcabamba la Vieja's setting in lowland jungle is unusual for an Inca settlement. It served as the capital of the neo-Inca state for over thirty years before Spanish forces invaded it in 1572.

temples and honored local *wakas*, but the northern quarter's meticulously planned road network linking great administrative cities overshadowed the religious complexes they contained. Qollasuyu and Kuntisuyu, on the other hand, with their smaller, less-centralized societies and sacred landscape, lent themselves to a less rigid system of roads and imperial installations. Resource distribution and population densities probably influenced the Incas' more gradual and discontinuous southern approach. Of course, both the upper and lower empire held elements of the symbolic and the systematic, but in lower Tawantinsuyu, the symbolic and the sacred appear foremost, while in Chinchaysuyu, the systematic and more "practical" features tend to dominate.

10 · Qollasuyu and Kuntisuyu: Herds, Metals, and Mountains of Sacrifice

168 Scholars generally concur that early expansion far beyond the Cusco heartland targeted the Titicaca basin. There, the Lupaqa and the Qolla (or Colla) had emerged as Tiwanaku's most notable successors, drawing their wealth from vast herds of camelids. It was this prosperity, as well as the region's powerful mythology, that attracted the Incas. When Cieza visited the territory of the Qolla on Lake Titicaca, from which Qollasuyu got its name, he observed that "the region…is the largest in all Peru," although he never saw the vast reach of Inca control beyond the Qolla lands in what are now Bolivia, Argentina, and Chile. He also spoke of "great unsettled regions full of flocks [of llamas and alpacas]," recognizing the importance of camelids to the people of the *altiplano* of Qollasuyu and to the wealth of the empire.[1] A survey of 1567 confirmed Cieza's observation, estimating the camelid herds of the Lupaqa, neighbors of the Qolla and another principal lake kingdom, at more than 80,000 animals, noting, however, that the numbers had fallen since Inca times.[2]

Andean people regarded cloth as one of the most valuable commodities and produced the finest textiles from the hair of the alpaca, the long-haired llama, and the vicuña. To Inca—and Andean—eyes, Qollasuyu was therefore extremely wealthy. Taking their cue from Inca estimates of wealth, the Spaniards made the lake region one of only three Andean regions (another being Chincha, discussed in Chapter 8) whose wealth was reserved directly for the Spanish Crown.[3] While the pastures of northern Qollasuyu provided the ideal habitat for camelids, much of southern Qollasuyu's wealth lay underground. The empire tapped the region's plentiful sources of silver, copper, tin, and other ores to create the sumptuary objects offered to the shrines and to adorn the costumes of the elite.

Aside from its natural wealth, one of Qollasuyu's most striking features is its large number of religious and ceremonial sites and, particularly, the high incidence of human sacrifice on its sacred mountains. The snow-capped peaks of scores of mountains, most spectacularly Llullaillaco in Argentina, have yielded astonishingly well-preserved frozen offerings of children and young women, accompanied by rich grave goods. Just as herding and metals are rooted in

168 Map of the Qollasuyu and Kuntisuyu quarters of the Inca empire.

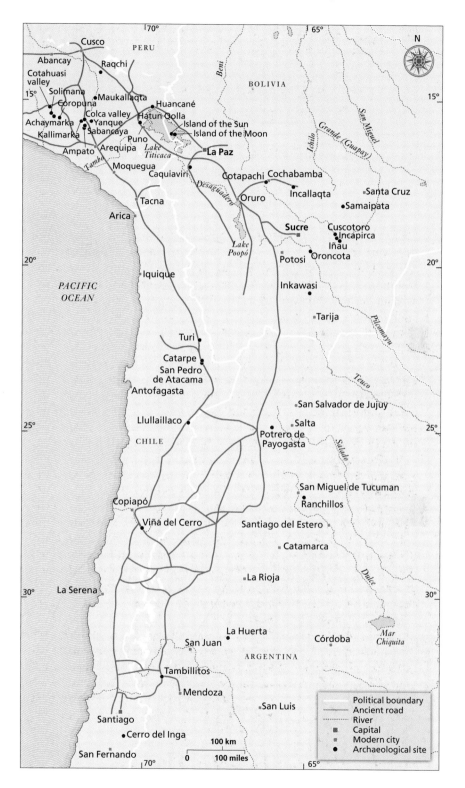

Qollasuyu's environment, human sacrifices at high altitudes are also closely connected to the geography due to the high snowline and relative accessibility of the peaks.[4]

While Kuntisuyu is the least known of the *suyu* divisions, its small size and apparent insignificance belies its importance, along with Qollasuyu, as one of the richest ceremonial *suyus*, embracing important regional and empire-wide religious centers, ranging from Paqariqtampu, the mythic origin place of the founding Incas, to the snow-clad volcanoes of Arequipa with their human sacrificial offerings. Fertile *puna* grasslands provided pasture for vast herds of wild and domesticated camelids, and the few Spanish descriptions of the region also note rich gold mines.

Places of imperial origin

The origin myths recounted in Chapters 2 and 5 relate Lake Titicaca in Qollasuyu and Paqariqtampu in Kuntisuyu to the mythic roots of the Incas. Researchers have documented major temples and pilgrimage routes on the Islands of the Sun and the Moon in Lake Titicaca and at the archaeological site of Maukallaqta (the ancient Paqariqtampu).[5] Iñak Uyu on the Island of the Moon and Maukallaqta share rare building features, suggesting that the Incas reserved special architectural embellishments to commemorate origin places.

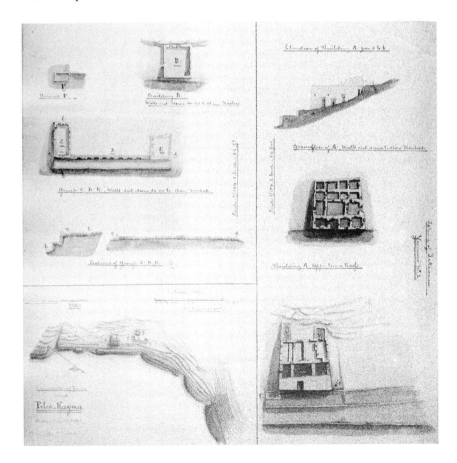

169 OPPOSITE Plan of Pilco Kayma on the Island of the Sun, Bolivia. The building is notable for its two-story construction and its large niches, some of which serve as entryways into inner chambers.

170 LEFT Triple-jambed niche at Pilco Kayma on the Island of the Sun.

One such embellishment is cell-like rooms arranged around three sides of a plaza; another is large and deep trapezoidal niches in the walls facing the plazas, with some of the niches serving as doorways to small inner chambers. Pilco   169
Kayma on the Island of the Sun also features large niches, some of which open into cell-like chambers.

In Pilco Kayma, however, the main building is a massive two-story structure, rather than a winged complex opening onto a plaza. Particularly noteworthy are the triple-jambed niches at the two island sites and at Maukallaqta, as well   170
as the quadruple-jambed niches at Iñak Uyu. While double-jambed doors and niches are common in most elite sectors of sites throughout Tawantinsuyu, niches with more than two jambs are exceedingly rare.

A sacred rock on the **Island of the Sun** in Lake Titicaca marked the sun's   171
birthplace, while the **Island of the Moon** housed a shrine to Quilla, the moon goddess. The sacred rock is a sandstone outcrop 18 ft (5.5 m) high and 260 ft (80 m) long. On the side facing the lake, "a curtain of cumbi [*qompi*], which is

171 The sacred rock on the Island of the Sun, Bolivia. One of the empire's most sacred shrines, the rock was once covered in gold sheet on the plaza-facing side and fine cloth on the side overlooking the lake.

the finest and most delicate piece [of cloth] that has ever been seen," covered the stone; while on the side facing the plaza "the entire concave part of it was covered with sheets of gold."[6] Excavations revealed the remains of a stone-lined canal leading from the sacred rock across the plaza, probably to drain the *chicha* beer that Cobo says was poured into a basin in front of the rock. The sacred stone outcrop and its adjacent stone basin, drain, and canal suggest that it may have been an *ushnu* complex (see page 120).[7]

On the Island of the Sun, the Incas embarked on one of the most ambitious building schemes and reorganization of sacred geography undertaken in Tawantinsuyu. They resettled the island's residents on the mainland, and replaced them with *mitmaq* colonists from all over the realm to serve the shrines and the pilgrims. At the Copacabana peninsula on the mainland, an administrative center controlled the flow of pilgrims, who came from afar bearing offerings of llamas, gold, silver, *Spondylus* shell, feathers, coca, and fine cloth. "Indians…from all the provinces of this kingdom"[8] staffed the facilities at Copacabana, and storehouses contained provisions and clothing for attendants and pilgrims. Before reaching Copacabana pilgrims had to pass through a gate "with watchmen and guards" at Yunguyu.[9]

Prior to embarking for the islands, the pilgrims fasted, abstaining from salt, meat, and hot peppers, and visited and prayed at local shrines. They sailed for the islands in reed boats, walking on paved roads to the sanctuaries. The chronicler Ramos Gavilán, writing around 1618, said that pilgrims approaching the sacred rock and its plaza had to pass through three gateways. The final gate marked the boundary of the sacred precinct, which was surrounded by a low wall. Pilgrims removed their shoes to enter the plaza, but not everyone could approach the sacred rock; lower-status pilgrims probably only went as far as the first entry gate. From the plaza, pilgrims observed solstice sunsets and sunrises, much as worshippers did in Cusco. Those not allowed to enter the plaza could observe the sun setting over the rock and plaza from an observation platform outside the sacred precinct.

The buildings on the Islands of the Sun and Moon are constructed from fieldstone joined with mud mortar, covered with a thick coat of earthen stucco. When Squier visited the Island of the Moon he noted traces of yellow paint on the temple of Iñak Uyu, and red, yellow, and white paint in the niches.[10] The Iñak Uyu apparently housed a statue of Quilla, the moon goddess that Cobo described as made of "gold from the waist up and silver from the waist down."[11]   172

It is somewhat surprising that the Incas did not use their famous dressed and fitted stone masonry for the main buildings on the Titicaca islands, given their importance; only one of the terraces at Iñak Uyu is constructed in this masonry style. In many respects the construction techniques of the sites contrast with the majesty of the great dressed stone palaces and temples of Cusco and many

172 Plan of the Iñak Uyu building on the Island of the Moon, Bolivia. It may have functioned as a moon temple served by female attendants and housed a statue of Quilla, the moon goddess, made of gold from the waist up and silver from the waist down.

places in Chinchaysuyu. Did the Inca architects and their Qolla construction teams consider it inappropriate to use their most elegant building styles and techniques in temples meant to tie them to their distant origins? There are, in fact, numerous decorative allusions to the lake region's earlier Tiwanaku culture, including the stepped tops of doorways and the stepped diamond motifs recessed in the walls. Both of the major islands in Lake Titicaca had been important religious centers for centuries before Tawantinsuyu, although early accounts indicate that the Incas razed the existing temples. It seems that the Incas deliberately alluded to the great Tiwanaku civilization that had flourished centuries earlier in what was now the putative land of their own origins. Sophisticated Inca architects built the ritual scenery that served as backdrops for pageants that recreated stories of long ago, legitimizing their own sacred origin—and thus their rule.

Located 21 miles (32 km) south–southwest of Cusco, Paqariqtampu (known today as **Maukallaqta**) is said to have housed the founding Inca Manco Qhapaq's oracle. At the base of a stone outcrop known as Puma Urqu lies the cave of Tampu T'uqu where Manco Qhapaq and his siblings were said to have emerged from below ground. Excavations and mapping at Maukallaqta recorded over 200 structures, aligned in a grid system.[12] Cobo, who visited Paqariqtampu several decades after its ransacking by Spaniards, noted that the Incas had built "a magnificent royal palace with a splendid temple…in order to make [Paqariqtampu] more famous."[13] Elegant gateways and cobbled streets underscore the site's importance, and the temple seen by Cobo may have been located in a sector that contains an unusually embellished courtyard, measuring just over 44 ft (some 13.5 m) across. Each of the courtyard's three walls is decorated by three triple-jambed niches, a feature shared with the Titicaca island sites. Although the tops are destroyed, archaeologists estimate that the niches once stood almost 10 ft (over 3 m) high. Like Iñak Uyu on Lake Titicaca's Island of the Moon, one of the niches in Maukallaqta's central courtyard is actually a doorway that led into an inner chamber which may have housed Manco's oracle.

As discussed in Chapter 5, Maukallaqta and the sites on the Islands of the Sun and Moon may relate to the Incas' hybrid origin myth. In Lake Titicaca they placed their origins in the broader story of the cosmos and justified the incorporation of a critical sacred region. By having their founding ancestors travel underground to re-emerge near Cusco at the cave by Maukallaqta, they sanctified the land in which they founded their capital.

On the road to Qollasuyu

In far northern Qollasuyu, south–southeast of Cusco, lie the lands of the Canchis and the Canas. According to the chronicles, the Canchis resisted the Incas, while the Canas became early and close allies. At Cacha in Canas territory, some 73 miles (118 km) from the capital on the principal road to Qollasuyu, the Incas built a monumental complex of buildings in stone and adobe enclosed by a wall. The central feature of this site, called **Raqchi** today, is a large rectangular building measuring 302 by 82 ft (92 by 25 m), commonly

173 Maukallaqta, the ancient Paqariqtampu, southwest of Cusco in the Kuntisuyu quarter of the empire, included over 200 structures. It is said to have housed the legendary founding Inca Manco Qhapaq's oracle in the inner chamber of a temple embellished with triple-jambed niches.

referred to as the "temple of Wiraqocha." The roof of this great structure was once supported by a central wall of stone and adobe reaching 39 ft (12 m) in height, with eleven columns arrayed on either side. In front of the "temple" extends an expansive plaza with cell-like groupings of rectangular buildings on its southern side. Behind these buildings, the Incas constructed 152 circular storehouses in orderly rows. To the north of the plaza rises a large rectangular platform. The entire complex was constructed on leveled and filled land and surrounded on three sides by the lava field of the Kinsach'ata eruption to the north (the Canas viewed the volcano as their origin place), with a shallow lake to the northwest.[14] Although Betanzos says an earlier shrine existed at Raqchi, Wayna Qhapaq apparently "re-endowed" the shrine—building the great hall and perhaps also six nearby *kancha* groups to house *aqlla*, the "chosen women."

174

175

The presence of a shallow lake and lava flow from a sacred mountain suggest a strong religious and ceremonial motivation for the site's construction and function. The storehouses, however, underscore economic dimensions. This combination of religious, political, economic, and ceremonial features is famil-

174 ABOVE The temple of Wiraqocha at Raqchi, south of Cusco on the Qollasuyu road, measures 302 by 82 ft (92 by 25 m). Its roof was once supported by a central wall made of stone and adobe with eleven columns arrayed on either side.

175 BELOW Plan of the temple of Wiraqocha at Raqchi.

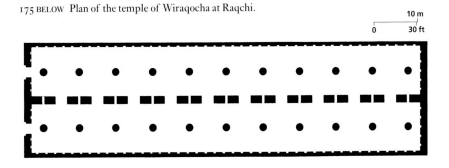

iar from the administrative centers explored in Chapter 8, but Qollasuyu's settlements put a greater emphasis on religion than those in the north. If we could only reconstruct the ceremonies that took place in the great "temple" and its adjoining plazas and platform, in view of the lake and volcano, we would have a much better understanding of the ties and possible tensions between the Inca rulers and their neighboring allies.

The lake kingdoms

Lake Titicaca is one of the world's highest and largest navigable bodies of water, surrounded by pastures of native *ichu* and other tender grasses that provide food for Andean camelids. These animals served as beasts of burden, as a food source—both fresh meat and freeze-dried *charki* (jerky)—and provided fiber for weaving. Lakeside weavers valued camelid fibers because they are warm and absorb dyes more readily than cotton.

Excavations of an Inca house at **Caquiaviri**, Bolivia, about 30 miles (50 km) south of the lake, uncovered Inca pottery pre-dating the mid-fifteenth century.[15] This is consistent with dates from several other regions and suggests that the Incas began incorporating the lake area into the empire earlier than previously thought. As we have suggested, the process may have been more gradual and less strictly military than frequently portrayed. Early overtures may have included exchanges of gifts, feasts, and perhaps even women (see page 45). In any case, the evidence implies that the lake region and its peoples became early and vitally important participants in Tawantinsuyu.

A survey of ancient lakeshore settlements near the modern town of Juli, Peru, documented hundreds of sites dating from Inca and pre-Inca times. It revealed the massive impact of Inca policies on the region as many pre-Inca towns and villages were abandoned, while some villages became larger settlements.[16] Overall, Inca rule witnessed a substantial population increase, significantly greater than would have occurred naturally, indicating that the Incas moved large numbers of *mitmaq* colonists into the area. The survey suggests that people stressed terrace agriculture, lakeside urbanized areas, and, of course, pastures for camelids. As in other regions, the Incas exploited local resources and conditions to produce and transport the goods, such as camelid fiber, that fueled the state economy and nourished its craving for cloth.

The two best-known ancient Lake Titicaca region peoples are the Lupaqa, who were early and important allies of the Incas, and the Qolla. Modern towns cover **Chucuito**, the Lupaqa capital, and **Hatun Qolla**, the principal Qolla city, making it difficult to map and study them. Survey and excavations at Hatun Qolla and survey in the Chucuito area found little evidence for pre-Inca occupation.[17] Chronicler Garci Diez de San Miguel's account of 1567 states that Qhari and Kusi, the dual leaders of the two Lupaqa divisions, lived in Chucuito. If Chucuito was indeed a newly built Inca center, it represents a rare case where local leaders resided in an Inca administrative installation, rather than in a settlement pre-dating incorporation into Tawantinsuyu. The layouts of Chucuito and Hatun Qolla feature long rectangular blocks, a plan shared with some sites in the Cusco region and perhaps the ceremonial core of Cusco itself. It is not clear whether this pattern of settlement planning pre-dates the Incas, but if it did the Incas borrowed it for some of their own settlements.

As noted, not only the Incas, but also earlier societies maintained colonies in myriad ecological zones. Diez de San Miguel described the colonies established by the Lupaqa in the warm valleys located between Chucuito and the Pacific coast, noting that they dated from pre-Inca times. Although the lake kingdoms held vast wealth in camelid herds, their homeland did not permit any significant production of maize and other temperate crops, which they acquired from enclaves of their own people who settled in warm lands as many as ten days distant from Chucuito.[18] The climate and resource distribution of northern Qollasuyu forced people to acquire warm weather products from greater distances than their contemporaries in Chinchaysuyu.

The warm foothills and the jungle frontier

East of the high plains and Lake Titicaca lie the temperate valleys of the Andean foothills. Well suited to maize production, they proved crucial for an empire reliant on royal hospitality, and the Incas invested heavily in economic, political, military, and religious initiatives to incorporate the region into Tawantinsuyu. These included four principal efforts: an ambitious resettlement program by Wayna Qhapaq in the Cochabamba valley, a massive imperial installation at Incallaqta, the monumental ceremonial site of Samaipata, and a chain of "forts" and other installations geared to securing tropical resources from largely uncooperative tribes living along the empire's eastern fringe.

Colonial lawsuits have revealed details of the bold project spearheaded by Wayna Qhapaq in Bolivia's Cochabamba valley to increase maize production.[19] The documents describe how Wayna Qhapaq's predecessor had already expelled some of the local inhabitants from valuable farmland in the valley. Wayna Qhapaq replaced them with an estimated 14,000 state workers. These *mitmaq* and *mit'a* laborers included maize farmers and storehouse overseers from many regions, supervised by two Inca administrators and a hierarchy of *kurakas*. They also brought in silversmiths from the Ica region of Chinchaysuyu. Maintaining and organizing this especially large workforce underscores the innovative and complex nature of Wayna Qhapaq's project.

More than 2,000 storehouses poised above the valley's edge, mainly at the site of **Cotapachi**, bear witness to this massive investment. The storehouses are relatively small, usually less than 10 ft (3 m) in diameter, and their upper walls appear to have been built largely of earth that has been eroded away. The building remains are extremely shallow, and the majority of excavations revealed no evidence that the storehouses were ever used. Cotapachi is believed to date to shortly before the European conquest, and Wayna Qhapaq's scheme to supply prestige food to an expanding Tawantinsuyu may not have been fully implemented. While the Inca sites in and around the Cochabamba valley are connected to one of Wayna Qhapaq's most crucial economic projects in Qollasuyu, the large Inca installations in the Bolivian foothills and *yungas* ("warm lands") had other functions.

Incallaqta and Samaipata are the most impressive of the sites that formed part of a chain of installations near Tawantinsuyu's eastern frontier, where the Andes meet the tropical forest. The tropical forest was home to peoples who raided along the border region, resisting Spanish settlers and no doubt their Inca predecessors as well. Other settlements in this restless region include **Cuscotoro, Incapirca, Iñau, Incahuasi** and, slightly farther west, **Oroncota**.[20] Such settlements probably served more as multi-functional Inca outposts than as strictly military installations, although their defensive walls doubtless protected them from raids. While Oroncota most likely did not have a primarily

176 Incallaqta, Bolivia, boasts one of the largest single-room roofed buildings ever built in Tawantinsuyu, seen here in the center of the photograph flanking a large double plaza. In front of the hall, which had twelve doorways, was a flattened and carved rock that served as an *ushnu*.

military function, Cuscotoro does have several clear military-defensive features and was reputedly captured by a fierce group of indigenous Chiriguano led by the Portuguese adventurer Alejo García, who reached the eastern frontier of Tawantinsuyu around 1522, a decade before Pizarro arrived at Cajamarca. Cuscotoro's 2,300-ft-long (700 m) wall connects two summits. Researchers have recorded the remains of two *kallankas*, as well as the foundations of round and rectangular storerooms and piles of sling stones.

Located some 80 miles (130 km) east of Cochabamba, **Incallaqta** is set majestically between two streams on a high river terrace. Walls, once plastered with mud and painted red, surround the central sector and most of the steep hill on which it stands. The central sector features a series of long rectangular buildings, as well as some compounds on the eastern side. A *kallanka* fronts a   176 large double plaza. Enclosing more than 16,000 sq ft (1,500 sq m), it is one of the largest single-room roofed buildings recorded in Tawantinsuyu. In front of the central doorway of the *kallanka*, a large rock surrounded by a wall served as an *ushnu*, with the platform in the shape of an inverted step pyramid.[21]

177 RIGHT The carved sandstone outcrop of Samaipata, Bolivia, features double zigzag and straight channels.

178 BELOW View looking east of the Samaipata outcrop, with its more than 100,000 sq ft (10,000 sq m) of carved surface.

Just west of the great hall, the Incas built a row of three smaller buildings, each with its own walled forecourt. Several other structures, lacking forecourts, lie to the northeast.

Incallaqta's location, surrounding wall, and orderly rows of rectangular buildings suggest a military function, and the long buildings may have housed soldiers. Although there is little doubt that the Incas designed Incallaqta to accommodate relatively large numbers of people, the lack of substantial documentary or archaeological evidence makes it difficult to determine the site's exact function. Some scholars have suggested that it served as an administrative center, others that Incallaqta played a primarily military role, protecting Tawantinsuyu's eastern flank, while still others believe that it was one of the "new Cuscos" that replicated the capital's sacred space.[22]

Samaipata, located some 75 miles (120 km) southwest of Santa Cruz de la Sierra, is one of the most intriguing Inca installations in Bolivia's Andean foothills. There, Inca stone carvers transformed an enormous sandstone outcrop into over 110,000 sq ft (10,000 sq m) of niches, seats, and channels— the largest known example of rock carving in Tawantinsuyu.[23] The outcrop's most prominent feature is three long, double zigzag channels forming chains of rhomboids. The channels recall *pacchas*, Inca ceramic, carved stone, or wooden vessels in which a stream of maize beer or other liquid flowed between two channels before emerging as one from the vessel's spout. Many anthropologists believe that the flow and mixing of liquids in the two channels served as a metaphor for the relationship between two groups that meet periodically to celebrate, exchange goods, even to fight, before each going its own way. Did the maize beer, water, or other liquids that once coursed through Samaipata's channels mimic the relationship between the Incas and local groups?

Seats, niches, and animal forms dominate the imagery carved around the sides of the outcrop. Their similarity to carvings found in the Cusco region leave little doubt that they were created under Inca direction, although it seems likely that various carvers worked over a significant span of time, rather than executing the carving as a single planned design. Some of the variations in the carvings suggest ritual differences.[24] Do these disparities reflect changes in religious practices over time? Or do they relate to religious differences among the local groups incorporated into the Inca empire? Or do they simply signal the multiple religious rituals that formed part of the imperial ceremonial calendar? Large halls and other buildings at Samaipata suggest housing for transients, and while future research may discover a broader role for the site, it was clearly a very important religious-ceremonial center.

Southern Qollasuyu's mineral wealth

Most scholars believe that the Incas incorporated the outermost reaches of Tawantinsuyu (Chile, Argentina, and Ecuador) shortly before Francisco Pizarro and his men arrived to cut short the empire's advance. As discussed in Chapter 2, however, recent radiocarbon dates challenge the view that these outlying lands—especially in Qollasuyu—were late additions to the empire, and point instead to "conquest" as part of an ongoing process that began relatively early and often required only minimal effort across broad stretches of geography. Archaeological research in Chile and Argentina sketches a tentative, but nevertheless remarkable, view of Inca expansion by, at least, the early fifteenth century.[25]

Nevertheless, there are two obstacles to tracking evidence of the Inca presence in far southern Qollasuyu. First, colonial officials began compiling documents considerably later in the south, due in large part to intense local resistance to the Spanish occupation. Secondly, the size of the Inca settlements and their architecture has biased some interpretations of the intensity of Inca rule in southern Qollasuyu. Inca builders placed much less emphasis on fine monumental architecture in this area than they did farther north, especially in Chinchaysuyu. Even within Qollasuyu, the more southerly sites fail to match the scale and complexity of Incallaqta and Samaipata in Bolivia.

Recent research also reveals, however, that in addition to its early date, Inca penetration south was highly ambitious. The Incas established relationships with dozens of local groups and built scores of settlements. This vast network provided Cusco's ruling elite with important commodities, mainly metallic ores. Thus, the earlier view of rapid military conquest is being replaced with a model of strong, but uneven, alliances with numerous local groups. The varying nature of the alliances lends the Inca presence a patchwork quality, signaling adjustments to distinct local circumstances. While this strategy is not substantially different from the one used farther north, the smaller scale of southern Qollasuyu's polities produced a particularly broken and varied political landscape. In addition, although there is evidence of fortification, it is limited mainly to areas in the eastern foothills where the Incas and their allies sought to protect themselves from belligerent neighbors, a pattern similar to the one seen along the Bolivian frontier.

179   Many Inca sites in far northern Argentina are large and impressive, especially **La Huerta** in the Humahuaca valley, which straddled a major Inca road and included plazas as well as more than 500 rooms, among them several public buildings. Although La Huerta's initial construction pre-dates Inca times, evidence of Inca-period use is extensive. Located at 8,900 ft (2,700 m), the settlement flanks apparent maize fields, a focus of the Inca occupation.[26] The Calchaqui valley, in the province of Salta, also demonstrates Inca interest in areas with agricultural potential. Sites in the Calchaqui region contain ample evidence for the production of metal, cloth, ceramics, and shell objects. At major sites, such as **Potrero de Payogasta**, artisans apparently worked under the supervision of Inca functionaries.[27]

As the Inca road headed south through the Mendoza river valley to the ends of the empire, austral winter snows probably prevented travel along the road as it traversed high-altitude passes, connecting way-stations such as **Ranchillos** and **Tambillitos**. Ranchillos contains more than 100 structures, while Tambillitos is the southernmost way-station recorded in Tawantinsuyu.[28]

179   The large walled plaza at Nevados de Aconquija, Argentina. An upright *ushnu* stone once stood in the center of the plaza.

West through Kuntisuyu

The smallest of the *suyu* divisions, Kuntisuyu extended south–southwest from Cusco to the Pacific coast, bordered to the north by the bay of Chala and Lake Parinacochas, and to the south by the region of Arequipa. The main road to Kuntisuyu left Cusco just below *puma chupan*, marked by a *ceque* shrine known as Uxi, and headed south–southwest for the mythic origin site of Paqariq-tampu.[29] The Kuntisuyu road afforded the closest route between Cusco and the Pacific coast, and probably served as the route that provided the Inca ruler with fresh fish, for "although this city [Cusco] is over seventy leagues from the sea, the fish was brought to him very fresh in [fewer] than two days."[30]

A major feature of Kuntisuyu is the Colca valley, famed for its elaborate terracing systems, most of which pre-date Inca times. The Incas established marriage links with herding communities of Aymara-speaking Collagua, who occupied the middle and upper valley. Herding activity appears to have increased in Inca times, and they exploited the Collagua's close ties with the *altiplano* and their links to regional exchange systems. In the lower valley, occupied by the Quechua-speaking Cabana, the Incas expanded existing terrace and irrigation systems to increase maize production, and they appear to have manipulated Collagua–Cabana relations, elevating the position of the Collagua, with whom they enjoyed close relations.[31]

The Collagua settlement of **Yanque**, which covered some 45 acres (18 hectares), appears to have been the upper valley's leading Inca administrative center; it may also have controlled the entire valley.[32] Aside from the remains of one building of finely worked stone, most of Inca Yanque is now buried beneath colonial buildings. Three other sites in the upper valley, occupied before the Incas, contain small plazas flanked by *kallankas*, suggesting that they may have served as secondary centers in Inca times. Some settlements in the lower valley contain intrusive Inca buildings, such as *kallankas* and an *ushnu* flanking a plaza at **Kallimarka**, which may point to closer Inca management of maize production.

Inca control over the Cotahuasi valley to the west, however, seems to have been somewhat more tenuous and fraught by uprisings. Nevertheless, the valley's strategic role as a corridor between the highlands and the coast, as well as its rich gold, silver, and copper mines and its sources of rock salt, ochre, and obsidian, spurred Inca interest in the area.[33] Unlike the Colca valley, where close political ties with the Incas allowed local lords to enjoy relative independence, Inca control over Cotahuasi appears to have been more direct, reflected by the construction of an administrative center covering almost 19 acres (some 7.5 hectares).[34]

More importantly, perhaps, the Colca and Cotahuasi valleys served as gateways to mountaintop shrines, among the most sacred in the empire. Many of the southern Peruvian peaks had been venerated long before the Inca conquest of the region, but in typical Inca fashion, the lords of Cusco allowed local people to continue worshipping the mountains and endowed the most important shrines—particularly those that served as *guacas pacariscas* or "origin places"—with herds and *mitmaq* colonists, even elevating some regional shrines to pilgrimage centers of empire-wide importance.

180 One of these was Coropuna, towering over 21,000 ft (6,400 m), the highest mountain in southwestern Peru. Cieza described it as "a lofty hill that was always covered with snow"[35] and ranked its temple as the fifth most important sanctuary in Tawantinsuyu. It received rich *qhapaq hucha* sacrificial processions (see Chapter 5), and offerings to it included twelve-year-old children, Andean goose and flamingo feathers, coca leaves, *Spondylus* shell, guinea pigs, raw meat, and *sanco* (a paste of maize flour and blood).[36] An illustration by the native chronicler Felipe Guaman Poma de Ayala shows people offering children and animals to the mountain. Gifts to snow-clad volcanoes, especially those with views of the ocean, "the mother of all waters," were believed to summon rain, and by extension, ensure the fertility of crops and herds. Indeed, chroniclers noted the area's abundant camelid herds, and wild vicuñas graze in the volcano's shadow today. Cieza says that the Inca rulers and the "leading nobles" visited its temple "making gifts and offerings…and it is held to be a fact that of the gifts…made to this temple there are many loads of gold and silver and jewels… And as the snow is so deep, they cannot climb to the summit. This temple had many flocks and farms and Indians to serve it, and "chosen women."[37]

The religious significance of the area for the Incas is corroborated by a survey that located more than thirty-five Inca sites: fifteen in the *puna* west and

180 Vicuñas pause below Coropuna in southern Peru, regarded by the Incas as one of the most sacred mountains. Coropuna's temple and oracle were located at nearby Maukallaqta, which covered some 75 acres (30 hectares).

south of Coropuna, several on the flanks of Solimana (including Muyu Muyu which may have served as the *waka*-oracle of Solimana) and over twenty in the nearby, more temperate Cotahuasi, Andaray, Pampacolca, and Chuquibamba valleys.[38] Equally remarkable is that within this relatively small area, five or six of the *puna* settlements and two or three valley sites contain plazas and *ushnus*, a number comparable only to those found on the road linking Cusco west to the coast. The leading *puna* settlement, apparently the seat of Coropuna's oracle and temple, appears to have been **Maukallaqta** (or "old town," a common name for abandoned Inca settlements, not to be confused with the Inca origin site near Cusco). Another candidate is **Achaymarka**, situated at over 13,000 ft (4,000 m), halfway between Coropuna and Solimana volcanoes. It fronts an important Inca road and contains over 200 structures surrounding a walled plaza, measuring 525 by 360 ft (160 by 110 m), which is flanked by a 10-ft-high (3 m) *ushnu* on its south side.[39] Achaymarka's *ushnu* is oriented northwest rather than toward Coropuna, suggesting that while it played an important role in Inca ritual, it probably did not serve as the seat of Coropuna's temple and oracle.[40]

Located at around 11,800 ft (3,600 m) on the slopes of Coropuna, Maukallaqta probably also functioned as the ceremonial and administrative center for the immediate area. It covers almost 75 acres (over 30 hectares) and includes more than 100 stone structures, as well as a monumental pre-Inca platform that is 525 ft (160 m) long and 157 ft (48 m) wide. Next to it the Incas built an *ushnu*. Both of these platforms offer spectacular views of Coropuna. Five *kallankas*—the largest of which is 184 ft (56 m) long and 33 ft (10 m) wide—flanked a plaza.[41] Some 3 miles (5 km) from Maukallaqta, researchers recorded around twenty structures that may have served as storehouses. Maukallaqta also functioned as a burial ground for its devotees, as the remains of three cemeteries (including *chullpas*, above-ground burial structures) demonstrate. One *chullpa*, though looted, contained spinning and weaving implements such as spindle whorls, needles, and loom parts, as well as textile and yarn remains.[42] The quantity of weaving tools, as well as fragments of dress pins and fine Cusco wares, suggests that the *chullpa* may have contained the bodies of *aqlla*—the "mamaconas" mentioned by Cieza as having "served" Coropuna.

Qollasuyu in Chile: mines and farmland

The chain of Inca sites and roads traversing the great *altiplano* and stretching down to the lower reaches of the Andes into northwest Argentina is paralleled by a less ambitious string of settlements and roads heading west of the Andean cordillera. Although it lacks great monumental sites, there is abundant evidence for a strong Inca presence. Once again, the Incas concentrated on the region's ore deposits and agricultural potential, and there is very little evidence of direct military conquest. Instead, they took advantage of selective collaborations with friendly groups, and the result is an uneven political landscape marked by pockets of strong Inca influence, connected by roads that crossed through areas uninhabited or populated by less cooperative peoples.

Northern Chile boasts more than 150 sites with evidence of strong Inca ties, including **Turi**, located on the Atacaman cordillera's snowcap-watered slopes. There, the Incas leveled part of an existing settlement beside the main road, and built a large rectangular, enclosed plaza with a *kallanka*.[43] A defensive stone wall with a large gate surrounds more than 600 structures. Somewhat farther south lies **Catarpe**, composed of eastern and western sectors, each containing about a hundred structures; the eastern sector features a double plaza. While often described as a *tampu* or way-station, Catarpe was large enough to have also housed administrators and craft workers, and some scholars believe it served as an administrative center.[44]

The Atacama desert is a great expanse of sand and salt flats, framed to the east by a chain of volcanoes. One of the most barren places on earth, it created

181

181 Turi, in Chile's Atacama desert, flanks the Inca road. Built within an earlier settlement, the Inca plaza and *kallanka* hall are in the center of the photograph. An *ushnu* may have been located in the center of the plaza.

a formidable obstacle to Inca expansion south. Nevertheless, roads and way-stations eased access to new mineral deposits and, ultimately, valuable farm-land. Long stretches of Inca road—at times almost 10 ft (3 m) wide—cross the Atacama.[45] Every so often, heaps of stones by the roadside served as markers to reassure travelers that they had not strayed from the road. The area's many pre-historic mines, most of them far from regular water sources, point to interest in the region long before the Incas.

As the Inca road advanced southward, it entered the more hospitable lands of the Diaguita, who joined forces with the expanding Incas, even adopting Inca stylistic features in their own pottery styles. Scholars' opinions differ on the extent of the Diaguita's role in administering and controlling areas south of the Atacama desert. But if the close relationship between the two art styles is any indication, they collaborated closely—regardless of whether the Incas imposed administrators from the Cusco region or left the Diaguita largely in control. Diaguita–Inca style ceramics found in the Copiapó and Aconcagua regions even farther south suggest that the Incas administered these areas through their Diaguita allies. There, too, metals and metallurgy attracted the Incas, as confirmed by the foundations of what appear to be smelting furnaces found in the **Viña del Cerro** complex, 53 miles (85 km) southeast of Copiapó in north-central Chile.[46]

The Aconcagua and Maule valleys feature several fortified Inca sites. Spanish sources disagree on the exact location of the empire's southern boundary, but recent research pinpoints **Cerro del Inga**, 60 miles (95 km) south of Santiago, the Chilean capital, as the southernmost of the chain of Inca forts.[47] The sociopolitical organization of groups living along the southern frontier differed substantially from that of the Incas, the Diaguita, and other recently incorporated peoples.[48] As the string of forts suggests, these differences may have engendered conflict with peoples unwilling to collaborate.

South of the Maule river, researchers have documented Inca-style copper axes and ceramics, indicating contact with Araucanian groups. Although it is difficult to discern whether these contacts were direct or indirect, they do suggest the onset of economic and social relations, even though there was no pretension of real imperial control.[49] Nevertheless, the nature of the contacts between the Incas and the peoples they sought to integrate illuminate how the empire expanded.

In spite of the many settlements that speak of an Inca presence and their relatively early radiocarbon dates, the imperial integration of southernmost Qollasuyu—northwestern Argentina and central Chile—appears tentative. This cautious approach, in which the Incas aimed selectively at more collaborative peoples and at particular economic resources, implies gradual expansion. Rather than relying on lightning military conquests and bureaucrats backed by garrisons, the Incas depended on economic measures, religion, and an infrastructure of roads and buildings as their vocabulary of expansion. Although in many cases contact had been long established, actual incorporation was ongoing. When the Incas encountered resistance, they most often responded by inserting themselves slowly into a new region using ceremony, diplomacy, and gifts rather than outright force. Nevertheless, as the preliminary evidence from south of the Maule river suggests, the search for additional resources, collaborations, and sources of labor was never-ending.

Human offerings to sacred peaks

Human life regularly became the most valuable offering the Incas made to their sacred world. As we have seen, mountain worship was common in Inca religion, and over 100 ceremonial sites on peaks towering over 16,400 ft (5,000 m), mainly in Qollasuyu and Kuntisuyu, contain evidence of human sacrifice. Some scholars[50] feel that mountain worship was more important in the southern part of the empire, but others[51] believe that the paucity of mountain sacrifice sites in the north is the result of the lower snowline on mountains nearer the Equator and the technical climbing challenges that this posed for the Incas.

As noted in Chapter 5, the Incas celebrated cyclical and special *qhapaq huchas*, the gift-bearing processions headed by children and young women destined for sacrifice. Some commemorated major events in an Inca emperor's life (illness, war, death, succession, the birth of a son). Others marked natural disasters such as droughts, earthquakes, or volcanic eruptions. People regarded the chosen children (aged four to ten), and young women (often *aqlla*, around fifteen years old), as messengers from their people to the sacred mountains, which controlled the forces of nature and were often viewed as ancestors. While the sacrifice itself may have been the critical moment of the *qhapaq hucha*, the elaborate processions and multiple ceremonies that preceded it were of greater religious and political significance. Processions of children or young women intended for sacrifice, the priests, and, sometimes, the children's parents passed through various regions making offerings to sacred places. Not all parents considered sacrifice an honor; Cobo notes that some parents were "happy to see [their daughters] seduced at a very early age; this way the girls were safe...since virginity was a prerequisite for selection."[52] Local people often joined the processions as they passed, and the priests leading the procession were said to have walked with their heads lowered, looking straight ahead.[53] The local participants changed at borders between regions, and in this sense the processions helped define political boundaries.

The Incas built way-stations or staging points near the bases of the sacred mountains for the pilgrims, the chosen children, and the ritual specialists. Farther up the mountain, they set up small camps of stone and thatch to house the children and the priests charged with carrying out the rite. The sacrifice ceremony usually took place on the summit, but occasionally it was performed on lower ledges of especially steep peaks such as Llullaillaco.

Archaeologists have unearthed remarkable details of the rites that took place on these frozen sanctuaries.[54] One such sanctuary is **Ampato** volcano in Kuntisuyu, which served as one of the principal sacred mountains of the Colca valley. The other, **Llullaillaco** in Salta province, Argentina, straddling the 182, 183 Chilean border, is the best-preserved *qhapaq hucha* complex and, at 22,110 ft (6,739 m), the world's highest archaeological site.

The 1995 eruption of Sabancaya melted the snow on Ampato's summit, causing a ceremonial platform on the summit ridge to collapse and expose the body of a young woman.[55] Wearing fine garments and plumed headgear, she was accompanied by offerings of silver, gold, and *Spondylus* figurines. Below PLS 75, 76 the summit archaeologists recorded the remains of a base camp, as well as other campsites, llama corrals, and trails. The infrastructure and remains of grass, pottery, leather, wool, sandals, and wooden posts suggest that the summit's ceremonial sites were used more than once, marking multiple *qhapaq hucha* events. Further excavations on Ampato unearthed three more children—two girls and a boy, ranging in age from eight to ten. Both girls wore feather headdresses and were accompanied by fine pottery, wooden drinking vessels, and weaving implements, and both had been struck by lightning in their tombs. The sacrifices appear to have taken place during a drought or a volcanic eruption as the summit was ice-free when the children were buried.

The young woman (about fourteen to sixteen years old) interred on Llullail- PL. 80 laco in Argentina is perhaps the most perfectly preserved mummy ever found.[56] The area around Llullaillaco lacked permanent settlements and water, making the logistics of staging such an elaborate procession and sacrifice daunting indeed. In fact, the closest Inca administrative center to Llullaillaco is Catarpe in Chile's San Pedro de Atacama oasis, over 120 miles (200 km) to the north. The girl wore rich garments and an exquisite feather headdress fashioned of white plumes. Draped over a shoulder, excavators found a man's tunic embel- PL. 89

182 Excavations on the summit of Llullaillaco, which straddles the Argentine-Chilean border, revealed the frozen remains of three sacrificed children, a boy and two girls.

183 An Inca *tampu* or way-station en route to the summit of Llullaillaco, at 22,110 ft (6,739 m) the world's highest archaeological site.

lished with a classic pattern known as the Inca key design. Fine tunics were often given by the ruler to *kurakas*, leading to speculation that the woman's father may have been a *kuraka*. Like the young woman of Ampato, she was buried with fine gold, silver, and *Spondylus* figurines. Only female figurines have so far been found with young women, and generally the offerings found with young women and girls are considerably finer and more varied than those found with the boys. Boys were often interred with a male figurine and, lined up behind it, camelid figurines, possibly suggesting a caravan or herd.

Near the summit, but in separate tombs, a young boy (around eight years old) and a young girl accompanied Llullaillaco's young woman. Next to the body of the boy archaeologists uncovered two pairs of sandals and a woven sling. The boy wore a red tunic, moccasins, a bunch of white feathers held in place by a sling, and a broad silver bracelet. His offerings, in addition to the male and llama figurines, included a necklace of *Spondylus* pendants. Four female figurines festooned with plumed headgear accompanied the young girl, who wore a metal head ornament. She had been struck by lightning.

It is difficult to imagine a ritual act more horrifying, that would impress itself more strongly on the mind, than a human sacrifice. Such an act is almost unimaginably appalling to our contemporary sensibilities. But once accepted as a way of gratifying the natural and supernatural worlds and of coping with and perhaps preventing calamity, it might attract awe—and obedience to the state religion that sponsored it.

PL. 79

PL. 85

Why were Chinchaysuyu and Qollasuyu different?

Inca strategies for integrating Chile and northwestern Argentina into the empire contrast dramatically with the empire's tactics for expanding northward into what is today Ecuador. There, expansion had a more definitive and hands-on approach, accompanied by the almost immediate building of imperial cities, overseen by the Inca emperor himself. These differences at the opposite ends of the empire suggest the general distinctions between upper and lower Tawantinsuyu.

Whatever the ultimate cause of these differences, the Incas applied varying strategies in integrating the opposite ends of the empire. These distinctions signal the grandest expression of the pervasive dualism so integral to the Incas—and to Andean society in general. Do the differences convey centuries-old cultural dissimilarities rooted in the legacies of the Wari and Tiwanaku empires? Do the distinctions reflect cultural differences between incorporated peoples themselves, or do they indicate imperial manipulation, designed to make local groups fit into the Incas' own dual conception of Tawantinsuyu? Further research is needed to clarify how these features and tendencies varied among the divisions, how they were balanced in each of the four parts separately—and, ultimately, in the "four parts together."

Our final chapter describes the last moments of Tawantinsuyu and its aftermath. Because the Spanish invasion cut short Tawantinsuyu's advance, we will never know whether the Spanish invaders found an empire at a period of turbulent growth or one that had reached its natural boundaries.

11 · The Fall: Bearded Men from across the Sea

Encouraged by news of the rapid fall of the fabulously wealthy Aztec empire, a group of Spanish soldier-adventurers based in Panama launched in the mid-1520s a series of expeditions along South America's west coast. Their leader, Francisco Pizarro, had heard reports of a rich "tribe" referred to as Virú or Birú. (That name, apparently derived from a valley called Virú on Peru's north coast, eventually became "Peru.")

After a failed voyage in 1524, Pizarro sailed again in 1525 to seek the "tribe." Just south of the Equator, his pilot Bartolomé Ruíz captured a large balsa raft rigged with cotton sails and manned by a crew of some twenty men. The raft carried a cargo of gold and silver objects, semi-precious stones and fine garments "beautifully worked with elaborate craftsmanship... All this," the sailors told Ruíz, they planned to exchange "for some sea shells [*Spondylus*] of which they make beads of a reddish and white color."[1] Several sailors jumped overboard to avoid capture but Ruíz seized three men to learn Spanish and serve as interpreters.

Armed with the report of the balsa raft and its riches, Pizarro convinced the Spanish Crown to name him governor and captain-general of Peru. In late 1530–early 1531, he made landfall near Tumbes, on Peru's north coast. He realized that he had stumbled on a major civilization, but it was a civilization in the throes of a succession dispute between two brothers, Atawallpa and Waskar, sons of Wayna Qhapaq. For Tawantinsuyu, the timing of the dispute, like the epidemics that preceded it, would prove catastrophic.

Foreign disease

While Spanish ships explored the coast of western South America in the early 1520s, Wayna Qhapaq was consolidating recently incorporated areas of northernmost Tawantinsuyu. As he oversaw the construction of new settlements, he heard that strangers had been spotted along the coast. But foreign diseases were making their inexorable way south and Wayna Qhapaq died before ever seeing the strangers. Some historians believe that as many as three pandemics—smallpox, measles, and influenza—killed hundreds of thousands of indigenous people before Pizarro actually set foot on South American soil. Because indigenous peoples had no natural immunities to foreign germs, mortality rates were extremely high.[2]

Wayna Qhapaq and his designated heir both died sometime between late 1524 and 1528, victims of the pandemics. A succession struggle between Atawallpa and Waskar ensued. As we have seen, this was not the first dispute to threaten the foundations of Tawantinsuyu or its ruling elite. Royal successions could be chaotic affairs, marked by intrigue, palace coups, provincial revolts, and even assassinations. But this dispute would prove different from earlier ones.

Because of the empire's vast size, the war that followed Wayna Qhapaq's death assumed almost continental proportions, and it probably would have taken longer to settle than previous conflicts. From Pizarro's standpoint, the timing of his landfall could not have been better. As one observer noted, "If the land had not been divided by the wars...we could not have entered or conquered it unless over a thousand Spaniards had come simultaneously."[3] Since neither Atawallpa nor Waskar had consolidated power, the foreigners themselves became a competing force jockeying for dominance. Taking a cue from his countryman, Hernán Cortés in Mexico, Pizarro eventually persuaded many of those who had not supported Atawallpa to cast their lot with the Europeans.

A tragic encounter

In late 1532, Pizarro, accompanied by some 150 men on foot and on horseback, set off for Cajamarca. He had learned that a victorious Atawallpa was camped not far from the city. In a typical display of Andean diplomatic courtship, Atawallpa dispatched an emissary bearing gifts for Pizarro, and invited the Spaniards to join him in Cajamarca. Pizarro, perhaps briefed in Andean gift-giving traditions, sent Atawallpa a fine shirt and two Venetian glass goblets.

The Spaniards marched unimpeded from the coast through the Andean foothills, reaching Cajamarca on November 15, 1532. From the edge of the valley they beheld a city whose square, observed Pizarro's secretary Francisco de Xerez, "is larger than any in Spain." Beyond the city, Xerez saw the cotton tents of Atawallpa's camp, which "extended for a league... There appeared to be more than thirty thousand men." A paved causeway led across the valley to the thermal baths of Konoj, where Atawallpa was fasting at his "pleasure house," the royal compound enclosing a garden and thermal bath, described in Chapter 8.[4]

After agreeing to meet Atawallpa the following day, the Spaniards returned to the lodgings that the Incas had provided for them in Cajamarca. Naturally suspicious and alarmed by the size of Atawallpa's camp, Pizarro speculated that Atawallpa schemed to have them killed, although there is no concrete evidence that this was the case. Rather, the events suggest that Atawallpa was engaged in ceremonial diplomacy, exploring how best to treat the interesting foreigners. The Spaniards, of course, also faced an unpredictable situation. They decided to capture Atawallpa the following day, planning to conceal themselves and their horses in the long buildings that fronted the plaza.

The next day, Atawallpa's 2,000-strong retinue entered the square, accompanied by the sound of flutes and conch shell trumpets. Fernández de Oviedo, another eyewitness, described squadrons of Indians dressed in a red and white check livery, some sweeping the road and placing fine cloth in the emperor's path, others dancing and singing, and still others festooned with gold and silver breastplates, medallions, and crowns. "They wore so much gold and silver that it was astonishing how much it shone in the sun."[5] In their midst came 184 Atawallpa, "richly dressed, with a crown on his head and a collar of large emeralds around his neck...[carried] in a litter lined with multicolored parrots' feathers and decorated with gold and silver plate... Behind him came two more litters and two hammocks containing persons of importance...followed by many more who wore gold and silver crowns and marched in bands."[6] While Atawallpa's entourage certainly numbered in the thousands, few of them appear to have been armed.

After the priest accompanying Pizarro's expedition read the so-called Requirement (a document that demanded Atawallpa acknowledge the Christian god and the Spanish king as supreme), Atawallpa—speaking through an interpreter who probably missed many of the nuances of the exchange—asked to see the friar's breviary. A Spanish eyewitness reported that the ruler leafed through the book and then "his face a deep crimson...threw it angrily down among his men."[7] This act of blasphemy—in the eyes of the Spaniards—provided justification for the attack. As Spaniards rushed from their hiding places, the square soon reverberated with a cacophony "of shots and...trumpets and...horses with their rattles... The Indians were thrown into confusion and panicked. The Spaniards fell upon them and began to kill."[8]

In the midst of the melee, the Spaniards reached Atawallpa's litter and "they began to kill the bearers. But as fast as one fell several more came... [The 185 Spaniards] attacked the litter with great fury, seizing Atawallpa by the hair...and dragging him roughly...until he fell out."[9] According to Xerez, throughout the slaughter "no Indian raised a weapon against a Spaniard."[10] The slaughter lasted about two hours. Hundreds of Atawallpa's men died; many more were wounded.

The clash of empires

As with so many other cases of European "conquest," the outcome of the encounter between Pizarro's rough band of invaders and the Incas had a certain inevitability, determined by the confrontation of differing political customs, religions, technologies, and methods of warfare. The Spanish aim was to invade, gather the spoils of war, and then occupy and control the land and its inhabitants. Religion—in large part—served as the justification, or at least the pretext, for the invasion and later control of the populace.

The circumstances surrounding Tawantinsuyu's rapid fall to a small group of Spaniards, and the actions and reactions of conquerors and conquered alike, are best understood if we analyze them from an Andean as well as a Spanish perspective. The Spaniards' point of view is most familiar to us because most accounts of the conquest are based on their writings. A careful reading of the Spanish sources, however, reveals nuances of the indigenous perspective, couched in distinctive Andean conventions and ritual.

The Incas appear vulnerable and almost rash compared to the Europeans. Why, for instance, did Atawallpa, whose forces vastly outnumbered the invaders,

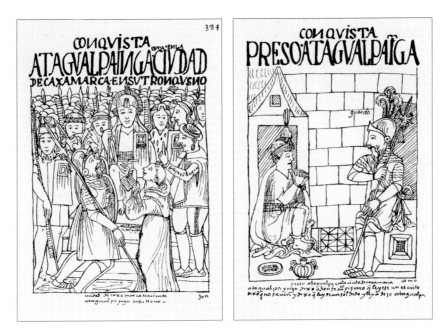

184 LEFT The Inca ruler Atawallpa sits atop the *ushnu* at Cajamarca in northern Peru surrounded by his warriors, the Spanish conquistador Francisco Pizarro, and the Dominican friar Vicente Valverde.

185 RIGHT Atawallpa is taken prisoner after being captured in Cajamarca's main plaza.

not kill the Spaniards outright before Pizarro captured him? Did he believe they were *viracochas*, or gods who had emerged from the sacred ocean? Although some have dismissed the *viracocha* label as Spanish propaganda, others feel that the first people who saw the Spaniards emerge from their ships did actually believe this, though they soon realized that they were only mortal. Titu Cusi, son of the rebel Vilcabamba ruler Manco Inca, explained that the indigenous peoples called the Spaniards *viracochas* "because [they] were very different in their dress and appearance…and also because [they] rode very large animals with silver feet…and because they had *yllapas*. This is the name we use to refer to thunder…because [they] thought the harquebuses were thunder from the sky."[11] All the while, Atawallpa appears to have been engaged in Andean diplomacy and perhaps even hoped to recruit the Spanish "warriors"— equipped with novel weapons and technologies such as steel swords and body armor and especially horses. Compared to Pizarro's men, Atawallpa's army was lightly armed, but most importantly, the surprise factor of the Spanish ambush in Cajamarca did not conform to Andean codes of warfare, which was structured and ritualized.

Inca traditions of conquest and expansion differed dramatically from those of the Spaniards. As we have seen, the Incas used diplomatic, ceremonial, and economic incentives as their primary tools of conquest. If these tactics failed, they certainly could raise large armies, and their reprisals against those who opposed them could be harsh, as this song suggests: "Let us drink from the skull of the traitor, adorn ourselves with a necklace of his teeth, play the melody of the *pinkullu* with flutes made from his bones, beat the drum made from his skin, and thus we will dance."[12]

But unlike the outright invasion and direct domination practiced by the Spaniards, the Incas juggled a series of shifting alliances with local peoples and regional shrines. This left them singularly vulnerable to European strategies of military conquest, domination, and colonization.

New-found wealth

Gold served as Europe's standard of exchange and was the immediate motivation of many of the Spaniards' acts and decisions. The riches they found in Atawallpa's camp the morning after his capture surpassed expectations. They "were amazed at so many fine gold and silver vessels... The gold vessels alone that Atawallpa carried with him weighed more than sixty thousand pesos."[13]

185   Imprisoned in Cajamarca's sun temple, Atawallpa feared being killed by his captors. Noting the Spaniards' fixation on precious metals he offered them tantalizing tribute in the form of a room filled once with gold and twice with silver. In February 1533, at Atawallpa's suggestion, Pizarro dispatched several Spaniards to Cusco to hasten the shipment of the tribute.

As the Inca ruler languished in captivity, he learned that his half-brother and rival, Waskar, had been captured in Cusco by Atawallpa loyalists and had been en route to Cajamarca when an escort killed him (some say under Atawallpa's orders). According to several eyewitnesses, one of Atawallpa's most treasured trophies was a drinking vessel fashioned from a human skull plated in gold, with a silver straw emerging from the skull's clenched teeth. When asked whose head it was, Atawallpa replied that it belonged to Atoq, one of Waskar's generals, and that he drank from it to remind himself of the wars Waskar had waged against him. "He [Atoq] said that he would drink from my head. And I killed him and I drink from his head."[14]

In May 1533, Pizarro ordered his men to begin melting down the gold, later dividing it among his followers after setting aside the customary royal fifth for the Crown. One observer who saw the gold plundered from Cusco by the advance expedition recalled "about five hundred plates of gold torn from some house wall in Cusco...a seat of very fine gold...a fountain all of gold...and many other pieces such as vases, jars and plates."[15] "Some house wall" refers to the empire's holiest shrine, the Qorikancha, or golden enclosure; the fountain and seat too had once graced the Qorikancha.

But Atawallpa underestimated the Spaniards' insatiable greed for gold; the enormous cache of precious metals amassed in Cajamarca merely stimulated their appetite for more. He must have also realized that the Spaniards would not release him, even though he had fulfilled his obligations. Perhaps Atawallpa believed that the Spaniards would treat him both as captive and honored guest, much as the Incas did with many leaders of defeated groups—as long as they collaborated, they were secure and retained their ceremonial trappings, and even some of their former power.

Atawallpa also misjudged the expansionist designs of the realm from across the ocean, and the Europeans' ability to bring reinforcements and settlers attracted by the new-found wealth. The precious metals sparked a gold rush in Cajamarca, where "if a man owed another something he paid with a lump of gold, without weighing the gold."[16] Eyewitness reports of the conquest circulated through Spain and the newly established Spanish colonies in Mexico and the Caribbean, triggering a wave of fortune-seekers bound for Peru. A concerned Spanish official in Puerto Rico alerted authorities in Spain that "with the news from Peru, not a citizen would remain if he were not tied down."[17]

As the Spaniards melted down the gold and silver, they deliberated Atawallpa's fate. Some believed his death would facilitate the conquest; others argued that he might prove more useful as an imprisoned puppet. Unfounded rumors of a rescue by Atawallpa loyalists ultimately forced Pizarro to order the ruler's execution. On July 26, 1533, in a plaza that once served as a stage for feasting sponsored by generous rulers, Atawallpa was "brought out of his prison and led into the middle of the square, to the sound of trumpets intended to proclaim his treason and treachery, and was tied to a stake."[18] After the once powerful Inca ruler accepted baptism to avoid burning at the stake, he was garroted to death. 186

A month after Atawallpa's death, the Spanish forces left Cajamarca for Cusco. At first their march was uneventful, but once they reached Hatun Xauxa they encountered the first resistance: a bloody battle with Inca troops that saw casualties on both sides. To the south, the Inca army occupying Cusco was determined to thwart the Spanish advance, burning down suspension bridges, villages, and storehouses. Nevertheless, after another battle at Vilcaswaman,

186 LEFT Atawallpa is killed by his Spanish captors, July 26, 1533.

187 RIGHT Manco Inca rebels against the Spanish invaders (1536), setting fire to Cusco.

the sacred city at the junction of the Qhapaq Ñan and the road leading to the
Pacific coast, the Spaniards succeeded in reaching the Apurímac river, which
they had to ford as the great bridge had been cut down (see page 95). After a
final battle where an eyewitness recalled finding "all the warriors waiting for us
at the entrance to the city,"[19] the Inca troops vanished, allowing the Spaniards
to enter Cusco unhindered on November 15, 1533.

Inca resistance and decline

A month later, Francisco Pizarro named Manco Inca, one of Wayna Qhapaq's
sons, puppet ruler of Tawantinsuyu. As Manco donned the *mascaypacha*, the
headdress of crimson and gold tassels that symbolized Inca kingship, Cusco
witnessed one of its last Inca celebrations. Thousands of people crowded into
the city's main square; even the mummies of the dead ancestors, including that
of Wayna Qhapaq, joined the revelry.

Nevertheless, the euphoria over Manco's coronation was short-lived. The
gold-hungry Spaniards began a campaign of harassment, accusing Manco of
stashing treasure. Manco realized that it would be impossible to live under
Spanish rule and he escaped, only to be captured and jailed. Released from
prison in January 1536, Manco, with the help of the Willaq Umu, the high
priest of the sun, began recruiting men. Within months, Inca troops—the
chroniclers say that there were between 100,000 and 200,000 (probably an
exaggeration, since both numbers were used in sixteenth-century Spain to
denote "many")—had mobilized near the Urubamba valley.

187 By early May, the Inca warriors had encircled Cusco. "So many troops came
there that they covered the fields," recalled Francisco Pizarro's cousin, Pedro.
"By day they looked like a black carpet...and by night there were so many fires
that it resembled nothing less than a very clear sky filled with stars."[20] Manco
launched his main attack on Cusco from Saqsawaman. "Suddenly, a large
number of men appeared everywhere around Cusco and closed in on the city
with much noise from their whistles, horns, and trumpets, as well as loud war
cries."[21] For days, Manco's warriors fired an unrelenting barrage of sling
stones, "like a dense hail,"[22] on the Spaniards and their indigenous auxiliaries
holed up in the city. The missiles included red-hot sling stones wrapped in
cotton cloth that set fire to the city's thatched roofs.[23]

Nevertheless, Manco and his soldiers never succeeded in switching from the
ritualized Inca-style of battle to that of the Spaniards. The Spaniards used
siege tactics, building ladders to scale Saqsawaman's walls. They took advantage of the Incas' cyclical and ritual approach to warfare, for the indigenous
army considered the full moon a propitious time to fight and "in all their sieges
or wars are accustomed to stop fighting at the new moon and carry out their
sacrifices."[24] Indeed, the fall of Saqsawaman to Pizarro's forces apparently
coincided with the new moon on May 19, 1536.[25]

By the end of May, the Spaniards had regained control over Cusco. Manco
and his army withdrew to the Urubamba valley, converting Ollantaytambo
into their headquarters and engaging the Spaniards in pitched battles. Alerted
to the arrival of Spanish reinforcements, Manco escaped over the Panticalla

pass to Vitcos in the province of Vilcabamba, which became the de facto capital of the rebellious Incas. From his Vilcabamba stronghold, Manco instigated a second uprising in 1538.

Manco's rebellion triggered a wave of defiant Inca nationalism. From the forested fastness of Vilcabamba, Manco's guerrillas "sallied forth in all directions,"[26] raiding Spanish caravans on the Cusco–Lima road. Manco's spies kept him abreast of events in an increasingly chaotic Spanish Peru. The instability culminated, in 1541, with the murder of Francisco Pizarro by the son of rival conquistador Diego de Almagro. In 1542, seven Spanish fugitives from the Almagro faction joined Manco in Vitcos. The Spanish deserters, however, soon grew restless, and plotted to kill Manco, reckoning that Spanish authorities in Cusco would forgive them their earlier treachery. In mid-1544, during a game of horseshoe quoits, one of the men fatally stabbed Manco. The Spanish renegades fled, but were later caught and killed.

Manco's followers took his embalmed body to Vilcabamba la Vieja. His son, Sayri Tupac, was too young to govern, and regents administered the exiled court. The Incas settled into life at Vilcabamba la Vieja, where, in relative isolation, they revived Inca traditions and ceremony. In 1548, however, Spanish officials initiated diplomatic overtures, sending gifts and offers of rich estates. By 1557, Sayri Tupac had come of age, and was crowned Inca. He accepted the Spanish proposal to settle in the Urubamba valley, where he lived off the income of his estates. After Sayri Tupac died in 1561 he was succeeded by Titu Cusi. Negotiations between the two sides continued and the Spanish authorities dispatched several emissaries. Titu Cusi appeared compliant and in 1566 he signed the Treaty of Acobamba, allowing missionaries to enter Vilcabamba, although he prevented them from reaching Vilcabamba la Vieja. Exasperated with their treatment, the friars burned the shrine of Yurak Rumi near Vitcos, which infuriated Titu Cusi.

The arrival of the Viceroy Toledo in 1570 sealed the fate of the Vilcabamba Incas, for the Viceroy had resolved to end Inca rule. Toledo made a final attempt at diplomacy, unaware that Titu Cusi had died in mid-1571, replaced by his brother, Tupac Amaru. Toledo dispatched 250 Spanish soldiers and 1,500 indigenous auxiliaries to Vilcabamba. Although they skirmished with Inca soldiers as they advanced toward Vilcabamba la Vieja, they could not be stopped and reached the last Inca capital in June 1572 where they succeeded in capturing Tupac Amaru, the mummies of Manco Inca and Titu Cusi, as well as the golden image of the sun, known as Punchao. They marched Tupac Amaru to Cusco in chains, where he underwent a three-day summary trial, converted to Catholicism, and was beheaded in Cusco's main plaza.

Tupac Amaru's death signaled the end of Inca resistance to Spanish rule. The fall of Vilcabamba la Vieja, the final, luxurious center of an empire in exile, marked the end of Tawantinsuyu.

Notes

Chapter 2 (pp. 20–31)
1 Glowacki 2002
2 Mannheim 1991, Torero 1974
3 McEwan 1991, 1996
4 Bauer and Covey 2002
5 Bauer 2004
6 McEwan, Chatfield, and Gibaja 2002
7 Bauer 2004
8 Bauer and Covey 2002
9 Bauer 2004, Bauer and Covey 2002, Covey 2006
10 Sarmiento 1999, p. 45
11 Sarmiento 1999, p. 55
12 Bauer and Kellett 2010
13 González Carré 1992
14 González Carré 1992
15 Sarmiento 1999, p. 91
16 Rostworowski 1995
17 Zuidema 1999
18 Cieza 1959, p. 188
19 Niles 1999
20 Cobo 1979, p. 252
21 Rostworowski 1999, J. Rowe 1958
22 Pärssinen 1992
23 Pärssinen 1992
24 Murra 1986
25 D'Altroy 2003, 2007

Chapter 3 (pp. 32–47)
1 Murúa 2001, p. 198
2 D'Altroy 2002, Pärssinen 1992, J. Rowe 1946
3 Urton and Brezine 2007
4 Julien 1988
5 Ortiz de Zúñiga 1967, pp. 45, 54
6 Pärssinen 1992
7 Urton 2008
8 Cobo 1979, p. 200
9 Hartmann 1972, Topic and Topic 1987, Ziółkowski 1996
10 Arkush and Stanish 2005, Topic and Topic 1987
11 John Topic, personal communication 2006
12 Ziółkowski 1996
13 Hartmann 1972, Sallnow 1987, Urton 1993
14 Cieza 1959, p. 226
15 Murra 1986, p. 52
16 Murra 1986
17 Hartmann 1972
18 Betanzos 1996, p. 120
19 Cieza 1959, p. 57
20 Cieza 1959, p. 191
21 Betanzos 1996, p. 52
22 Murúa 1946, p. 191, quoted in Silverblatt 1987, p. 92
23 Silverblatt 1987

Chapter 4 (pp. 48–64)
1 Murra 1980
2 Murra 1979

3 A. Rowe 1984
4 Cieza 1959, p. 68
5 Baudin 1928
6 Cieza 1959, p. 178
7 Lechtman 1984
8 Guaman Poma 1980, p. 310
9 Garcilaso 1966, p. 57
10 Cummins 2002
11 Cieza 1959, pp. 342–44
12 Murra 1962
13 J. Rowe 1979

Chapter 5 (pp. 65–76)
1 Estete 1872, p. 82
2 Cieza 1959, p. 329
3 Betanzos 1996, pp. 44–45
4 Gose 1996
5 Cieza 1959, p. 138
6 Cieza 1959, p. 184
7 Betanzos 1996, p. 291
8 Sarmiento 1999, p. 176
9 Betanzos 1996, p. 232
10 Blas Valera 1950, p. 136, quoted in Silverblatt 1987, p. 47
11 Cobo 1990, p. 32
12 Albornoz 1989, p. 20
13 Bauer 1987–89, 1991
14 Cobo 1990, p. 74
15 Cieza 1959, p. 150
16 Cobo 1990, p. 134
17 Cieza 1959, p. 280
18 Cieza 1959, p. 31
19 Cieza 1959, p. 172
20 Aveni 1981, Zuidema 1977
21 Bauer and Dearborn 1995
22 Bauer and Stanish 2001, Dearborn, Seddon, and Bauer 1998
23 Garcilaso 1966, p. 118
24 Garcilaso 1966, pp. 118–19
25 Garcilaso 1966, p. 119
26 Dearborn and Schreiber 1986
27 Polo 1916, Chapter 1, quoted in Urton 1981, p. 169
28 Urbano and Duviols 1989, p. 477
29 Cieza 1959, p. 191
30 Cobo 1990, p. 155
31 Cobo 1990, p. 156
32 Molina 1989, p. 127, quoted in MacCormack 1991, pp. 200–1
33 Salomon and Urioste 1991, p. 112
34 Cieza 1996, p. 200
35 Ceruti 1999
36 Betanzos 1996, p. 77
37 Cobo 1990, p. 156
38 Bauer 1998, J. Rowe 1979, Zuidema 1964
39 Bauer 1998
40 Murúa 1946, p. 48, quoted in Silverblatt 1987, p. 43
41 J. Rowe 1960
42 Molina 1989, p. 127, quoted in MacCormack 1991, p. 201
43 Segovia 1968, p. 82ff, quoted in Hemming 1983, p. 172

Chapter 6 (pp. 77–101)
1 Cieza 1959, p. 64
2 Humboldt 1850
3 Protzen and Nair 1997
4 J. Rowe 1946
5 Niles 1999
6 Hyslop 1990
7 Rostworowski 1995
8 Coben 2006, Lee 1992
9 Cobo 1990, p. 227
10 Squier 1973, p. 395
11 Cieza 1959, p. 114
12 Lee 1988
13 Morris 1981
14 van de Guchte 1990
15 van de Guchte 1990
16 van de Guchte 1990
17 Protzen 1993
18 Protzen 1985
19 Acosta 1987, p. 279
20 Lee 1986
21 Cobo 1990, p. 229
22 Garcilaso 1966, p. 464
23 Cieza 1959, p. 138
24 Ochsendorf 2004
25 Cieza 1959, p. 305
26 Cieza 1959, p. 140
27 Cobo 1979, p. 226
28 Hyslop 1984
29 Xerez 1872, p. 29
30 Sancho 1986, p. 90
31 Squier 1973, pp. 546–48
32 Bauer 2006
33 Cieza 1959, p. 134
34 Espinoza 1970, Spurling 1992
35 Murra 1978
36 Spurling 1992
37 Cieza 1959, p. 70
38 Xerez 1872, p. 60
39 A. Rowe 1978, J. Rowe 1979
40 Cobo 1990, p. 225
41 P. Pizarro 1986, pp. 67–68
42 P. Pizarro 1986, p. 99
43 P. Pizarro 1986, p. 99
44 Cieza 1959, p. 71
45 Cobo 1990, p. 215
46 Xerez 1872, p. 60
47 Cobo 1990, p. 216
48 Cobo 1990, pp. 215–16
49 Lechtman 2007
50 Pärssinen 1992
51 Cieza 1959, p. 328
52 Cieza 1959, p. 114
53 Lechtman 2007
54 Cieza 1959, p. 156

Chapter 7 (pp. 102–32)
1 Bauer 2004
2 Sancho 1917, pp. 153–54, quoted in Bauer 2004, p. 110
3 Cobo 1990, p. 51
4 Hyslop 1990, Sherbondy 1994
5 Betanzos 1996, p. 69
6 Betanzos 1996, p. 74

7 Zuidema 1983
8 Niles 1987, J. Rowe 1968
9 Bauer 2004
10 *Noticia del Perú* 1938, p. 241, in Gasparini and Margolies 1980, p. 58
11 Cieza 1959, p. 203
12 de las Casas 1909, p. 674, quoted in J. Rowe 1968, p. 62
13 Molina [Bartolomé de Segovia] 1943, p. 33, quoted in Gasparini and Margolies 1980, p. 49
14 Hyslop 1990
15 J. Rowe 1968, p. 60
16 Garcilaso 1966, p. 422
17 Cieza 1959, p. 148
18 Garcilaso 1966, p. 428
19 Polo 1965, pp. 118–19
20 Farrington and Raffino 1996
21 Betanzos 1996, p. 48
22 Albornoz 1987, p. 26
23 Betanzos 1996, p. 169
24 Betanzos 1996, p. 136
25 Sancho 1872, p. 192, quoted in Hemming 1983, p. 119
26 Hyslop 1990
27 Protzen 1993
28 Sancho 1872, p. 192, quoted in Hemming 1983, p. 119
29 Murúa 1946, p. 181, quoted in Silverblatt 1987, p. 60
30 Garcilaso 1966, p. 426
31 Murúa 1946, pp. 165–66
32 Cieza 1959, p. 145
33 Cieza 1959, p. 146
34 J. Rowe 1944
35 Anonymous conqueror 1929, p. 5, quoted in J. Rowe 1944, pp. 37–38
36 P. Pizarro 1986, p. 92
37 Cieza 1959, p. 146
38 Mena 1934, p. 256, quoted in MacCormack 1991, p. 65
39 P. Pizarro 1986, pp. 90–91
40 Estete 1924, pp. 54–56, quoted in Hemming 1983, p. 127
41 Sancho 1917, pp. 155–57, quoted in Bauer 2004, p. 100
42 Garcilaso 1966
43 Garcilaso 1966
44 Cieza 1959, pp. 153–54
45 Bauer 2004
46 Cieza 1959, p. 153
47 Protzen 1987–89
48 Bauer 2004
49 P. Pizarro 1986, p. 104
50 Sancho 1917, pp. 193–94, quoted in Hyslop 1990, p. 54
51 Cieza 1959, p. 153
52 P. Pizarro 1986, p. 54
53 J. Rowe 1997, p. 277
54 Garcilaso 1966, p. 303
55 Niles 1999, 2004, Niles and Batson 2007
56 Betanzos 1996, p. 170
57 Betanzos 1996, p. 159
58 Betanzos 1996, p. 159
59 Nair 2003
60 Protzen 1993

61 J. Rowe 1990
62 Pärssinen 1992

Chapter 8 (pp. 133–85)
1 Heffernan 1996
2 van de Guchte 1990
3 Cieza 1959, p. 135, Farrington and Zapata 2003
4 Cieza 1959, p. 134
5 P. Pizarro 1986, p. 82
6 Hemming and Ranney 2010
7 van de Guchte 1990
8 Oberti 1997
9 Lechtman 1976
10 Santillana 2011
11 Cieza 1959, Santillana 2011
12 Cieza 1959, p. 127
13 Cieza 1959, p. 127
14 Cieza 1959, p. 127
15 Carbajal 1965, pp. 218–19
16 Gasparini and Margolies 1980
17 Cieza 1959, Santillana 2011
18 González Carré and Pozzi Escot 2002
19 Gasparini and Margolies 1980, Protzen and Harris 2005
20 Morris and Santillana 2007, Protzen and Morris 2004
21 Morris n.d. (2006)
22 Protzen and Morris 2004, Protzen 2008
23 Rostworowski 1970
24 Lechtman 2007
25 Curatola 1997, Morris and Santillana 2007
26 Lumbreras 2001
27 Alcalde et al. 2010
28 Duviols 1967, Rostworowski 1992
29 Cieza 1959, p. 346
30 Santillán 1968, pp. 14–15
31 Menzel 1959
32 Rostworowski 1978–80
33 Rostworowski 1978–80
34 Cieza 1959, pp. 342–43
35 Cieza 1959, p. 339
36 Menzel and Riddell 1954/1986; Menzel 1959
37 Menzel and Riddell 1954/1986; Menzel 1959
38 Canziani 1995
39 Canziani 1995
40 Salomon and Urioste 1991, p. 113
41 Patterson 1985, Xerez 1872, pp. 136–37
42 Estete 1872, p. 83
43 Estete 1872, p. 123
44 Cieza 1959, p. 136
45 Duviols 1997
46 D'Altroy 2002
47 Toledo 1940, p. 19, quoted in D'Altroy 1992, p. 78
48 Cieza 1959, p. 114
49 D'Altroy 2002
50 D'Altroy and Hastorf 1984, LeVine 1992
51 Cieza 1959, p. 172
52 H. Pizarro 1872, pp. 125, 126
53 Estete 1872, p. 90

54 Cieza 1959, p. 114
55 Cieza 1959, p. 112
56 Cieza 1959, p. 112
57 LeVine 1992, Matos 1994
58 Matos 1994
59 Matos 1994
60 Cieza 1959, p. 109
61 Morris 1998
62 Morris and Thompson 1985
63 Cieza 1959, pp. 101–2
64 Topic and Topic 1993
65 Topic, Topic, and Melly 2002, Topic 2008
66 Topic, Topic, and Melly 2002, Topic 2008
67 Cieza 1959, p. 95
68 Xerez 1872, p. 60
69 Yupanqui 2005, p. 7
70 Xerez 1872, pp. 45–46
71 P. Pizarro 1986, p. 32
72 Xerez 1872, p. 48
73 Xerez 1872, p. 61
74 Xerez 1872, p. 61
75 Shimada 1990
76 Hayashida 2003
77 J. Rowe 1948
78 Cabello de Valboa 1951, p. 332
79 Cieza 1959, p. 328
80 Cieza 1959, p. 329
81 Cieza 1959, p. 322
82 Cieza 1959, p. 321
83 Mackey 2003, 2010
84 Mackey 2010
85 Mackey 2003
86 Heyerdahl et al. 1995
87 Cummins 2002
88 Heyerdahl et al. 1995
89 Hayashida 1994, 1999
90 Hayashida 1999
91 Mena 1968, p. 136
92 Ruíz de Arce 1933, p. 419
93 Cieza 1995, p. 170
94 Mena 1987, p. 136
95 Hocquenghem and Peña Ruíz 1993
96 Hocquenghem 1994a
97 Church and von Hagen 2008
98 Lerche 1995
99 Espinoza 1967
100 Pärssinen 1992
101 Schjellerup 1997
102 Vasquez de Espinosa 1969
103 Polo 1940, p. 170, quoted in LeVine 1992, p. 18
104 von Hagen 2002, 2007, von Hagen and Guillén 1998
105 Urton 2001, 2007
106 Schjellerup 1997
107 Cieza 1998, p. 182
108 Trujillo 1968, vol. 2, p. 20, quoted in Hocquenghem 1994b, p. 58
109 Astuhuamán 1995, 1999
110 Xerez 1872, p. 28
111 Diez 1964, p. 105
112 Salomon 1987
113 Salomon 1987
114 Cieza 1959
115 Hyslop 1990
116 Cieza 1959, p. 70

117 Cieza 1959, p. 70
118 Cabello de Valboa 1951, p. 365
119 Ogburn 2004
120 Cieza 1959, p. 70
121 Murúa 1946, p. 103, quoted in Ogburn 2004, p. 425
122 Ogburn 2004
123 Protzen, personal communication 2006
124 Hocquenghem 1993
125 Cieza 1996, p. 157
126 Odaira 1998
127 Hyslop 1990
128 Salomon 1987
129 Connell et al. 2003, Gifford et al. 2002, Hyslop 1990
130 Gifford et al. 2002
131 Sarmiento 1999, p. 162
132 Sarmiento 1999, p. 164
133 Sarmiento 1999, p. 167
134 Sarmiento 1999, p. 167
135 Cieza 1959, Caillavet 2000
136 Cieza 1959, p. 20
137 Cieza 1959, p. 121

Chapter 9 (pp. 186–209)
1 Garcilaso 1966, p. 823
2 Cieza 1959, p. 143
3 Cobo 1979, p. 136
4 Cobo 1979, p. 137
5 Pärssinen 1992
6 Lyon 1984
7 Hornborg 2005, Renard-Casevitz 1981
8 Pärssinen 1992, Siiriäinen and Pärssinen 2003
9 Pärssinen 1992
10 Pärssinen 1992, Siiriäinen and Korpisaari 2002, Pärssinen and Siiriäinen 2003
11 H. Bingham 1913, p. 408
12 A. Bingham 1989, pp. 19–20
13 H. Bingham 1913, p. 542
14 Burger 2004, Hyslop 1990
15 Burger 2004, Gasparini and Margolies 1980
16 Gasparini and Margolies 1980
17 Reinhard 2002
18 Dearborn and Schreiber 1986, Reinhard 2002
19 Salazar and Burger 2004, Salazar 2007
20 Burger 2004
21 Valencia 2004
22 Salazar 2004
23 Verano 2003
24 Burger 2004, Verano 2003
25 H. Bingham 1930, p. 233
26 Burger 2004
27 Rostworowski 1963, p. 155
28 Drew 1984
29 Rostworowski 1963, p. 158
30 Ocampo 1907, p. 216
31 Lee 2000
32 Ocampo 1907, p. 216
33 Lee 2000
34 Yupanqui 2005, p. 53
35 Calancha 1978, p. 1800

36 Calancha 1978, p. 1827
37 H. Bingham 1913, p. 520
38 Lee 1997
39 Frost et al. 2002
40 Rodríguez de Figueroa 1913, pp. 178–80, quoted in Lee 2000, pp. 85–86
41 Lee 2000
42 H. Bingham 1913, pp. 196–97
43 Murúa 2001, pp. 287–89
44 Lee 2000
45 Betanzos 1996, p. 299
46 Murúa 2001, p. 288

Chapter 10 (pp. 210–33)
1 Cieza 1959, p. 270
2 Diez de San Miguel 1964
3 Murra 1975
4 Ceruti 1999, Reinhard and Ceruti 2011
5 Bauer 2004, Bauer and Stanish 2001
6 Cobo 1990, p. 97
7 Bauer and Stanish 2001
8 Cobo 1990, p. 94
9 Cobo 1990, p. 94
10 Squier 1973, p. 362
11 Cobo 1990, p. 95
12 Bauer 1987–89, 1991
13 Cobo 1990, p. 107
14 Sillar and Dean 2002
15 Pärssinen and Siiriäinen 1997
16 Stanish 1997
17 Hyslop 1990, Julien 1983
18 Murra 1975
19 Wachtel 1982
20 Alconini 2004, Lee 1992, Pärssinen and Siiriäinen 1998
21 Coben 2006
22 Coben 2006
23 Hyslop 1990, Trimborn 1959
24 Meyers 2007
25 D'Altroy, Williams, and Lorandi 2007, Raffino 1993, Williams and D'Altroy 1999
26 Raffino 1993
27 Williams and D'Altroy 1999
28 Hyslop 1984
29 Bauer 1998
30 Cobo 1979, p. 230
31 Doutriaux 2002
32 Wernke 2006
33 Jennings and Yépez 2008
34 Ziółkowski 2005
35 Cieza 1959, pp. 151–52
36 Guaman Poma 1980, pp. 272–73
37 Cieza 1959, pp. 151–52
38 Ziółkowski 2005, Ziółkowski and Sobczyk 2010
39 Reinhard 1999a
40 Ziółkowski 2005, Ziółkowski and Sobczyk 2010
41 Ziółkowski 2005
42 Wołoszyn 2000–1
43 Aldunate 2001
44 Niemeyer and Schiappacasse 1988
45 Hyslop 1984
46 Niemeyer, Cervellino, and Muñoz 1983

47 Rossen et al. 2010
48 Aldunate and Cornejo 2001
49 Dillehay and Gordon 1998
50 Schobinger 2001
51 Reinhard and Ceruti 2011
52 Cobo 1979, p. 238
53 Molina 1989
54 Ceruti 2003, Reinhard 2005, Schobinger 2001
55 Reinhard 1996, 1997, 2005
56 Ceruti 1999, Reinhard 1999, Reinhard and Ceruti 2011

Chapter 11 (pp. 234–41)
1 Xerez 1985, pp. 179–80
2 Cook 1998
3 P. Pizarro 1986, p. 50
4 Xerez 1872, pp. 45, 50
5 P. Pizarro 1986, p. 37
6 Estete 1919, quoted in Hemming 1983, p. 39
7 Estete 1919, quoted in Hemming 1983, p. 41
8 P. Pizarro 1986, p. 39
9 P. Pizarro 1986, p. 39
10 Xerez 1872, pp. 55–56
11 Yupanqui 2005, pp. 9–11
12 Guaman Poma 1980, p. 287
13 Zárate 1947, p. 105
14 De Mesa 1940, p. 200, quoted in Niles 1999, p. 62
15 Lothrop 1938
16 Xerez, in Hemming 1983, p. 74
17 "Los oficiales de Puerto Rico al Emperador, San Juan, 26 de febrero de 1534," *Cartas del Perú*, p. 100, quoted in Spalding 1984, p. 910
18 Sancho 1872, p. 27, quoted in Hemming 1983, p. 78
19 Ruíz de Arce 1933, p. 368, quoted in Hemming 1983, p. 110
20 P. Pizarro 1986, p. 124
21 Yupanqui 2005, p. 105
22 *Relación de los sucesos*, p. 392, quoted in Hemming 1983, p. 193
23 Hemming 1983
24 Anonymous 1934, quoted in Ziółkowski 1996, p. 11
25 Ziółkowski 1996
26 Cieza 1959, p. 121

Boxes
pp. 34–35: "cords and knots," Miguel de Estete, cited in Urton 2002, p. 6; "way of counting," Cieza 1959, p. 105; "measured and recorded," Garcilaso 1966, pp. 269–70; "remembered their history," Garcilaso 1966, p. 332; "twenty or thirty," Garcilaso 1966, p. 331; "fraud or deceit," Cieza 1959, p. 177.
pp. 122–23: "as a god," Cobo 1979, p. 111; "their eyes lowered," Garcilaso 1966, p. 307; "hard and stiff," Garcilaso 1966, p. 307; "to be alive," Acosta, in Garcilaso 1966, p. 307; "it to Cuzco," Betanzos 1996, p. 185.

Further Reading

ACOSTA, JOSÉ DE. *Historia natural y moral de las Indias*, Crónicas de América, no. 34, ed. by JOSÉ ALCINA FRANCH. Madrid, 1987 [1590].

ALCALDE, JAVIER, CARLOS DEL AGUILA, FERNANDO FUJITA, and ENRIQUE RETAMOZO. "'Plateros' precoloniales tardíos en Tambo de Mora, valle de Chincha (siglos XIV-XVI)," *Arqueología y Sociedad*, vol. 21, pp. 171–84, 2010.

ALCONINI, SONIA. "The Southeastern Inka Frontier against the Chiriguanos: Structure and Dynamics of the Inka Imperial Borderlands," *Latin American Antiquity*, vol. 15, no. 4, pp. 389–418, 2004.

ALDUNATE, CARLOS, VICTORIA CASTRO, and VARINIA VARELA. "Antes del Inka y después del Inka: Paisajes culturales y sacralidad en la puna de Atacama, Chile," in PETER KAULICKE, GARY URTON, and IAN FARRINGTON (eds), *Identidad y transformación en el Tawantinsuyu y en los Andes coloniales: Perspectivas arqueológicas y etnohistóricas*, pp. 9–26. *Boletín de Arqueología PUCP*, no. 7, 2003.

ALDUNATE, CARLOS, and LUIS E. CORNEJO (eds). *Tras la huella del Inka en Chile*. Santiago: Museo Chileno de Arte Precolombino, 2001.

ANON. *The Conquest of Peru as Recorded by a Member of the Pizarro Expedition*. Reproduced from the copy of the Seville edition of 1534 in the New York Library and trans. by JOSEPH H. SINCLAIR, New York, 1929.

ARKUSH, ELIZABETH, and CHARLES STANISH. "Interpreting Conflict in the Ancient Andes: Implications for the Archaeology of Warfare," *Current Anthropology*, vol. 46, no. 1, pp. 3–28, 2005.

ASTUHUAMÁN GONZÁLEZ, CÉSAR. "Asentamientos Incas en la sierra de Piura," *Sequilao*, vol. 4, no. 8, pp. 85–124, 1995.

————"Los Incas en el extremo Noroeste del Perú," *Comunidad: Tierra–Hombre–Identidad*, vol. 3, pp. 38–44, 1999.

AVENI, ANTHONY F. "Horizon Astronomy in Incaic Cuzco," in R. A. WILLIAMSON (ed.), *Archaeoastronomy in the Americas*, pp. 305–18. Los Altos (CA): Ballena Press, 1981.

BAUDIN, LOUIS. *A Socialist Empire: The Incas of Peru*, trans. by KATHERINE WOODS. Princeton (NJ): D. Van Nostrand Co., 1961 [1928].

BAUER, BRIAN S. "Recent Archaeological Investigations at the Sites of Maukallaqta and Puma Orco, Department of Cuzco, Peru," *Ñawpa Pacha*, vols 25–27, pp. 207–50, 1987–89.

————"Pacariqtambo and the Mythical Origins of the Inca," *Latin American Antiquity*, vol. 2, no. 1, pp. 7–26, 1991.

————*The Sacred Landscape of the Inca: The Cusco Ceque System*. Austin: University of Texas Press, 1998.

————*Ancient Cuzco: Heartland of the Inca*. Austin: University of Texas Press, 2004.

————"Suspension Bridges of the Inca Empire," in WILLIAM H. ISBELL and HELAINE SILVERMAN (eds), *Andean Archaeology III: North and South*, pp. 468–93. New York: Springer, 2006.

BAUER, BRIAN S., and ALAN R. COVEY. "State Development in the Inka Heartland (Cuzco, Peru)," *American Anthropologist*, vol. 10, no. 3, pp. 846–64, 2002.

BAUER, BRIAN S., and DAVID S. P. DEARBORN. *Astronomy and Empire in the Ancient Andes: The Cultural Origins of Inca Sky Watching*. Austin: University of Texas Press, 1995.

BAUER, BRIAN S., and LUCAS C. KELLETT. "Cultural Transformation of the Chanka Homeland (Andahuaylas, Peru) during the Late Intermediate Period (A.D. 1000–1400)," *Latin American Antiquity*, vol. 21, no. 1, pp. 87–111, 2010.

BAUER, BRIAN S., and CHARLES STANISH. *Ritual and Pilgrimage in the Ancient Andes: The Islands of the Sun and the Moon*. Austin: University of Texas Press, 2001.

BETANZOS, JUAN DE. *Narrative of the Incas*, trans. and ed. by ROLAND HAMILTON and DANA BUCHANAN. Austin: University of Texas Press, 1996 [1551–57].

BINGHAM, ALFRED M. *Portrait of an Explorer: Hiram Bingham, Discoverer of Machu Picchu*. Ames: Iowa State University Press, 1989.

BINGHAM, HIRAM. "In the Wonderland of Peru," *National Geographic*, vol. 24, no. 4, 1913.

————*Machu Picchu: A Citadel of the Incas*. New York: Hacker Art Books, 1979 (reprint of the 1930 edition)

BURGER, RICHARD L. "Scientific Insights into Daily Life at Machu Picchu," in RICHARD L. BURGER and LUCY C. SALAZAR (eds), *Machu Picchu: Unveiling the Mystery of the Incas*, pp. 85–108. New Haven (CT) and London: Yale University Press, 2004.

CABELLO DE VALBOA, MIGUEL. *Miscelánea antártica: Una historia del Perú antiguo*. Lima: Instituto de Etnología, 1951.

CAILLAVET, CHANTAL L. "Etnías del norte: etnohistoria e historia de Ecuador," *Travaux de l'IFEA*, vol. 106, 2000.

CALANCHA, ANTONIO DE LA. *Corónica Moralizada de la Orden de San Agustín en el Perú*, vol. 5, ed. by IGNACIO PRADO PASTOR. Lima, 1978 [1638].

CANZIANI, JOSÉ. "Las lomas de Atiquipa: arqueología y problemas de desarrollo regional," *Gaceta Arqueológica Andina*, no. 24, pp. 13–33, 1995.

CARBAJAL, PEDRO DE. "Descripción fecha de la Provincia de Vilcas Guamán...año de 1586," in M. JIMÉNEZ DE LA ESPADA (ed.), *Relaciones Geográficas de Indias-Perú*, Biblioteca de Autores Españoles, vol. 183, pp. 205–19. Madrid: Ediciones Atlas, 1965 [1586].

CASAS, BARTOLOMÉ DE LAS. *Apologética histórica de las Indias*, Nueva Biblioteca de Autores Españoles, vol. 13. Madrid: Bailly-Baillière e Hijos, 1909.

CERUTI, MARÍA CONSTANZA. *Cumbres sagradas del noroeste argentino: avances en arqueología de alta montaña y etnoarqueología de santuarios de altura andinos*. Buenos Aires: EUDEBA, 1999.

————"Elegidos de los dioses: identidad y estatus en las víctimas sacrificiales del volcán Llullaillaco," in PETER KAULICKE, GARY URTON, and IAN FARRINGTON (eds), *Identidad y transformación en el Tawantinsuyu y en los Andes coloniales: Perspectivas arqueológicas y etnohistóricas*, pp. 263–76. *Boletín de Arqueología PUCP*, no. 7, 2003.

CHURCH, WARREN B., and ADRIANA VON HAGEN. "Chachapoyas: Cultural Development at an Andean Cloud Forest Crossroads," in HELAINE SILVERMAN and WILLIAM H. ISBELL (eds), *Handbook of South American Archaeology*, pp. 903–26. New York and London: Springer, 2008.

CIEZA DE LEÓN, PEDRO DE. *The Incas*, trans. by HARRIET DE ONIS. Norman: University of Oklahoma Press, 1959 [1553].

————*Crónica del Perú, Segunda Parte*, ed. by FRANCESCA CANTÚ. Lima: Fondo Editorial, Pontificia Universidad Católica del Perú, 1996 [1553].

————*The Discovery and Conquest of Peru: Chronicles of the New World Encounter*, trans. and ed. by ALEXANDRA PARMA COOK and NOBLE DAVID COOK. Durham (NC) and London: Duke University Press, 1998.

COBEN, LAWRENCE S. "Other Cuzcos: Replicated Theaters of Inka Power," in TAKESHI INOMATA and LAWRENCE S. COBEN (eds), *Archaeology of Performance: Theaters of Power,*

Community, and Politics, pp. 223–60. Lanham (MD) and Oxford: Altamira Press, 2006.

COBO, BERNABÉ. *History of the Inca Empire: An Account of the Indians' Customs and their Origin, together with a Treatise on Inca Legends, History, and Social Institutions*, trans. by ROLAND HAMILTON. Austin and London: University of Texas Press, 1979 [1653].

———*Inca Religion and Customs*, trans. by ROLAND HAMILTON. Austin: University of Texas Press, 1990 [1653].

CONNELL, SAMUEL V., CHAD GIFFORD, ANA LUCÍA GONZALEZ, and MAUREEN CARPENTER. "Hard Times in Ecuador: Inka Troubles at Pambamarca," *Antiquity*, vol. 77, no. 295, 2003.

COOK, NOBLE DAVID. *Born to Die: Disease and New World Conquest, 1492–1650*. Cambridge: Cambridge University Press, 1998.

COVEY, R. ALAN. *How the Incas Built their Heartland: State Formation and the Innovation of Imperial Strategies in the Sacred Valley, Peru*. Ann Arbor: University of Michigan Press, 2006.

CUMMINS, THOMAS B. F. *Toasts with the Inca: Andean Abstraction and Colonial Images on Quero Vessels*. Ann Arbor: University of Michigan Press, 2002.

CURATOLA, MARCO. "Guano: una hipótesis sobre el origen de la riqueza del señorío de Chincha," in RAFAEL VARÓN GABAI and JAVIER FLORES ESPINOZA (eds), *Arqueología, Antropología e Historia en los Andes: Homenaje a María Rostworowski*, pp. 223–39. Lima: Instituto de Estudios Peruanos, 1997.

D'ALTROY, TERENCE N. *Provincial Power in the Inka Empire*. Washington, DC, and London: Smithsonian Institution, 1992.

———*The Incas*. Malden (MA) and Oxford: Blackwell, 2002.

D'ALTROY, TERENCE N., and CHRISTINE A. HASTORF. "The Distribution and Contents of Inca State Storehouses in the Xauxa Region of Peru," *American Antiquity*, vol. 49, pp. 334–49, 1984.

D'ALTROY, TERENCE N., VERÓNICA I. WILLIAMS, and ANA MARÍA LORANDI. "The Inkas in the Southlands," in RICHARD L. BURGER, CRAIG MORRIS, and RAMIRO MATOS (eds), *Variations in the Expression of Inka Power*, pp. 85–134. Washington, DC: Dumbarton Oaks, 2007.

DEARBORN, DAVID S. P., and KATHARINA J. SCHREIBER. "Here Comes the Sun: the Cuzco–Machu Picchu connection," *Archaeoastronomy*, vol. 9, pp. 15–37, 1986.

DEARBORN, DAVID S. P., MATTHEW T. SEDDON, and BRIAN S. BAUER. "The Sanctuary of Titicaca: When the Sun Returns to Earth," *Latin American Antiquity*, vol. 9, no. 3, pp. 240–58, 1998.

DEARBORN, DAVID S. P., and RAYMOND E. WHITE. "The 'Torreón' at Machu Picchu as an Observatory," *Archaeoastronomy*, vol. 5, pp. 37–49, 1983.

DIEZ DE SAN MIGUEL, GARCI. *Visita hecha a la provincia de Chucuito, por Garci Diez de San Miguel en el año de 1567*. Lima: Casa de la Cultura del Perú, 1964 [1567].

DILLEHAY, TOM D., and AMÉRICO GORDON. "La actividad prehispánica de los Incas y su influencia en la Araucanía," in TOM D. DILLEHAY and PATRICIA J. NETHERLY, *La Frontera del Estado Inca*, pp. 183–96. Quito: Fundación Alexander von Humboldt and Editorial Abya-Yala, 1998.

DOUTRIAUX, MIRIAM. "Relaciones étnicas y económicas de poder: la conquista Incaica en el valle del Colca, Arequipa," in PETER KAULICKE, GARY URTON, and IAN FARRINGTON, *Identidad y transformación en el Tawantinsuyu y en los Andes coloniales: Perspectivas arqueológicas y etnohistóricas. Boletín de Arqueología PUCP*, no. 6, pp. 411–32, 2002.

DREW, DAVID. *The Cusichaca Project: the Lucumayo and Santa Teresa Valleys*. Oxford: BAR, International Series, no. 44, 1984.

DUVIOLS, PIERRE. "Un inédit de Cristóbal de Albornoz: La Instrucción para descubrir todas las guacas del Pirú y sus

camayos y haziendas," *Journal de la Société des Américanistes*, vol. 56, pp. 7–39, 1967.

———"Dónde estaba el santuario de Pariacaca?" in RAFAEL VARÓN GABAI and JAVIER FLORES ESPINOZA (eds), *Arqueología, Antropología e Historia en los Andes: Homenaje a María Rostworowski*, pp. 643–49. Lima: Instituto de Estudios Peruanos, 1997.

ESPINOZA SORIANO, WALDEMAR. "Los señoríos étnicos de Chachapoyas y la alianza hispano-chacha," *Revista Histórica*, vol. 30, pp. 224–333, 1967.

———"Los mitmas yungas de Collique en Cajamarca, siglos XV, XVI, y XVII," *Revista del Museo Nacional*, vol. 36, pp. 9–57, 1970.

ESTETE, MIGUEL DE (attributed). *La relación del viaje que hizo el señor capitán Hernando Pizarro por mandado del señor Gobernador, su hermano, desde el pueblo de Caxamalca a Parcama y de allí a Jauja*, in FRANCISCO DE XEREZ, *Verdadera Relación de la Conquista del Perú*, pp. 130–48. Madrid: Historia 16, 1985. English edition: "Report of Miguel de Astete on the Expedition to Pachacamac," in CLEMENTS R. MARKHAM (trans. and ed.), *Reports on the Discovery of Peru*, published for the Hakluyt Society, London, 1872 [1534].

FARRINGTON, IAN S., and RODOLFO RAFFINO. "Inka News from around the Empire," *Tawantinsuyu*, vol. 2, pp. 73–77, 1996.

FARRINGTON, IAN S., and JULINHO ZAPATA. "Nuevos cánones de arquitectura inka: investigaciones en el sitio de Tambokancha–Tumibamba, Jaquijahuana, Cuzco," in PETER KAULICKE, GARY URTON, and IAN FARRINGTON (eds), *Identidad y transformación en el Tawantinsuyu y en los Andes coloniales: Perspectivas arqueológicas y etnohistóricas. Boletín de Arqueología PUCP*, no. 7, pp. 57–78, 2003.

FROST, PETER, SCOTT GORSUCH, IVES BEJAR MENDOZA, and ALFREDO VALENCIA ZEGARRA. *Preliminary Report, NGS Qoriwayrachina Project*, 2001–2.

GARCILASCO DE LA VEGA, EL INCA. *Royal Commentaries of the Incas and General History of Peru*, trans. by HAROLD V. LIVERMORE. Austin and London: University of Texas Press, 1966 [1609].

GASPARINI, GRAZIANO, and LUISE MARGOLIES. *Inca Architecture*, trans. by PATRICIA J. LYON. Bloomington: Indiana University Press, 1980.

GIFFORD, CHAD, SAMUEL CONNELL, ANA LUCÍA GONZÁLEZ, and MAUREEN CARPENTER. "'Y el inga Guayna Capac derribado': Difficult Encounters in Pambamarca, Ecuador." Paper presented at the 21st Annual Northeast Conference on Andean Archaeology and Ethnohistory. Pittsburgh (PA): University of Pittsburgh, November 2002.

GLOWACKI, MARY. "The Huaro Archaeological Site Complex: Rethinking the Wari Occupation of Cuzco," in WILLIAM H. ISBELL and HELAINE SILVERMAN (eds), *Andean Archaeology I: Variations in Sociopolitical Organization*, pp. 267–85. New York and London: Kluwer Academic/Plenum, 2002.

GONZÁLEZ CARRÉ, ENRIQUE. *Los Señoríos Chankas*. Lima: Universidad Nacional San Cristóbal de Huamanga and Instituto Andino de Estudios Arqueológicos, 1992.

GONZÁLEZ CARRÉ, ENRIQUE, and DENISE POZZI ESCOT. "Arqueología y Etnohistoria en Vilcashuamán," in PETER KAULICKE, GARY URTON, and IAN FARRINGTON (eds), *Identidad y transformación en el Tawantinsuyu y en los Andes coloniales: Perspectivas arqueológicas y etnohistóricas. Boletín de Arqueología PUCP*, no. 6, pp. 79–105, 2002.

GOSE, PETER. "Oracles, Divine Kingship, and Political Representation in the Inka State," *Ethnohistory*, vol. 43, no. 1, pp. 1–32, 1996.

GUAMAN POMA DE AYALA, FELIPE. *El primer nueva corónica y buen gobierno*, ed. by JOHN V. MURRA, ROLENA ADORNO, and JORGE URIOSTE. Mexico City: Siglo Veintiuno, 1980 [ca. 1615].

GUCHTE, MAARTEN J. D. VAN DE. *Carving the World: Inca Monumental Sculpture and Landscape*. Unpublished Ph.D. dissertation, Department of Anthropology, University of Illinois at Urbana-Champaign. Ann Arbor (MI): University Microfilms, 1990.

HAGEN, ADRIANA VON. "Chachapoya Iconography and Society at Laguna de los Cóndores, Peru," in HELAINE SILVERMAN and WILLIAM H. ISBELL (eds), *Andean Archaeology II: Art, Landscape, and Society*, pp. 137–55. New York and London: Kluwer Academic/Plenum, 2002.

———"Stylistic Influences and Imagery in the Museo Leymebamba Textiles," in LENA BJERREGAARD (ed.), *Chachapoya Textiles: the Laguna de los Cóndores Textiles in the Museo Leymebamba, Chachapoyas, Peru*, pp. 41–62. Copenhagen: Museum Tusculanum Press, 2007.

HAGEN, ADRIANA VON, and SONIA GUILLÉN. "Tombs with a View," *Archaeology*, vol. 51, no. 2, pp. 48–54, 1998.

HAGEN, ADRIANA VON, and CRAIG MORRIS. *The Cities of the Ancient Andes*. London and New York: Thames & Hudson, 1998.

HARTMANN, ROSWITH. "Otros datos sobre las llamadas 'batallas rituales,'" in ROSALIA ÁVALOS DE MATOS and ROGGER RAVINES (eds), *Actas y Memorias del XXXIX Congreso Internacional de Americanistas*, vol. 6. Lima: Instituto de Estudios Peruanos, 1972.

HAYASHIDA, FRANCES. "Producción cerámica en el imperio Inka: Una visión global y nuevos datos," in IZUMI SHIMADA (ed.), *Tecnología y organización de la producción de cerámica prehispánica*, pp. 443–75. Lima: Fondo Editorial, Pontificia Universidad Católica del Perú, 1994.

———"Style, Technology, and Administered Production: the Manufacture of Inka Pottery in the Leche Valley, Peru," *Latin American Antiquity*, vol. 10, no. 4, pp. 337–52, 1999.

———"Leyendo el registro arqueológico del dominio inka: reflexiones desde la costa norte del Perú," in PETER KAULICKE, GARY URTON, and IAN FARRINGTON (eds), *Identidad y transformación en el Tawantinsuyu y en los Andes coloniales: Perspectivas arqueológicas y etnohistóricas. Boletín de Arqueología PUCP*, no. 7, pp. 305–19, 2003.

HEFFERNAN, KENNETH J. *Limatambo: Archaeology, History, and the Regional Societies of Inca Cusco*. Oxford: BAR, International Series, no. 644, 1966.

HEMMING, JOHN. *The Conquest of the Incas*. Harmondsworth: Penguin, 1983.

HEMMING, JOHN, and EDWARD RANNEY. *Monuments of the Incas*, revised and expanded edition. London and New York: Thames & Hudson, 2010.

HEYERDAHL, THOR, DANIEL H. SANDWEISS, and ALFREDO NARVÁEZ. *Pyramids of Túcume: the Quest for Peru's Forgotten City*. London and New York: Thames & Hudson, 1995.

HOCQUENGHEM, ANNE-MARIE. "Rutas de entrada del mullu en el extremo norte del Perú," *Bulletin de l'IFEA*, vol. 22, no. 3, pp. 701–19, 1993.

———"Los españoles en los caminos del extremo norte del Perú en 1532," *Bulletin de l'IFEA*, vol. 23, no. 1, pp. 1–67, 1994a.

HOCQUENGHEM, ANNE-MARIE, and MANUEL PEÑA RUÍZ. "La talla de material malacológico en Tumbes," *Bulletin de l'IFEA*, vol. 23, no. 2, pp. 209–29, 1994b.

HORNBERG, ALF. "Ethnogenesis, Regional Integration, and Ecology in Prehistoric Amazonia: Toward a System Perspective," *Current Anthropology*, vol. 46, no. 4, pp. 589–620, 2005.

HUMBOLDT, ALEXANDER VON. *Views of Nature, or, Contemplations on the Sublime Phenomena of Creation: With Scientific Illustrations*, trans. by ELISE C. OTTÉ and HENRY G. BOHN. London: Henry G. Bohn, 1850.

HYSLOP, JOHN. *The Inka Road System*. New York: Academic Press, 1984.

———*Inkawasi: the new Cuzco*. Oxford: BAR, International Series, no. 234, 1985.

———*Inka Settlement Planning*. Austin: University of Texas Press, 1990.

JENNINGS, JUSTIN, and WILLY YÉPEZ ÁLVAREZ. "The Inca Conquest and Consolidation of the Cotahuasi Valley of Southern Peru," *Ñawpa Pacha*, vol. 29, pp. 119–52, 2008.

JULIEN, CATHERINE J. *Hatunqolla: A View of Inca Rule from the Lake Titicaca Region*, Publications in Anthropology, vol. 15. Berkeley: University of California Press, 1983.

———"How Inca Decimal Administration Worked," *Ethnohistory*, vol. 35, pp. 257–79, 1988.

———*Reading Inca History*. Iowa City: University of Iowa Press, 2000.

LECHTMAN, HEATHER. "A Metallurgical Site Survey in the Peruvian Andes," *Journal of Field Archaeology*, vol. 3, no. 1, pp. 1–42, 1976.

———"Andean Value Systems and the Development of Prehistoric Metallurgy," *Technology and Culture*, vol. 25, pp. 1–36, 1984.

———"The Inka, and Andean Metallurgical Tradition," in RICHARD L. BURGER, CRAIG MORRIS, and RAMIRO MATOS, *Variations in the Expression of Inka Power*, pp. 313–56. Washington, DC: Dumbarton Oaks, 2007.

LEE, VINCENT R. "The Building of Sacsayhuaman," *Ñawpa Pacha*, vol. 24, pp. 49–60, 1986.

———*The Lost Half of Inca Architecture*. Wilson (WY): Sixpac Manco, 1988.

———*Investigations in Bolivia*. Wilson: Sixpac Manco, 1992.

———*Inca Choqek'iraw*. Wilson: Sixpac Manco, 1997.

———*Forgotten Vilcabamba: Final Stronghold of the Incas*. Cortez (CO): Sixpac Manco, 2000.

LERCHE, PETER. *Los Chachapoya y los símbolos de su historia*. Lima: P. Lerche, 1995.

LEVILLIER, ROBERTO. *Don Francisco de Toledo, supremo organizador del Perú: su vida, su obra (1515–1582)*, 3 vols. Madrid: Espasa-Calpe, 1935–42.

LEVINE, TERRY Y. "The Study of Storage Systems," in Terry Y. LeVine (ed.), *Inka Storage Systems*, pp. 3–28. Norman: University of Oklahoma Press, 1992.

LOTHROP, SAMUEL K. *Inca Treasure; as Depicted by Spanish Historians*, Frederick Webb Hodge Anniversary Publication Fund, vol. 2. Los Angeles: Southwest Museum, 1938.

LUMBRERAS, LUIS G. "Uhle y los asentamientos de Chincha en el siglo XVI," *Revista del Museo Nacional*, vol. 49, pp. 13–88, 2001.

LYON, PATRICIA J. "An Imaginary Frontier: Prehistoric Highland-Lowland Interchange in the Southern Peruvian Andes," in PETER D. FRANCIS, F. J. KENSE, and P. G. DUKE (eds), *Networks of the Past: Regional Interaction in Archaeology*. Calgary: University of Calgary Archaeological Association, 1984.

MACCORMACK, SABINE. *Religion in the Andes: Vision and Imagination in Early Colonial Peru*. Princeton (NJ) and Oxford: Princeton University Press, 1991.

MCEWAN, GORDON F. "Investigations at the Pikillacta Site: A Provincial Huari Center in the Valley of Cuzco," in WILLIAM H. ISBELL and GORDON F. MCEWAN (eds), *Huari Administrative Structures: Prehistoric Monumental Architecture and State Government*, pp. 93–119. Washington, DC: Dumbarton Oaks, 1991.

———"Archaeological Investigations at Pikillacta, a Wari Site in Peru," *Journal of Field Archaeology*, vol. 23, no. 2, pp. 68–86, 1996.

MCEWAN, GORDON F., MELISSA CHATFIELD, and ARMINDA GIBAJA. "The Archaeology of Inca Origins: Excavations at Chokepukio, Cuzco, Peru," in WILLIAM H. ISBELL and HELAINE SILVERMAN (eds), *Andean Archaeology I: Variations in Sociopolitical Organization*, pp. 287–301. New York and London: Kluwer Academic/Plenum, 2002.

MACKEY, CAROL. "La transformación socioeconómica de Farfán bajo el gobierno inka," in PETER KAULICKE, GARY URTON, and IAN FARRINGTON (eds), *Identidad y transformación en el Tawantinsuyu y en los Andes coloniales: Perspectivas arqueológicas y etnohistóricas. Boletín de Arqueología PUCP*, no. 7, pp. 321–53, 2003.

———"The Socioeconomic and Ideological Transformation of Farfán under Inka Rule," in MICHAEL A. MALPASS and SONIA ALCONINI (eds), *Distant Provinces in the Inka Empire*, pp. 221–59. Iowa City: University of Iowa Press, 2010.

MANNHEIM, BRUCE. *The Language of the Inka since the European Invasion*. Austin: University of Texas Press, 1991.

MATOS, RAMIRO. *Pumpu: Centro Administrativo Inka de la Puna de Junín*. Lima: Editorial Horizonte, 1994.

MENA, CRISTÓBAL DE. "La Conquista del Perú, llamada la Nueva Castilla," in ALBERTO M. SALAS, MIGUEL A. GUÉRIN, and JOSÉ LUIS MOURE (eds), *Crónicas iniciales de la conquista del Perú*, pp. 89–118. Buenos Aires: Plus Ultra, 1987 [1534].

MENZEL, DOROTHY. "The Inca Conquest of the South Coast of Peru," *Southwestern Journal of Anthropology*, vol. 15, pp. 125–42, 1959.

MENZEL, DOROTHY, and FRANCIS A. RIDDELL. *Archaeological Investigations at Tambo Viejo, Acarí Valley, Peru, 1954*. Sacramento: California Institute for Peruvian Studies, 1986.

MEYERS, ALBERT. "Toward a Reconceptualization of the Late Horizon and the Inka Period: Perspectives from Cochasquí, Ecuador, and Samaipata, Bolivia," in RICHARD L. BURGER, CRAIG MORRIS, and RAMIRO MATOS, *Variations in the Expression of Inka Power*, pp. 223–54. Washington, DC: Dumbarton Oaks, 2007.

MOLINA, CRISTÓBAL DE (EL CUSQUEÑO). "Relación de las Fábulas i Ritos de los Incas," in HENRIQUE URBANO and PIERRE DUVIOLS (eds), *Fábulas y mitos de los Incas*, Crónicas de América, no. 48, pp. 47–134. Madrid: Historia 16, 1989 [*ca*.1576].

MORRIS, CRAIG. "Tecnología y organización inca del almacenamiento de víveres en la sierra," in HEATHER LECHTMAN and ANA MARÍA SOLDI (eds), *Runakunap Kawsayninkupaq Rurasqankuna: La tecnología en el mundo andino*, pp. 327–75. Mexico City: UNAM, 1981.

———"Inka Strategies of Incorporation and Governance," in GARY M. FEINMAN and JOYCE MARCUS (eds), *Archaic States*, pp. 293–309. Santa Fe (NM): School of American Research, 1998.

———"Enclosures of Power: The Multiple Spaces of Inca Administrative Palaces," in SUSAN TOBY EVANS and JOANNE PILLSBURY (eds), *Palaces of the Ancient New World*, pp. 299–324. Washington, DC: Dumbarton Oaks, 2004.

———"Color Schemes of the Palace at Tambo Colorado," unpublished manuscript on file at the American Museum of Natural History, New York, n.d. (2006).

MORRIS, CRAIG, and ADRIANA VON HAGEN. *The Inka Empire and its Andean Origins*. New York and London: Abbeville Press, 1993.

MORRIS, CRAIG, and JULIAN IDILIO SANTILLANA. "The Inka Transformation of the Chincha Capital," in RICHARD L. BURGER, CRAIG MORRIS, and RAMIRO MATOS (eds), *Variations in the Expression of Inka Power*, pp. 135–64. Washington, DC: Dumbarton Oaks, 2007.

MORRIS, CRAIG, and DONALD E. THOMPSON. *Huánuco Pampa: An Inca City and its Hinterland*. London: Thames & Hudson, 1985.

MOSELEY, MICHAEL E. *The Incas and their Ancestors: The Archaeology of Peru*, revised edition. London and New York: Thames & Hudson, 2001.

MURRA, JOHN V. "Cloth and its functions in the Inca State," *American Anthropologist*, New Series, vol. 64, no. 4, pp. 710–28, 1962.

———*Formaciones económicas y políticas del mundo andino*. Lima: Instituto de Estudios Peruanos, 1975.

———"Los olleros del Inca: hacia una historia y arqueología del Qollasuyu," in F. MIRÓ QUESADA, FRANKLIN PEASE G.Y., and DANIEL SOBREVILLA (eds), *Historia, Problema y Promesa: Homenaje a Jorge Basadre*, pp. 415–23. Lima: Pontificia Universidad Católica del Perú, 1978.

———"Some contrasts between *Páramo* and *Puna* as zones of human habitation," in *Symposium sobre Páramos*. Mérida: Instituto Venezolano de Investigaciones Científicas, 1979.

———*The Economic Organization of the Inka State*. Greenwich (CT): JAI Press, 1980.

———"The Expansion of the Inka State: Armies, War, and Rebellions," in JOHN V. MURRA, NATHAN WACHTEL, and JACQUES REVEL (eds), *Anthropological History of Andean Polities*, pp. 49–58. Cambridge: Cambridge University Press, 1986.

MURÚA, MARTÍN DE. *Historia General del Perú*. Madrid: Dastín, 2001 [1590–98].

NAIR, STELLA E. *Of Remembrance and Forgetting: The Architecture of Chinchero, Peru from Thupa 'Inka to the Spanish Occupation*. Unpublished Ph.D. dissertation, Department of Architecture, University of California, Berkeley, 2003.

NIEMEYER, HANS, G. CERVELLINO, and E. MUÑOZ. "Viña del Cerro, expresión metalúrgica inca en el valle de Copiapó," *Creces*, vol. 4, no. 4, pp. 32–35, 1983.

NIEMEYER, HANS, and V. SCHIAPPACASSE. "Patrones de asentamiento incaicos en el Norte Grande de Chile," in T. D. DILLEHAY and P. NETHERLY (eds), *La frontera del estado inca*, pp. 141–80. Oxford: BAR, International Series, no. 442, 1988.

NILES, SUSAN A. *Callachaca: Style and Status in an Inca Community*. Iowa City: University of Iowa Press, 1987.

———*The Shape of Inca History: Narrative and Architecture in an Andean Empire*. Iowa City: University of Iowa Press, 1999.

———"Moya Place or Yours? Inca Private Ownership of Pleasant Places," *Ñawpa Pacha*, vols 25–27, pp. 189–206, 2004.

NILES, SUSAN A., and ROBERT N. BATSON. "Sculpting the Yucay Valley: Power and Style in Late Inka Architecture," in RICHARD L. BURGER, CRAIG MORRIS, and RAMIRO MATOS (eds), *Variations in the Expression of Inka Power*, pp. 185–222. Washington, DC: Dumbarton Oaks, 2007.

NOTICIA DEL PERÚ, in *Los cronistas de la conquista*, Biblioteca de la Cultura Peruana, 1st series, no. 2, pp. 195–251. Paris: Desclée de Brouwer, 1938.

OBERTI, ITALO. "Investigaciones preliminares en el Usno-Moq'o, Abancay," *Tawantinsuyu*, vol. 3, pp. 15–21, 1997.

OCAMPO, BALTASAR DE. *Account of the Province of Vilcapampa and a Narrative of the Execution of the Inca Tupac Amaru*, trans. by CLEMENTS R. MARKHAM, published for the Hakluyt Society, 2nd series, no. 22, Cambridge, 1907 [1610].

OCHSENDORF, JOHN. "Expansion and Construction in the Andes Mountains: The Role of Inca Suspension Bridges." Paper presented at the Annual Meeting of the Society of Architectural Historians, Providence (RI), April 16, 2004.

ODAIRA, SHUICHI. "El Mirador de Mollepungo: Un aspecto del control inca en la costa sur del Ecuador," *Tawantinsuyu*, vol. 5, pp. 145–52, 1998.

OGBURN, DENNIS E. "Power in Stone: The Long-Distance Movement of Building Blocks in the Inca Empire," *Ethnohistory*, vol. 51, no. 1, pp. 101–35, 2004.

ORTIZ DE ZÚÑIGA, IÑIGO. *Visita de la Provincia de León de Huánuco en 1562, Iñigo Ortiz de Zúñiga, visitador*, vol. 1, ed.

by JOHN V. MURRA. Huánuco: Universidad Nacional Hermilio Valdizán, 1967 [1562].

PÄRSSINEN, MARTTI. *Tawantinsuyu: The Inca State and its Political Organization*. Helsinki: Societas Historica Finlandiae, 1992.

PÄRSSINEN, MARTTI, and ARI SIIRIÄINEN. "Inka-style Ceramics and their Chronological Relationship to the Inka Expansion in the Southern Lake Titicaca Area (Bolivia)," *Latin American Antiquity*, vol. 8, no. 3, pp. 255–71, 1997.

——"Cuzcotoro and the Inca Fortification System in Chuquisaca, Bolivia," *Baessler-Archiv*, vol. 46, pp. 135–64, Berlin, 1998.

——*Andes Orientales y Amazonía Occidental: Ensayos entre la historia y la arqueología de Bolivia, Brasil y Perú*. La Paz: Producciones CIMA, 2003.

PATTERSON, THOMAS. "Pachacamac: An Andean Oracle under Inka Rule," in D. PETER KVIETOK and DANIEL H. SANDWEISS (eds), *Recent Studies in Andean Prehistory and Proto-history*, pp. 159–76. Ithaca (NY): Cornell University, 1985.

PIZARRO, PEDRO. *Relación del descubrimiento y conquista de los reinos del Perú*, ed. by GUILLERMO LOHMANN VILLENA. Lima: Pontificia Universidad Católica del Peru, 1986 [1571].

POLO DE ONDEGARDO, JUAN. "A Report on the Basic Principles Explaining the Serious Harm which Follows when the Traditional Rights of the Indians are not Respected," in *Information Concerning the Religion and Government of the Incas*, trans. by A. BRUNEL, JOHN V. MURRA, and SIDNEY MUIRDEN, pp. 53–196. New Haven (CT): Human Relations Area Files, 1965 [1567].

PROTZEN, JEAN-PIERRE. "Inca Quarrying and Stonecutting," *Journal of the Society of Architectural Historians*, vol. 44, no. 2, pp. 161–82, 1985.

——"The Fortress of Saqsa Waman: Was it ever finished?" *Ñawpa Pacha*, vols 25–27, pp. 155–76, 1987–89.

——*Inca Architecture and Construction at Ollantaytambo*. Oxford: Oxford University Press, 1993.

——"Times go by at Tambo Colorado," *Ñawpa Pacha*, vol. 29, pp. 221–40, 2008.

PROTZEN, JEAN-PIERRE, and DAVID HARRIS (eds). *Explorations in the Pisco Valley: Max Uhle's Reports to Phoebe Apperson Hearst, August 1901 to January 1902*. Contributions to the University of California Archaeological Research Facility, no. 63, Berkeley, 2005.

PROTZEN, JEAN-PIERRE, and CRAIG MORRIS. "Los colores de Tambo Colorado: una reevaluación," in PETER KAULICKE, GARY URTON, and IAN FARRINGTON (eds), *Identidad y transformación en el Tawantinsuyu y en los Andes coloniales: Perspectivas arqueológicas y etnohistóricas. Boletín de Arqueología PUCP*, no. 8, pp. 267–76, Lima, 2004.

PROTZEN, JEAN-PIERRE, and STELLA NAIR. "Who taught the Inca Stonemasons their Skills? A Comparison of Tiahuanaco and Inca Cut-Stone Masonry," *Journal of the Society of Architectural Historians*, vol. 56, no. 2, pp. 146–67, 1997.

RAFFINO, RODOLFO. *Inka: Arqueología, historia y urbanismo del altiplano andino*. Buenos Aires: Corregidor, 1993.

REINHARD, JOHAN. "Peru's Ice Maidens," *National Geographic*, vol. 189, no. 6, pp. 62–81, 1996.

——"Sharp Eyes of Science Probe the Mummies of Peru," *National Geographic*, vol. 191, no. 1, pp. 36–43, 1997.

——"Coropuna: Lost Mountain Temple of the Incas," *South American Explorers Journal*, vol. 58, no. 5, pp. 26–30, 1999a.

——"Frozen in Time," *National Geographic*, vol. 196, no. 5, pp. 36–55, 1999b.

——*Machu Picchu: The Sacred Center*, 2nd revised edition. Lima: Instituto Machu Picchu, 2002.

——*The Ice Maiden: Inca Mummies, Mountain Gods, and Sacred Sites in the Andes*. Washington, DC: National Geographic Society, 2005.

REINHARD, JOHAN, and MARÍA CONSTANZA CERUTI. *Inca Rituals and Sacred Mountains: A Study of the World's Highest Archaeological Sites*. Los Angeles: Cotsen Institute of Archaeology, 2011.

RENARD-CASEVITZ, FRANCE-MARIE. "Las fronteras de las conquistas en el siglo XVI en la montaña meridional del Perú," *Bulletin de l'IFEA*, vol. 10, nos 3–4, pp. 113–40, 1981.

ROSSEN, JACK, MARÍA TERESA PLANELLA, and RUBEN STEHBERG. "Archaeobotany of Cerro del Inga, Chile, at the Southern Inka Frontier," in MICHAEL A. MALPASS and SONIA ALCONINI (eds), *Distant Provinces in the Inka Empire*, pp. 14–43. Iowa City: University of Iowa Press, 2010.

ROSTWOROWSKI DE DIEZ CANSECO, MARÍA. "Dos manuscritos inéditos con datos sobre Manco II, tierras personales de los Incas y mitimaes," *Nueva Corónica*, vol. 1, pp. 223–39, 1963.

——"Mercaderes del valle de Chincha en la época prehispánica: Un documento y unos comentarios," *Revista Española de Antropología Americana*, vol. 5, pp. 135–78, 1970.

——"Huarco y Lunahuaná: Dos señoríos prehispánicos de la costa sur-central del Perú," *Revista del Museo Nacional*, vol. 44, pp. 153–214, 1978–80.

——*History of the Inca Realm*, trans. by HARRY B. ICELAND. Cambridge: Cambridge University Press, 1999.

ROWE, ANN P. "Technical Features of Inca Tapestry Tunics," *Textile Museum Journal*, vol. 17, pp. 5–28, 1978.

——*Costumes and Featherwork of the Lords of Chimor: Textiles from Peru's North Coast*. Washington, DC: Textile Museum, 1984.

——"Inca Weaving and Costume," *Textile Museum Journal*, vols 34–35, pp. 5–54, 1997.

ROWE, JOHN H. *An Introduction to the Archaeology of Cuzco*, Papers of the Peabody Museum of American Archaeology and Ethnology, Harvard University, vol. 27, no. 2, Cambridge (MA), 1944.

——"Inca Culture at the Time of the Spanish Conquest," in JULIAN STEWARD (ed.), *Handbook of South American Indians*, vol. 2, pp. 183–330. Washington, DC: United States Government Printing Office, 1946.

——"The Kingdom of Chimor," *Acta Americana*, vol. 6, pp. 26–59, 1948.

——"The Age Grades of the Inca Census," in *Miscellanea Paul Rivet Octogenario Dicata II. XXXI Congreso Internacional de Americanistas*, pp. 499–522. Mexico: Universidad Nacional Autónoma de México, 1958.

——"The Origins of Creator Worship among the Incas," in STANLEY DIAMOND (ed.), *Culture in History*, pp. 408–29. New York: Columbia University Press, 1960.

——"What Kind of Settlement was Inca Cuzco?" *Ñawpa Pacha*, vol. 5, pp. 59–77, 1968.

——"Standardization in Inca Tapestry Tunics," in ANN P. ROWE, ELIZABETH P. BENSON, and ANNE-LOUISE SCHAFFER (eds), *The Junius B. Bird Pre-Columbian Textile Conference*, pp. 239–64. Washington, DC: The Textile Museum and Dumbarton Oaks, 1979.

——"Machu Picchu a la luz de documentos del siglo XVI," *Histórica*, vol. 14, no. 1, pp. 139–54, 1990.

——"Las tierras reales de los Incas," in RAFAEL VARÓN GABAI and JAVIER FLORES ESPINOZA (eds), *Arqueología, Antropología e Historia en los Andes: Homenaje a María Rostworowski*, pp. 277–87. Lima: Instituto de Estudios Peruanos, 1997.

RUÍZ DE ARCE, JUAN. "Relación de servicios en Indias de don Juan Ruíz de Arce, conquistador del Perú," *Boletín de la Real Academia de Historia*, vol. 102, no. 2, pp. 327–84, 1933 [1543].

SALAZAR, LUCY C. "Machu Picchu: Mysterious Royal Estate in the Cloud Forest," in RICHARD L. BURGER and LUCY C.

SALAZAR (eds), *Machu Picchu: Unveiling the Mystery of the Incas*, pp. 21–48. New Haven (CT) and London: Yale University Press, 2004.

———"Machu Picchu's Silent Majority: A Consideration of the Inka Cemeteries," in RICHARD L. BURGER, CRAIG MORRIS, and RAMIRO MATOS, *Variations in the Expression of Inka Power*, pp. 165–84. Washington, DC: Dumbarton Oaks, 2007.

SALAZAR, LUCY C., and RICHARD L. BURGER. "Lifestyles of the Rich and Famous: Luxury and Daily Life in the Households of Machu Picchu's Elite," in SUSAN TOBY EVANS and JOANNE PILLSBURY (eds), *Palaces of the Ancient New World*, pp. 325–58. Washington, DC: Dumbarton Oaks, 2004.

SALLNOW, MICHAEL J. *Pilgrims of the Andes: Regional Cults in Cusco*. Washington, DC: Smithsonian Institution Press, 1987.

SALOMON, FRANK. "A North Andean Status Trader Complex under Inka Rule," *Ethnohistory*, vol. 34, no. 1, pp. 63–77, 1987.

SALOMON, FRANK, and SUE GROSBOLL. "Names and Peoples in Incaic Quito: Retrieving Undocumented Historic Process through Anthroponymy and Statistics," *American Anthropologist*, vol. 88, no. 2, pp. 387–99, 1986.

SALOMON, FRANK, and JORGE URIOSTE (eds). *The Huarochirí Manuscript: A Testament of Ancient and Colonial Andean Religion*. Austin: University of Texas Press, 1991.

SANCHO DE LA HOZ, PEDRO. "Relación," in HORACIO H. URTEAGA (ed.), *[1532–1533] Colección de libros y documentos referentes a la historia del Perú*, vol. 5, pp. 122–202. Lima: Sanmartí, 1917 [1532–33].

SANTILLÁN, HERNANDO DE. "Relación del origen, descendencia, política y gobierno de los Incas," in E. BARBA (ed.), *Crónicas peruanas de interés indígena*, Biblioteca de Autores Españoles, vol. 209. Madrid, 1968 [1563].

SANTILLANA, IDILIO. *Vilcas Huaman: Paisaje Sagrado e Ideología Inca*. Lima: Fondo Editorial, Pontificia Universidad Católica del Perú, 2011.

SARMIENTO DE GAMBOA, PEDRO. *History of the Incas*, trans. and ed. by CLEMENTS R. MARKHAM, published for the Hakluyt Society, 2nd series, no. 22, Cambridge, 1907 (reprinted by Dover Publications, 1999) [1572].

SCHJELLERUP, INGE. *Incas and Spaniards in the Conquest of the Chachapoya: Archaeological and Ethnohistorical Research in the North-eastern Andes of Peru*, GOTARC, Series B, Gothenburg Archaeological Theses 7, University of Gothenburg, Gothenburg, 1997.

SCHOBINGER, JUAN (ed.). *El santuario incaico del cerro Aconcagua*. Mendoza: Universidad Nacional de Cuyo, 2001.

SEGOVIA, BARTOLOMÉ DE. "Relación de muchas cosas acaecidas en el Perú...en la conquista y población destos reinos" [formerly attributed to Cristóbal de Molina de Santiago], in E. BARBA (ed.), *Crónicas peruanas de interés indígena*, Biblioteca de Autores Españoles, vol. 135, pp. 189–279. Madrid, 1965.

SHERBONDY, JEANETTE E. "Water and Power: The Role of Irrigation Districts in the Transition from Inca to Spanish Cuzco," in WILLIAM P. MITCHELL and DAVID GUILLET (eds), *Irrigation at High Altitudes: The Social Organization of Water Control Systems in the Andes*, Society for Latin American Anthropology Publication Series, vol. 12, pp. 69–97. Washington, DC: American Anthropological Association, 1994.

SHIMADA, IZUMI. "Cultural Continuities and Discontinuities on the Northern North Coast of Peru, Middle-Late Horizons," in MICHAEL E. MOSELEY and ALANA CORDY-COLLINS (eds), *The Northern Dynasties: Kingship and Statecraft in Chimor*, pp. 297–392. Washington, DC: Dumbarton Oaks, 1990.

SIIRIÄINEN, ARI, and ANTTI KORPISAARI, *Reports of the Finnish-Bolivian Archaeological Project in the Bolivian Amazon*. Helsinki: Department of Archaeology, University of Helsinki–Unidad Nacional de Arqueología de Bolivia, 2002.

SILLAR, BILL, and EMILY DEAN. "Identidad étnica bajo el dominio inka: una evaluación arqueológica y etnohistórica de las repercusiones del Estado Inka en el grupo étnico canas," in PETER KAULICKE, GARY URTON, and IAN FARRINGTON (eds), *Identidad y transformación en el Tawantinsuyu y en los Andes coloniales: Perspectivas arqueológicas y etnohistóricas. Boletín de Arqueología PUCP*, no. 6, pp. 205–64, Lima, 2002.

SILVERBLATT, IRENE. *Moon, Sun, and Witches: Gender Ideologies and Class in Inca and Colonial Peru*. Princeton (NJ) and Guildford: Princeton University Press, 1987.

SPALDING, KAREN. "The Crises and Transformation of Invaded Societies: Andean Area (1500–1580)," in FRANK SALOMON and STUART B. SCHWARTZ (eds), *The Cambridge History of the Native Peoples of the Americas*, vol. 3, South America, Part 1, pp. 904–72. Cambridge: Cambridge University Press, 1999.

SPURLING, GEOFFREY E. *The Organization of Craft Production in the Inka State: The Potters and Weavers of Milliraya*. Unpublished Ph.D. dissertation, Department of Anthropology, Cornell University. Ann Arbor: University Microfilms, 1992.

SQUIER, EPHRAIM GEORGE. *Peru: Incidents of Travel and Exploration in the Land of the Incas*. London: Macmillan, and New York: Harper and Brothers, 1877. Facsimile edition: AMS Press Inc, New York, for Peabody Museum of Archaeology and Ethnology, Harvard University, Cambridge (MA), 1973.

STANISH, CHARLES. "Nonmarket Imperialism in the Prehispanic Americas: The Inka Occupation of the Titicaca Basin," *Latin American Antiquity*, vol. 8, no. 3, pp. 195–216, 1997.

STONE-MILLER, REBECCA. *Art of the Andes: from Chavín to Inca*, 2nd edition. London and New York: Thames & Hudson, 2002.

TOLEDO, FRANCISCO DE, see LEVILLIER, ROBERTO.

TOPIC, JOHN R. "El santuario de Catequil: estructura y agencia. Hacia una comprensión de los oráculos andinos," in MARCO CURATOLA PETROCCHI and MARIUSZ S. ZIÓŁKOWSKI (eds), *Adivinación y Óraculos en el Mundo Andino Antiguo*, pp. 71–96. Lima: Pontificia Universidad Católica del Peru, 2008.

TOPIC, JOHN R., and THERESA TOPIC. "The Archaeological Investigation of Andean Militarism: some Cautionary Observations," in JONATHAN HAAS, SHELIA POZORSKI, and THOMAS POZORSKI (eds), *The Origins and Development of the Andean State*, pp. 47–55. Cambridge: Cambridge University Press, 1987.

———"A Summary of the Inca Occupation of Huamachuco," in MICHAEL A. MALPASS (ed.), *Provincial Inca: Archaeological and Ethnohistorical Assessment of the Impact of the Inca State*. Iowa City: University of Iowa Press, 1993.

TOPIC, JOHN R., THERESA LANGE TOPIC, and ALFREDO MELLY. "Catequil: the Archaeology, Ethnohistory, and Ethnography of a Major Provincial Huaca," in WILLIAM H. ISBELL and HELAINE SILVERMAN (eds), *Andean Archaeology I: Variations in Sociopolitical Organization*, pp. 303–36. New York and London: Kluwer Academic/Plenum, 2002.

TORERO, ALFREDO. *El quechua y la historia social andina*. Lima: Universidad Ricardo Palma, 1974.

TRIMBORN, HERMANN. "Archäologische Studien in den Kordilleren Boliviens," *Baessler Archiv: Beitrage zur Völkerkunde*, New Series, no. 2, Berlin, 1959.

TRUJILLO, DIEGO DE. "Relación del descubrimiento del Perú," in *Biblioteca Peruana: El Perú a través de los siglos*, vol. 2, pp. 9–103. Lima: Editores Técnicos Asociados, 1968 [1571].

URTON, GARY. *At the Crossroads of the Earth and Sky: An Andean Cosmology.* Austin: University of Texas Press, 1981.

———"Moieties and Ceremonialism in the Andes: The Ritual Battles of the Carnival Season in Southern Peru," in LUIS MILLONES and YOSHIO ONUKI (eds), *El Mundo Ceremonial Andino*, Senri Ethnological Studies, no. 37, pp. 117–42. Osaka: National Museum of Ethnology, 1993.

———"A Calendrical and Demographic Tomb Text from Northern Peru," *Latin American Antiquity*, vol. 12, no. 2, pp. 127–47, 2001.

———"An Overview of Spanish Colonial Commentary on Andean Knotted-String Records," in JEFFREY QUILTER and GARY URTON (eds), *Narrative Threads: Accounting and Recounting in Andean Khipu*, pp. 3–25. Austin: University of Texas Press, 2002.

———"The Khipus from Laguna de los Cóndores," in LENA BJERREGAARD (ed.), *Chachapoya Textiles: the Laguna de los Cóndores Textiles in the Museo Leymebamba, Chachapoyas, Peru*, pp. 62–68. Copenhagen: Museum Tusculanum Press, 2007.

———"Andean *Quipu*: A History of Writings and Studies on Inca and Colonial Knotted-String Records," in JOANNE PILLSBURY (ed.), *Guide to Documentary Sources for Andean Studies, 1530–1900*, vol. 1, pp. 65–86. Norman: University of Oklahoma Press, in collaboration with the Center for Advanced Study in the Visual Arts, National Gallery of Art, Washington, DC, 2008.

———"The Inca Khipu: Knotted-Cord Record Keeping in the Andes," in HELAINE SILVERMAN and WILLIAM H. ISBELL (eds), *Handbook of South American Archaeology*, pp. 831–44. New York and London: Springer, 2008.

URTON, GARY, and CARRIE BREZINE. "Information Control in the Palace of Puruchuco: An Accounting Hierarchy in a Khipu Archive from Coastal Peru," in RICHARD L. BURGER, CRAIG MORRIS, and RAMIRO MATOS (eds), *Variations in the Expression of Inka Power*, pp. 357–84. Washington, DC: Dumbarton Oaks, 2007.

VALENCIA ZEGARRA, ALFREDO. "Recent Archaeological Investigations at Machu Picchu," in RICHARD L. BURGER and LUCY C. SALAZAR (eds), *Machu Picchu: Unveiling the Mystery of the Incas*, pp. 71–84. New Haven (CT) and London: Yale University Press, 2004.

VASQUEZ DE ESPINOSA, ANTONIO. *Compendio y descripción de la Indias occidentales*, Biblioteca de Autores Españoles, vol. 231. Madrid, 1969 [1629].

VERANO, JOHN W. "Human Skeletal Remains from Machu Picchu: A Reexamination of the Yale Peabody Museum's Collections," in RICHARD L. BURGER and LUCY C. SALAZAR (eds), *The 1912 Yale Peruvian Scientific Expedition Collections from Machu Picchu: Human and Animal Remains*, pp. 65–118, Yale University Publications in Anthropology, no. 85. Distributed by Yale University Press, 2003.

WACHTEL, NATHAN. "The Mitimas of the Cochabamba Valley: The Colonization Policy of Huayna Capac," in GEORGE A. COLLIER, RENATO I. ROSALDO, and JOHN D. WIRTH (eds), *The Inca and Aztec States 1400–1800: Anthropology and History*, pp. 199–235. New York: Academic Press, 1982.

WERNKE, STEVE. "The Politics of Community and Inka Statecraft in the Colca Valley, Peru," *Latin American Antiquity*, vol. 17, no. 7, pp. 177–208, 2006.

WILLIAMS, VERÓNICA I., and TERENCE N. D'ALTROY. "El sur del Tawantinsuyu: Un dominio selectivamente intensivo," *Tawantinsuyu*, vol. 5, pp. 170–78, 1999.

WOLOSZYN, JANUSZ Z. "Tumba No. 7 del sitio Maucallacta," in MARIUSZ S. ZIÓŁKOWSKI and LUIS AUGUSTO BELAN FRANCO (eds), *Proyecto Arqueológico Condesuyos*, vol. 1 / *Andes – Boletín de la Misión Arqueológica Andina*, vol. 3, pp. 201–11. Warsaw: University of Warsaw, 2000–1.

XEREZ, FRANCISCO DE. "Report of Francisco de Xeres, Secretary to Francisco Pizarro," in CLEMENTS R. MARKHAM (trans. and ed.), *Reports on the Discovery of Peru*, published for the Hakluyt Society, London, 1872 [1534].

———*Verdadera Relación de la Conquista del Perú*, ed. by CONCEPCIÓN BRAVO, Crónicas de América, no. 14. Madrid: Historia 16, 1985 [1534].

YUPANQUI, TITU CUSI. *An Inca Account of the Conquest of Peru by Titu Cusi Yupanqui*, trans. by RALPH BAUER. Boulder: University Press of Colorado, 2005 [1570].

ZÁRATE, AGUSTÍN DE. *Historia del descubrimiento y conquista del Perú*, Biblioteca de Autores Españoles, vol. 26, pp. 459–574, 1947.

———"Historia del descubrimiento y conquista del Perú," *Biblioteca Peruana: El Perú a través de los siglos*, 1st series, vol. 2, pp. 105–413. Lima: Editores Técnicos Asociados, 1968 [1555].

ZIÓŁKOWSKI, MARIUSZ S. *La guerra de los wawqi: los objetivos y los mecanismos de la rivalidad dentro de la élite inka, siglos XV–XVI.* Quito: Ediciones Abya-Yala, 1996.

———"Apuntes sobre la presencia inca en la región de los Nevados Coropuna y Solimana," in MARIUSZ S. ZIÓŁKOWSKI, LUIS AUGUSTO BELAN FRANCO, and MACIEJ SOBCZYK (eds), *Proyecto Arqueológico Condesuyos*, vol. 3 / *Andes – Boletín de la Misión Arqueológica Andina*, vol. 6, pp. 27–64. Warsaw: University of Warsaw, 2005.

———"Coropuna y Solimana: Los Óraculos de Condesuyos," in MARCO CURATOLA PETROCCHI and MARIUSZ S. ZIÓŁKOWSKI (eds), *Adivinación y oráculos en el mundo andino antiguo*, pp. 121–59. Lima: Fondo Editorial, Pontificia Universidad Católica del Perú, and Instituto Francés de Estudios Andinos, 2008.

ZIÓŁKOWSKI, MARIUSZ S., and MACIEJ SOBCZYK. "Buscando el oráculo y santuario del Nevado Solimana," in MARIUSZ S. ZIÓŁKOWSKI, JUSTIN JENNINGS, LUIS AUGUSTO BELAN FRANCO, and ANDREA DRUSINI (eds), *Arqueología del Área Centro Sur-Andina, Actas del Simposio Internacional 30 de junio–2 de julio, 2005, Arequipa, Peru / Andes – Boletín del Centro de Estudios Precolombinos de la Universidad de Warsovia*, pp. 655–93. Warsaw University Press / Instituto Francés de Estudios Andinos, 2010.

ZUIDEMA, R. TOM. *The Ceque System of Cuzco*, trans. by Eva M. Hooykaas, International Archives of Ethnography, supplement to vol. 50. Leiden: E. J. Brill, 1964.

———"The Inca Kinship System: A New Theoretical View," in RALPH BOLTON and ENRIQUE MAYER (eds), *Andean Kinship and Marriage*, a special publication of the American Anthropological Association, no. 7. Washington, DC: American Anthropological Association, 1977.

———"The Lion in the City: Royal Symbols of Transition in Cuzco," *Journal of Latin American Lore*, vol. 9, no. 1, pp. 39–100, 1983.

———*Inca Civilization in Cuzco*, trans. by Jean-Jacques Decoster. Austin: University of Texas Press, 1999.

Sources of Illustrations

Index